CONNECTIONS ACROSS EURASIA

TRANSPORTATION, COMMUNICATION, AND CULTURAL EXCHANGE ON THE SILK ROADS

XINRU LIU

College of New Jersey

LYNDA NORENE SHAFFER

Tufts University, Emerita

Boston   Burr Ridge, IL   Dubuque, IA   New York
San Francisco   St. Louis   Bangkok   Bogotá   Caracas   Kuala Lumpur
Lisbon   London   Madrid   Mexico City   Milan   Montreal   New Delhi
Santiago   Seoul   Singapore   Sydney   Taipei   Toronto

The McGraw·Hill Companies

Higher Education

Published by McGraw-Hill, an imprint of The McGraw-Hill companies, Inc., 1221 Avenue of the Americas, New York, NY 10020. Copyright © 2007. All rights reserved. No part of this publication may be reproduced or distributed in any form or by any means, or stored in a database or retrieval system, without the prior written consent of The McGraw-Hill Companies, Inc., including, but not limited to, in any network or other electronic storage or transmission, or broadcast for distance learning.

This book is printed on acid-free paper.

1 2 3 4 5 6 7 8 9 0 DOC/DOC 0 9 8 7

ISBN-13: 978-0-07-284351-4
ISBN-10: 0-07-284351-9

Editor in Chief: *Emily Barrosse*
Publisher: *Lisa Moore*
Senior Sponsoring Editor: *Jon-David Hague*
Editorial Coordinator: *Sora Kim*
Production Service: *Valerie Heffernan, Carlisle Publishing Services*
Cover Design: *Srdjan Savanovic*
Senior Production Supervisor: *Richard DeVitto*
Composition: *10/13 Palatino*
Printing: *#45 New Era Matte, R. R. Donnelley & Sons*

Library of Congress Cataloging-in-Publication Data

Liu, Xinru.
   Connections across Eurasia : transportation, communications, and cultural exchange along the Silk Roads / Xinru Liu, Lynda Norene Shaffer.
      p. cm.
   Includes bibliographical references and index.
   ISBN 0-07-284351-9
   1. Eurasia—Commerce—History. 2. Silk Road—History. 3. Silk industry—Eurasia—History. I. Shaffer, Lynda, 1944- II. Title.

HC420.3.L58 2007
388.095—dc22   2006048523

www.mhhe.com

TABLE OF CONTENTS

 PREFACE

Our volume, entitled *Connections Across Eurasia: Transportation, Communication, and Cultural Exchange on the Silk Roads,* is a study of the Eurasian silk trade. It begins in the second century BCE and ends almost fifteen centuries later with the consolidation of the Eurasia-wide conquests of the Mongol confederacy. By focusing on the silk trade, one of the most important topics in the history of economic exchange, we explore some of the most significant technological and cultural exchanges that transpired during these centuries. One of the more obvious lessons that can be drawn from this volume is that cultural exchanges fueled by improvements in transportation and communications are by no means new in the modern world. Although the speed with which today's cultural exchanges take place is unique, such exchanges have been a significant part of the past for many millennia. Indeed, they have been so pervasive in the past that today much of what people perceive to be an indigenous part of their own local or regional culture was at one point, in whole or in part, an import from some other place.

Given its long history and the number of places involved, studying the Eurasian silk trade is one of the most useful ways to illuminate a significant part of world history. The majority of world history texts and courses proceed from region to region in order to introduce the unique features of each region's past, thereby identifying the participants in world historical events. We appreciate the usefulness of this approach and the necessary information that it imparts. However, a topical approach, such as this study of the silk trade, also has its advantages. In particular, a study focused on such a long-lasting trade of Eurasia-wide dimensions helps to identify and illuminate those events whose impacts and consequences were sufficiently widespread to merit a significant place in world history. By abandoning an organization based on region and instead using a chronological organization that emphasizes the most significant transitions in this trade, events are placed within a context that comes at least somewhat closer to a world historical perspective. Hopefully this approach will make some small contribution to the ongoing effort to better conceptualize and periodize world history.

Chapter One emphasizes that the Eurasian silk trade began as a frontier trade between the rulers of China, a sedentary urban-agricultural empire, and the Yuezhi confederacy, an alliance of nomadic peoples who raised horses on a part of the Central Asian steppe. Thus, it began as a trade between the peoples of two quite different ecological zones. The further internationalization of the silk trade occurred only after the Yuezhi were defeated by the Xiongnu, a rival confederation of nomads, and fled westward to present-day Afghanistan. Thereafter, silk very quickly made its way to the eastern shores of the Mediterranean, after passing through numerous different cultural regions on its way.

Chapter Two begins around the first century CE. The Yuezhi were still the most important silk traders and they had acquired an empire that included much of Central Asia, including all the territory between the Chinese frontier and Afghanistan, all of present-day Pakistan, and much of northern India. Mahayana Buddhists were attracted to this highly commercialized kingdom, and it was there that many of the distinct features of Mahayana Buddhism developed, prior to its spread along the silk roads to eastern Asia. It was also in the first century BCE that Roman Empire sailors based in Egyptian ports began sailing to ports in northwestern India where they could purchase the silks that the Yuezhi-Kushan had brought from China.

Chapter Three discusses the developments during the Kushan Empire and immediately thereafter on the overland routes through deserts. It emphasizes the multicultural societies that flourished both in and around the Takla-Makan Desert in present-day China's Xinjiang Uighur Autonomous Region and in the deserts between Parthia and the Roman Empire's eastern frontier. The routes through the Takla Makan Desert were altogether new. They were also treacherous. Nevertheless, traders were willing to take their chances in this bone-dry land of shifting sands since they did not have to worry about being attacked by horseback-riding raiders. Unlike the oases towns of the Takla Makan Desert, the caravan cities in the western Eurasian deserts between Parthia and the Roman Empire's eastern frontier were not created by the silk trade. They already had long histories before traders began using them to deliver silk to the Roman Empire. The silk trade, nevertheless, contributed to their prosperity, especially in the case of Palmyra, and added new layers to their multicultural heritage.

Chapter Four discusses developments that began in the third century with the emergence of the Sasanid Empire in Iran. It defeated the Parthians and took over much of the Kushan Empire in Central Asia. Many traders from the Kushan Empire then migrated to the oases of the Takla Makan Desert, especially its southern rim, where Buddhist institutions flourished by the third century. Indeed, by this time, Buddhist monasteries facilitated the trade all the way from Afghanistan to northeastern China. After the demise of the Parthians, the Sogdians, whose homes were in present-day Uzbekistan, became one of the primary movers of the trade between Iran and China, and many of them settled in the oases towns along the northern rim of the Takla Makan oases.

This chapter illuminates the close relationship that developed between religion and empire, primarily the Zoroastrian religion in Iran, Christianity in Byzantium, and Mahayana Buddhism in China. Although Buddhism was never the official religion in China, as Zoroastrianism was in Sassanian Iran and Christianity became in the Byzantine Empire, it was favored and promoted by many of the short-lived regional dynasties during the centuries when China was divided among numerous regional kingdoms. Even after China's reunification, especially during the first 200 years of the Tang dynasty, Buddhism's place in China did resemble that of an official religion. The chapter is principally focused on the ways in which both the political powers and the religious institutions used silk to enhance their positions and to display their grandeur.

Chapter Five describes the impact that the Muslim caliphates had on the silk trade. In spite of the fact that their expansion was accomplished by military means, after the hostilities ended the silk trade prospered and grew ever larger. By this time sericulture, the production of silk threads and yarns from the cocoons of silk worms, was well established in Byzantium and many parts of the Muslim world, and thus China no longer had a monopoly on the production of silk raw materials. This development, however, did not diminish the trade in Chinese silk. Islam's positive attitude toward trade and traders, the Muslim system of partnerships that provided investment funds to traders, and other innovations such as embroidered silk "trademarks" that identified the origin of textiles all contributed to the continuing growth of the silk trade. The extension of Muslim power into Central Asia also facilitated the spread of paper, another product of Chinese origin, along the silk roads and throughout the lands of the caliphate.

Chapter Six focuses on the maritime trade routes that silk traveled and their ever-increasing significance. Although silk had been shipped westward from ports in northeastern India to ports on the Red Sea beginning in the first century CE, that route lost much of its significance some time after the fall of the Kushan Empire. Also the silk that supplied that early route was brought from China to India by overland routes. It was not until the fifth century CE that silk began to travel in significant quantities from China to the Indian subcontinent by an overseas route. The sailors who developed this route were Southeast Asians, and by the seventh century Iranian and Arab ships were also using this route to sail back and forth between India and China.

By the tenth century a major transition was underway. The maritime routes were becoming increasingly important, so much so that by the twelfth century they had become more significant than the land routes. The beginning of this transition in the tenth century was marked by two major developments. Prior to the tenth century the preeminent maritime destination within the Muslim lands had been the Persian Gulf, but beginning in the tenth century this was no longer true, and ports on Egypt's Red Sea coast had become preeminent. The other major development was that Chinese ships had joined the Southeast Asians, Iranians, and Arabs on the routes between China and India.

By the eleventh century Chinese ships were sailing with compasses, yet another Chinese invention. Apparently the use of the compass spread steadily along the various maritime routes, for by the thirteenth century it could be found on ships sailing the Mediterranean Sea. By the twelfth century the significance of the maritime routes had surpassed the overland routes. Not only were they carrying more silk, but they also made it possible for bulkier and heavier items to become a significant part of the cargo on the same routes that silk traveled. Horses and camels, used on the overland routes, were limited in the number of heavy chests filled with porcelain that they could carry. Ships, on the other hand, could take these chests on in large numbers. The nature of the trade was also changing in that it was no longer just a luxury trade. Such items as horses and rice were also on the ships that carried the silk.

Chapter Seven begins in the thirteenth century with the Mongol conquests of much of Eurasia and ends in the fourteenth century. Unlike the conquests of the Muslim cavalries, the Mongolian conquests destroyed many of the most significant overland routes that silk had followed for more than a millennium, as well as the commercial infrastructure that had grown up along them. The Mongol conquests brought an end to the previous significance of the overland routes that had carried silk for almost a millennium and a half. There still were some land routes, but they generally had moved northward onto the steppe and their growth was largely dependent upon the effort to supply Mongol capitals and summer camps located on the steppe. Meanwhile the sea routes south of Eurasia continued to prosper and grow in importance. We end by discussing maritime developments in the Mediterranean and then along Europe's western coast that would eventually lead to the Portuguese rounding of the southern tip of Africa and their arrival on the maritime routes that silk was traveling.

ACKNOWLEDGMENTS

Both of us would like to thank the McGraw-Hill Series editors for their assistance on this project. Robert Strayer's encouraging words were much appreciated, and Kevin Reilly's thoughtful critiques of the organization and presentation of this volume led to significant improvements in the final version. The contributions of the two outside reviewers, Jerry Bentley of the University of Hawaii and Stephen Gosch of the University of Wisconsin–Eau Claire, also made significant contributions to the manuscript. Steven Gosch, who is an expert on the silk roads, provided us with detailed comments, all of which we put to good use.

Xinru Liu

Lynda Norene Shaffer

Lynda Shaffer would particularly like to thank Kevin Reilly, who despite the distance between their universities, has been one of her closest colleagues for the last 25 years. His contributions to the formation of the World History Association, his dedication to the growth of the Association since 1982, and especially to the development of scholarship in world history has been exceptional. She also wants to thank Xinru Liu for asking her to join this project. The depth and breath of Professor Liu's knowledge in world history is awe-inspiring, and it has been a privilege to work with her.

Xinru Liu would first like to thank Thomas Allsen, who held lunch meetings almost every teaching day with her and other adjunct teachers at The College of New Jersey. The topic of the meetings was Central Asia, and he participated in these discussions until 2003, when he retired. He encouraged her to take up this project and helped her draft the proposal and the first chapter. She is also grateful to Lynda Shaffer, who took over all the revisions and details after we finished the manuscript, since Professor Liu was busy with her first full-time teaching job in the United States.

NOTE FROM THE SERIES EDITORS

World History has come of age. One of the prominent features of the World History movement has been the unusually close association of its scholarly and its teaching wings. Teachers at all levels have participated with university-based scholars in the development of this new field.

The McGraw-Hill series—Explorations in World History—operates at this intersection of scholarship and teaching. It seeks to convey the results of recent research in World History in a form wholly accessible to beginning students. It also provides a pedagogical alternative to or supplement for the large and inclusive core textbooks, which are features of so many World History courses. Each volume in the series focuses briefly on a particular theme, set in a global and comparative context. And each of them is "open-ended," raising questions and drawing students into the larger issues that animate World History.

When one thinks of ancient trade between Europe and Asia, one thinks of the silk road. In this history of the silk road, the reader quickly learns that there was more than one "road" between China and Europe, that some of the most well-worn routes were on what the Chinese called the "Southern Ocean," and that far more people than Chinese and Europeans were involved. For this volume, Xinru Liu, a leading scholar of the ancient trade networks of Eurasia, and Lynda Shaffer, an important world historian and scholar of the Chinese past, team up to explain not only the workings of the silk roads but also the remarkable histories of the societies and peoples who fostered Eurasian trade and communication in the almost two millennia before 1500 CE. This is a story full of memorable merchant adventurers, of intrepid travelers, of sophisticated societies long forgotten, of states and cities rising and falling, and of religions transplanted. As a study in the early history of "globalization," it's also a primer on tomorrow's news.

Kevin Reilly
Robert Strayer

THE ECOLOGICAL CONTEXT FOR THE EMERGENCE OF THE EURASIAN SILK ROADS

CHAPTER OUTLINE

The Silk

Three Interrelated Ecological Zones

Inside the Urban-Agricultural Zone

Inside the Pastoral Zone

Inside the Taiga Forest Zone

Exchanges among the Zones

The Significance of Horses

TIMELINE

Silk in China

4800–3000 BCE

Yangshao (Painted Pottery) culture. Silkworms found in archaeological sites.

16th–11th centuries BCE

China's Shang dynasty.
The character for silk is found on oracle bones.

First millennium BCE

Early Chinese texts.
Folk songs refer to silk weaving and silk textiles.

Interrelated ecological zones in Eurasia

From ca. 8000 BCE

Localization within three ecological zones: the urban-agricultural, the pastoral, and the Taiga Forest. Plant domestication in urban-agricultural zone and animal domestication in pastoral zone.

ca. 6000 BCE	Cows and other animals domesticated in pastoral zone.
ca. 4000 BCE	Horse domesticated in pastoral zone.
Fourth to second millennium BCE	Emergence of early urban civilizations in agricultural zone.
By 1750 BCE	Charioteers appear on the steppe.
1700–1500 BCE	Charioteeers begin to overrun urban-agricultural zone. Appearance of early empires thereafter including: Mycenae in Greece (ca. 1600 BCE) China's Shang dynasty (16th–11th centuries BCE) Vedic peoples in India (ca. 1500 BCE)
ca. 600 BCE	Cavalries appear on the steppe.
ca. 200 BCE	The ecological frontier between steppe and sown. Urban-agricultural from east to west: Qin-Han China, India's Mauryan Empire, Parthia. Hellenistic kingdoms, and Rome: Pastoralists from east to west: Xiongnu, Yuezhi, and Sakas/Scythians.

Traders first began to carry silk, a lustrous, smooth, supple yet tough textile, westward out of China in the second century BCE. Prior to this time silk had long been abundant in China and practically unknown outside its frontiers. This was mainly because China had been relatively isolated from the other large urban-agricultural civilizations on the Eurasian landmass due to the formidable mountains and deserts that separated it from the others. Among these mountains are the Himalayas and the Karakorum, which together include the ten highest peaks in the world, ranging from 29,028 to 26,545 feet above sea level. Furthermore, some of the most used passes through them are as high as 18,000 feet above sea level. Although several deserts also separated the other urban-agricultural centers in Eurasia from each other, those deserts were not so difficult to cross as the ones near China. A thousand years before the silk roads emerged, caravans of one-humped dromedary camels had already been providing reliable transportation among them. Yet it was not until the silk roads emerged that the geographic obstacles west of China were surmounted and China's interactions with the other agricultural civilizations became significant.

The roads going in and out of China that crossed these geographical obstacles were new in the second century BCE. However, once the traders reached various parts of central Asia, Iran, and India, they traveled roads that were already long established. Thus, from the very beginning of the trade, silk was carried westward for many thousands of miles, thereby linking together for the first time the eastern and western ends of the vast Eurasian landmass, the Earth's largest expanse of *terra firma*. The land routes would maintain their significance for about fourteen centuries, and the overseas routes for even longer, creating unprecedented connections and exchanges, both commercial and cultural, between Eurasia's eastern and western shores, and among all those who lived in between.

The peoples who participated in the creation and development of the routes were numerous and diverse. They included both urban and agricultural peoples who lived within the empires that stretched across the Eurasian landmass, as well as nomadic peoples who lived on the grasslands north of the empires, moving their herds and their homes from one place to another according to the seasons and the local circumstances. Both of these populations would be major players in the development of the silk trade. In addition, south of the empires lay the southern seas and oceans, where sailors of many different origins had long before pioneered various maritime routes through the Persian Gulf and the Red Sea, thereby linking India to both Mesopotamia and Egypt. Sailors on the Red Sea and the Arabian Sea, for example, would play an important role in the earliest maritime silk route, which emerged in the first century CE, connecting Indian ports (to which the silk was brought overland) with the eastern territories of the Roman Empire, one of the most important markets for Chinese silk. And several centuries later sailors from Southeast Asia would develop a sea route that went between Sri Lanka and China, significantly increasing the commercial traffic between India and China.

THE SILK

Although silk was only one of many products that traders carried along these routes, it is not surprising that historians now refer to these networks as the silk roads. Silk played a crucial role in the origins of some of the most critical routes and it became one of the most important products on all of the roads that the silk traders used. What is surprising is that when the first silk roads emerged, silk was not a new product, at least not in China. In the second century BCE its production had already been a Chinese preoccupation for more than a thousand years. However, throughout all that time it had remained exclusively a Chinese product and was unknown beyond China's frontiers.

Silk was one of the very first textiles ever produced in China and can be dated back to the earliest years of its civilization. Silkworms have been found at an archaeological site in northern China that belongs to the Yangshao (or Painted Pottery) culture, which is dated from 4800 to 3000 BCE. At another site dated to the Shang dynasty (sixteenth to the eleventh centuries BCE) archaeologists have found the character for silk written on oracle bones. In addition, some of China's earliest texts (which date from the early first millennium BCE) include folk songs that refer to silk weaving and silk textiles.

By the time the silk roads emerged, silk had long been the most common and the most ordinary textile in China. Although today, as in the past, people outside China still think of silk only as an expensive luxury, in China it was not just a luxury material. It was used to clothe both ordinary people and the elites. While it is true that government workshops did produce elaborate and exquisite silk textiles such as brocades, tapestries, and intricately embroidered materials that common people could not afford (and during some dynasties were not allowed to wear), village women produced great quantities of less expensive varieties of silk cloth, and these were used by the overwhelming majority of the people to make their everyday, ordinary clothing. (Although today cotton is ubiquitous in China and has replaced silk as the most common textile, it was totally unknown there prior to the development of the silk roads. Cotton was first produced on the Indian subcontinent, and was introduced to China via the silk roads as a foreign-made luxury product. The cotton plant was not grown in China until many centuries after the silk roads emerged.)

Like many materials that humans have used to cover themselves, silk is made from an animal product, but it is unique in that its filaments come not from a fellow mammal, but from an insect, the larva of the silk moth. Each silkworm (the larva) produces a single extraordinarily long filament, a single strand of silk, in order to wrap itself inside a cocoon, from which the adult moth eventually emerges, provided that the cocoon is not used to make silk. In fact, it is the unusual length of the filaments that makes silk yarn and thus silk cloth so smooth, lustrous, and strong. Although there are many species of silk moths, the Chinese over many centuries selected out the one species that made the strongest and longest filament.

Harvesting these filaments was a difficult, arduous task. While the men were tending crops in the fields, the village women saved silk moth eggs and tended mulberry trees. In the spring, the eggs would hatch out into worms, which have a voracious appetite for the early, tender leaves of the mulberry tree. The process of keeping the worms fed day and night lasted about one and a half months, by which time the insects were ready to spin the silk filaments that would form their cocoons. The women then attached the worms to fake tree branches so that they dangled from the branch, ensuring that they would spin their silk filaments into cylindrical cocoons. When the cocoons were finished, they boiled them so that the filament could be unwound. This was accomplished by teasing out the end of the strand while the cocoon was floating on steaming water, and then pulling on it until the cocoon was completely unraveled. This process required intensive labor, much skill, and was very hard on the women's fingers. The filaments were then rolled up, spun into yarn, and the yarn was woven into cloth.

Floss, another silk product, was made by placing worms that were ready to spin on a flat surface where they could not wrap themselves into a cylindrical cocoon. Instead, the worms' filaments spread out over the surface and built up soft fluffy wads of silk. (Silk floss bears no resemblance to the plastic strings now used for dental hygiene.) This material was used to stuff quilted fabrics, which were made into bedding or robes and jackets. Along with the various sorts of silk cloth, some of the floss was traded locally. It was also traded to the steppe nomads on China's northern frontier where floss (as well as the quilted bedding and clothing made with it) were much appreciated during the freezing cold winters on the northern grasslands.

THREE INTERRELATED ECOLOGICAL ZONES

The Eurasian silk roads, the roads that would carry China's silks westward, arose amidst an economic, social, and political context that had been evolving for thousands of years, at least since the emergence of the Eastern Hemisphere's first urban-agricultural civilizations from the fourth to the second millennium BCE. Three of these early civilizations were in Eurasia—in Mesopotamia along the Tigris and Euphrates rivers (in present-day Iraq), along the Indus River (in present-day Pakistan), and along the Yellow River (in present-day China). Yet another was in northeastern Africa along the Nile (in present-day Egypt). Since the early Egyptian civilization was adjacent to the Eurasian landmass and connected to it by a narrow land passage as well as by Red Sea sailors, it became an integral part of the Eurasian experience, and the story of the Eurasian silk roads cannot be told without it.

In the vicinity of each of these early areas of urban civilization there were three distinct but interdependent ecological zones—the agricultural, the pastoral, and the forested. This ecological divide occurred soon after the end of the last Ice Age approximately 10,000 years ago. Thus, the emergence and development of a different way of life within each of these zones predated the emergence of the urban civilizations by many millennia. People within all three ecological zones had long been adapting to and changing their own habitats and had begun to take advantage of the distinct resources within each of these environments.

In both hemispheres, in places where climate, soils, and water supplies made agriculture fruitful, people who would become farmers domesticated wild plants and subsequently became more sedentary, which is to say, more closely tied to their fields of rooted, immobile plants. In contrast, almost exclusively in the Eastern Hemisphere and especially on the Eurasian steppe, people carried out another sort of domestication, the domestication of the wild grass-eating animals that flourished there. Wild cattle, horses, and sheep, for example, had thrived on these grasslands, and like the farmers in sedentary lands who became dependent upon their domesticated plants, the herders of the Eurasian steppe became dependent for their food supply upon their domesticated animals. The peoples of the forests also became localized, depending upon forest products available in their areas. Thus, they became expert hunters of wild animals, gathered plants and their products, and also collected and traded useful stones and minerals.

INSIDE THE URBAN-AGRICULTURAL ZONE

In urban areas large numbers of people live in close proximity to each other, much too close together for every family to grow its own food, raise domesticated animals, or supply other sorts of needs within the urban boundaries. Thus, the earliest urban civilizations arose in places where nearby agricultural areas could produce a food surplus large enough to support an urban population. In order to carry out their usual economic functions, as well as to fulfill other sorts of needs and obligations, the city dwellers had to exchange their services or trade goods for the supplies that came from the agricultural areas. Thus, the ancient cities were centers for trade and exchange from their very origin.

In addition, people in the urban-agricultural zones required goods that had to be brought from faraway places. This was particularly true with regard to minerals such as copper and tin. Both the city dwellers and the farmers that lived nearby were also dependent upon pastoral peoples who lived on the vast Eurasian steppe where they tended their domesticated herds. The pastoralists supplied animals for agricultural labor and transportation and animal products such as meat and leather. In addition, peoples who lived in the forests north of the steppe possessed products that city people desired such as gold, high-quality furs, and amber (a fossilized tree resin that was made into beads).

Among the three distinct ways of life that the ecological zones supported, it was agriculture that was the most secure. Even though natural disasters brought about by prolonged droughts, floods, and pests caused massive famines from time to time, farmers and their governments were often wise enough to store food grains in times of good harvests in order to relieve the miseries of misfortunes and ensure survival in bad times. Furthermore, a well-structured government could transport food from regions of good harvests to famine-stricken areas to provide minimal life support. Also, the markets in agricultural societies accumulated grains that could be purchased and transported to areas where crops had failed.

Inside the Pastoral Zone

The Eurasian steppe lies north of the urban-agricultural zone, with its eastern end on the Mongolian plateau directly north of China and its western end in Eastern Europe, on the plains of Hungary. It is an enormous expanse of grasslands only occasionally interrupted by mountains and deserts. In comparison to what historians have learned about the ancient urban and agricultural zone, relatively little is known about the peoples who lived on the Eurasian steppe, especially in the millennia that preceded the emergence of the silk roads in the second century BCE. Although the archaeological record indicates that all the groups had similar material cultures as well as similar belief systems, the texts from ancient writers make clear that they spoke quite different languages. None of the steppe peoples had a written language until much later, so what historians do know comes mainly from descriptions of them written by outsiders from the sedentary agricultural societies. Other information about them comes from various present-day academic pursuits, such as linguistic studies of the names of tribes and places, archaeology carried out on the steppe, and anthropological studies of present-day tribes.

The steppe people who maintained herds of animals were nomads, a term that refers to people who move frequently from place to place. They lived in portable tents, and within their own territories, they moved their herds and themselves on a regular basis to take advantage of the locales where the grazing was good and sources of water were reliable. At roughly the same time that farmers in the agricultural areas had been domesticating plants, they had been domesticating animals. And like the farmers' knowledge of plants and their agricultural skills, the nomads' knowledge of animals and their pastoral skills had been developing over many millennia prior to the emergence of the urban civilizations.

Due to the steppe's more northern and significantly drier location, it was not well suited for cultivation. Its frost-free growing season was short, and precipitation was limited. The lack of abundant rainfall also meant that forests did not flourish there. The grasslands of the steppe, however, were ideally suited for pastoralists with their herds of domesticated grazing animals. In the driest areas Bactrian camels, the two-humped variety, were the most common domesticated animals. Along the mountains' foothills, pastoral peoples drove their livestock—cattle, yaks, or sheep— from lowland to highland or vice versa according to the season. Throughout most of the Eurasian steppe, however, it was the peoples with great herds of horses on the open steppe who were predominant.

Because the peoples of the grasslands became dependent on domesticated grazing animals rather than plants, they were much more mobile than farmers. The health of their animals required them to move their herds and their own homes, which were portable, on a regular basis. Usually these movements were seasonal and, in any case, they were designed to position their herds in the best possible place at any given time. Even though they usually did not use any single location throughout the year and generally did not mark their boundaries, they knew intimately all the lands they used. They would defend their possession of these lands and their right to exclude interlopers from them year-round, whether or not they were actually living at a particular place when an intruder appeared. This was especially the case if intruders failed to properly acknowledge the pastoralists' rights immediately upon arrival in their territory and thus did not receive permission to be on their lands.

The horse-raising nomads pitched their tents on the grasslands wherever they were staying for the season, and sustained themselves with dairy products and meat, along with whatever plant foods were available. The tents, covered with animal skins or felt, were durable and weather-resistant, providing comfortable homes wherever they might go. Most of the tents were sparsely furnished, but some, especially after the silk trade began, were made into magnificent, palatial rooms where the chiefs held court. To please themselves, impress guests, and demonstrate wealth, status, and power, the walls could be hung with beautiful textiles and the floors covered with sumptuous carpets. Although the nomads produced some woolen textiles themselves, they often had more wool than they could weave on their relatively small portable looms. In good years the steppe communities also had plenty of animals and animal products such as wool and furs, which they could trade for the products of the agricultural zone, returning to the steppe with fine tapestries, carpets, and other sorts of cloth. Their winter coats, for example, were made from their own sheep skins, with the fur on the inside and the inner side of the skin on the outside. The outside of the coat was then covered with some textile, often one that came from the agricultural zone.

The mobility of the nomads appears to have fostered an extraordinary amount of cultural exchange among the various tribes and confederacies, so much so that archaeologists often find it nearly impossible to tell which steppe sites belonged to which nomads. Although each group moved within its own territorial boundaries during normal times, they were much inclined toward trade, and often made contact with each other to exchange goods. Also, to avoid an imminent danger (natural or political) they could quickly pack up their tents and herd their livestock away at a moment's notice. Fighting over resources or for political dominance among the tribes also prompted many migrations. This mobility resulted in frequent encounters, and thus new ideas or beliefs, as well as elements of material culture (including utensils, tools, housing, clothing, and the designs on them) could spread from one end of the steppe to the other in very little time. While it is true that nomads packed up their belongings and took everything along with them when they moved, leaving very little behind for archaeologists to study, the more basic problem in steppe archaeology is that the material cultures of the different nomads were so much alike.

Conditions on the steppe varied significantly. The Mongolian plateau, at its eastern end, was the highest in altitude and also the driest region. In general, the further west one went, the altitude became lower, precipitation increased, the grass grew higher, and more livestock could be supported. Thus, when a group decided to leave their territory and move elsewhere, they tended to migrate westward, going in the direction that the grass became more abundant. As a result, throughout much of history, the western edge of the steppe, that is, the grasslands of Hungary, tended to be the receiving end of the largest number of waves of nomad migrations, peaceful or otherwise.

Compared to the people in the agricultural zone, the livelihood and the lives of peoples of the pastoral steppe were less secure than those in the agricultural zone. Although the nomads much preferred their highly mobile way of life and did not envy the farmers who were tied to a particular spot by their immobile crops, they were fundamentally more vulnerable. Their migrations from one place to another could be an ordeal fraught with mortal dangers. In addition, unlike the farmers' grains, their meat and dairy products could not be stored for long. Sustained droughts or winter storms could decimate their herds and leave the people truly desperate. In such situations they either had to appeal to the generosity of other tribes, or take what they needed from other tribes or from farming villages on the frontier.

The earliest agricultural empires on the Eurasian landmass were somewhat distant from each other and had relatively little contact with each other until sometime after 1000 BCE. As mentioned earlier, the much more mobile pastoral peoples on the steppe had so much contact with each other that their archaeological remains are remarkably similar. The nomads also were often in contact with two or more of the agricultural empires, and thus they established sporadic and tenuous but sometimes significant links among them even in very ancient times. Furthermore, it is now clear to historians that the nomads also served as north-south go-betweens, providing the products of the Taiga Forests, which were near the Arctic Circle, to the agricultural areas and vice versa.

INSIDE THE TAIGA FOREST ZONE

On the northern edge of the steppe, not far from the Arctic Circle, were dense coniferous forests known as Taiga Forests. Neither agriculture nor pastoralism was possible in this environment. Nevertheless, there were peoples who understood the virtues of the place, took advantage of what it offered, and sustained themselves by hunting the forest-dwelling animals, gathering the products of forest plants, and collecting various useful or attractive stones and minerals. Even though their way of life survived into modern times, very little is known about these peoples until long after the silk roads emerged. Like the pastoralists they did not have a written language, and unlike the pastoralists, they did not live on or near the frontiers of the urban agricultural zone where scholars wrote about the neighboring peoples.

The peoples of the Taiga Forest had numerous contacts with the nomads, but no one recorded their lives or even their existence. Nevertheless, there must have been trade between the forest people and the nomads since rare furs from sables and bears made their way to China. Although the nomads, themselves, were excellent hunters, these furs came only from the northern forests, and thus the only way that nomads could have acquired them was through trade with the forest peoples. Other forest products that were sought by the nomads were gold and fossilized resins such as amber. Even though these items were highly valued, they did not come with trademarks or labels indicating their origins, so the city dwellers who possessed them associated them with the steppe nomads and remained oblivious to their true origins.

Another way historians have learned about contacts between the horse-back-riding nomads and the peoples of the Taiga Forest is from numerous gold plates that have been found on the steppe and nearby. The Siberian portion of the Taiga Forest was a major source of gold nuggets and there are numerous ancient gold plates that portray forest scenes even though they were found in areas associated with nomads. (These plates are known as Scythian plates, since they were first associated with nomads known as Scythians, who lived on the western part of the steppe.) The most common motifs on these plates are animals. Although some of the plates portray the domesticated animals of the steppe such as horses, sheep, and cows, a common subject on the earliest plates are reindeer, and on some of the later plates there are many wild forest animals such as leopards, eagles, and bears. The natural habitat of these animals was limited to the very northern edge of the steppe, in the transition area between the grasslands and the forest. Later still, the horse took the dominant place in this Scythian art form.

Historians believe that some nomads were originally forest people who had made the transition from hunting and gathering in the forests to pastoralism on the steppe. One reason they believe this is that some steppe tribes trace their ancestry back to totem animals such as the deer, the wolf, or the reindeer, a common custom in the forest areas, but not on the steppe. Also in historical times some nomadic tribes seem to have appeared on the steppe suddenly, out of nowhere, first appearing as a formidable force. The Mongols, a powerful confederacy that arose in the late twelfth century CE, are one example of such a group, and they trace their mythic ancestry to a male wolf and a doe, which suggests that they were originally from the forested zone. Historians of the steppe have also suggested that the Mongols may not have been the first steppe power whose original home was within the Taiga Forest zone. There may have been others who suddenly appeared on the steppe during the first millennium BCE, but it is impossible to identify them because there is so little information about forest or steppe peoples from that time period.

EXCHANGES AMONG THE ZONES

It was the various peoples' mutual desires for each other's products, many of which came from a specific ecological niche—urban-agricultural, pastoral, or forested—that shaped the various patterns of trade and communication among them. While the cities in the agricultural zone, the nomadic herders on the grasslands, and the hunters and gatherers in the forests all controlled their own specialized resources and produced for their own basic needs, they also needed or desired some products from other zones to improve their quality of life. Around each of the urban centers, the dynamics of the interchanges among the different ecological zones was one of the major forces stimulating the formation of regional networks of trade and communications. By the last centuries BCE these sorts of regional networks had become highly elaborated and were a significant part of the context from which the silk roads emerged.

Although mutual needs and desires stimulated this interaction among the peoples of the various ecological zones, the contacts that resulted did not necessarily create good relations among them. The customs and beliefs of the peoples within each zone were different, and encounters often created conflicts. Furthermore, contact was generally limited to a few intermediaries. The rest of the population within a zone knew little about their trading partners or the societies from which they came. With few exceptions, urban people in antiquity were not aware of the history and cultures of other peoples, neither those of the surrounding agricultural and pastoral communities (whom they often considered inferior) nor those of peoples living farther away (whom they often thought of as barbarian). As the urban civilizations, along with their nearby agricultural populations, developed and expanded, their contacts with other societies increased and there were more conflicts among them. Although scholars, who were only a miniscule part of the urban population, began to record increasing amounts of information about other peoples' products and customs, conflicts arose nevertheless and often caused the urban centers to attempt to control larger areas by military means. Empires emerged and expanded, and expeditions took soldiers to remote regions.

THE SIGNIFICANCE OF HORSES

Sometime around 6000 BCE cattle became one of the first domesticates on the Eurasian steppe, and by sometime around 4000 BCE peoples on the steppe had domesticated horses. Initially its importance was due mostly to its milk and its meat, but eventually, from a world historical perspective, the horse's greatest significance became its use as a means of transportation, especially military transportation. Not long after 2000 BCE the horse would become the power source par excellence for militaries, and would remain so for almost 4,000 years, first as a result of the horse-drawn chariot and later due to the development of cavalries. It was not until very recently, in the last part of the eighteenth century CE, that steam engines diminished the military significance of horses. And it was not until the late nineteenth and early twentieth century, about one hundred years ago, that horses truly lost their military significance due to the growing availability of vehicles with gasoline engines.

The appearance of the horse-drawn chariot sometime around 1750 BCE brought about a major military revolution all across Eurasia. Historians have little knowledge of where or how peoples in antiquity first put together this combination of cart mechanics and horse power, but it is clear that whoever's armies possessed the horse-drawn chariots soon began to enjoy military superiority. Prior to this time, most sedentary, agricultural peoples, which is to say those not living on or near the Eurasian steppe, were not familiar with horses, but soon thereafter armies led by charioteers began leaving the steppes and crossing into many agricultural areas.

Between 1700 and 1500 BCE charioteers overran much of Southwest Asia ("the Middle East"), and thereafter agricultural peoples who lived near the steppe also began to use the horse-drawn chariot to establish empires. On the shores of the Mediterranean, by 1600 BCE Mycenaean charioteers would play a major role in establishing the cultural and geographic foundations of what became classical Greece. The charioteers of the Shang dynasty (sixteenth to eleventh centuries BCE) gained ascendancy over the Yellow River valley of northern China, thereby establishing the groundwork for China's imperial foundations. At roughly the same time the chariot-riding Vedic peoples (ca. 1500 BCE) came to dominate the more northern parts of the Indian subcontinent. Eventually the Vedic people settled on the Indian subcontinent as farmers and by the sixth century BCE Vedic culture was evolving into Brahmanism, which subsequently had a significant impact throughout the subcontinent.

At roughly the same time that great urban-agricultural empires began to rise and fall south of the Eurasian steppe, the peoples of the grasslands also began to coalesce, creating large political structures called confederacies. Nomad confederacies were quite different from the armies of the sedentary empires. Unlike the typical ruler of a sedentary empire, a leader on the steppe could not conscript soldiers. However, a charismatic, talented leader with a reputation for military success and skillful diplomacy could attract an increasingly large group of followers. Other steppe leaders might ally with him voluntarily, or their followers might leave them in order to join the man whose reputation was growing.

Furthermore, it sometimes happened that after a battle, the victor might invite the defeated leader and his followers to join the victorious force. Although at times such an invitation might be considered coercive and would not necessarily lead to complete trust among all parties, there was no dishonor involved in leaving a defeated leader and joining the victor. Thus, a talented leader could become the head of a large confederacy, a grand alliance, that included many different lineages and even unrelated pastoral peoples with quite different languages, religions, and traditions. The allegiance of such tribes to the confederacy remained conditional, however, and if the confederacy suffered a serious defeat or if the charismatic leader died, tribes or individuals would regroup under another strong leader, should one appear. They considered their relationship to be one with the leader, personally, and not necessarily with his tribe or the confederacy.

Around 600 BCE, about a millennium after the appearance of the horse and chariot, cavalries appeared on the steppe, bringing about a second military revolution that relied on horses. Warriors no longer rode in chariots behind a horse, but on the horse's back, with bow and arrows close at hand. With the coming of such cavalries, the skills that steppe pastoralists learned from childhood in order to manage and protect their herds were just as useful for military purposes. Peoples of the steppe thereafter developed formidable military power, in large part due to their horses numbers and their equestrian skills, and the steppe's military capabilities would be essentially uncontainable by the sedentary societies for more than 2,000 years.

At about the same time the cavalries appeared, farmers in most of Eurasia's urban-agricultural zones began to rely more heavily on draft animals for plowing and transportation. This development brought about an even more complicated relationship between the agricultural societies and the nomadic peoples on the steppe. Since the agricultural areas could not supply the demand for these animals locally, either in terms of quantity or quality, the importation of horses and other draft animals from the steppe became a major concern for both farmers and governments. As long as the agricultural societies could produce a surplus of plant foods, textiles, and other goods, they could easily trade these products for the nomadic pastoralists' animals. However, just when the farmers began to need increasing numbers of these animals, the nomads and their cavalries were becoming increasingly formidable. First the nomads and then the empires began to defend their interests and their territories with cavalries of horseback-riding archers, and tensions between these two zones increased.

The mobility of the nomads on the Eurasian steppe, as well as their propensity for exchange, was quite remarkable in the ancient world. Their mobility also made it possible for them to overrun agricultural areas and settle there as either rulers or subjects. Waves of nomads from the steppe would shock the urban-agricultural parts of the Eurasian world several times in recorded history. Historians know much more about the encounters of nomads and sedentary peoples after 600 BCE, when the written record is more voluminous, and it was during this time when cavalries prevailed, that this story of trade and communications along the steppe-sown frontier begins.

It was also within this context that the Eurasian silk trade emerged. This trade in Chinese silks would bring about exchanges of peoples, goods, and knowledge throughout the Eurasian landmass as well as North Africa, and, not surprisingly, this trade would have an impact on all of the ecological regions and all of the peoples in the lands between China and the Mediterranean. Nor should it be surprising to learn that nomadic peoples of the steppe would be the principal instigators behind the emergence of the silk roads. Thereafter, China and its frontiers would no longer be the only place in the world where silk was known, and China would no longer be isolated from the other urban-agricultural areas. For the first time there would be significant, sustained exchanges, commercial and cultural, between China and the peoples involved in the long-distance trade networks that stretched westward all the way to the Mediterranean Sea.

TIMELINE

Fifth century BCE Nomad cavalries become a serious threat to China's steppe frontier.

403–221 BCE Warring States period, during which seven kingdoms competed for imperial hegemony in China.

325–299 BCE Reign of King Wuling of Zhao, one of the warring kingdoms. He transformed his army of charioteers into cavalries.

221 BCE The state of Qin, after defeating the other Warring States, created a single Chinese empire.

221–210 BCE The reign of Qin Shihuangdi. He oversaw the construction of the first Great Wall, built for defense against the steppe cavalries of the Xiongnu. Horses for his cavalries were acquired from the Yuezhi, and the emperor gave the Yuezhi chief Luo a rank in the Qin court equal to that of his highest ministers.

207 BCE The Qin dynasty is overthrown.

206 BCE–221 CE The Han dynasty. During the early part of the dynasty its rulers, out of weakness, appeased the Xiongnu nomads by giving them large quantities of silks and food grains.

140–87 BCE The reign of Han Wudi. By this time the Han is militarily strong. Emperor Wudi extends the Great Wall to Yumen.

139 BCE Emperor Wudi sends Zhang Qian out onto the steppe to find the Yuezhi, hoping to form a military alliance with them against the Xiongnu. Taken prisoner by the Xiongnu, he is held for ten years.

Ca. 130 BCE Due to defeat by the Xiongnu, the Yuezhi flee westward, and settle in what was once Bactria.

129 BCE Zhang Qian finds the Yuezhi in Bactria, then known to the Indians as Tuhara. Stays approximately one year.

126 BCE	Zhang Qian finally makes his way back to China and reports to Emperor Wudi about the Western Regions.
104 BCE	Emperor Wudi sends an army under General Li Guangli to Ferghana to acquire additional "heavenly horses." Along with the horses, alfalfa and grape vines were introduced to China.
48–33 BCE	Reign of Emperor Yuandi. He established an alliance with one of the Xiongnu leaders. To mark the significance of the alliance, he presented the Xiongnu leader Huhanxie a Chinese wife, Wang Zhaojun, a royal princess from his own harem.

THE ORIGINS OF THE SILK ROADS: SILKS AND HORSES ON THE CHINESE FRONTIER

> **GETTING STARTED ON CHAPTER ONE:** What was the nature of the relationship between steppe pastoralists and farming villages on China's northern frontier? What role did horses and silk play in the dynamic between steppe and sown? What policies did the Qin and Han dynasties develop to deal with problems on this frontier? What sort of cultural exchanges occurred across this frontier? How did people in other parts of Eurasia discover the value of silk?

CHAPTER OUTLINE

Steppe vs. Sown on the Chinese Frontier

The Xiongnu, the Yuezhi, and the Chinese

The Yuezhi-Kushan in Tuhara (Formerly Bactria)

The Political, Cultural, and Symbolic Significance of Horses, Chariots, and Silk

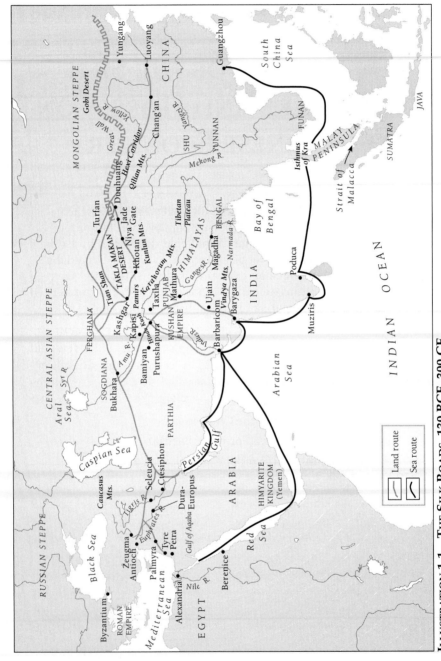

ILLUSTRATION 1-1 THE SILK ROADS, 130 BCE–300 CE

(Source: Used with permission from *Traditions and Encounters* (2nd ed.), by Jerry H. Bentley and Herbert F. Zieglar. Copyright 2003 by McGraw-Hill.)

STEPPE VS. SOWN ON THE CHINESE FRONTIER

Cross-cultural trade among peoples of diverse ecological environments is a common occurrence, especially when they do not live too far apart and the routes are reliable at least some of the time. This was certainly the case on the frontier between urban-agricultural China and the pastoral steppe. The pastoralists came to the frontier with horses for China's elites, donkeys and other animals needed by farmers, wool, leather, and other animal products in short supply in China, as well as precious stones such as jade, which could be found in the mountain ranges on and near the grasslands. Chinese who lived relatively near this frontier generally came with food grains, such as millet and wheat, and silk products to exchange for the steppe products. In the second century BCE when the silk roads emerged, this frontier trade, in one form or another, was already many millennia old. And, one might add, even though the silk roads lost much of their significance several centuries ago, the frontier trade across this ecological divide has persisted in China, even to the present day.

As early as the fifth century BCE, hostilities had become endemic all along the Chinese frontier and it was within this context of both hostilities and trade that the first silk roads emerged. The earliest roads were overland routes that carried Chinese silks westward from this frontier to other urban-agricultural centers of Eurasia, thereby beginning the processes that would end China's relative isolation from the other major urban-agricultural centers. For more than twelve centuries, until about 1100 CE when maritime routes took precedence, such overland routes would continue to carry the bulk of the traffic in Chinese silks.

THE XIONGNU, THE YUEZHI, AND THE CHINESE

The origin of the earliest silk roads was rooted in the complicated relationships between urban-agricultural China and two different pastoral peoples from the Eurasian steppe. The Chinese called one of these peoples by the name Xiongnu. They lived on the grasslands directly north of China in present-day Mongolia and spoke a language related to later Turkic languages. For much of history these grasslands on the Mongolian highlands were actually the home of Turkic, not Mongolian-speaking peoples, but because the Mongolian-speaking peoples were the last to live there, and remain there today, it is now referred to as the Mongolian plateau. Chinese historians recorded the names of Xiongnu rulers and various Xiongnu terms such as *Shanyu*, the word for chief. Nevertheless, the number of Xiongnu words occurring in Chinese documents are far too few even to begin to re-construct the language. It is also clear from the Chinese records that the Xiongnu were not just one tribe, but a powerful confederation of many tribes, and it is unlikely that all of these tribes spoke the same language. Just as in later times, when there is much more detailed information, tribes speaking different languages either voluntarily joined or, after a defeat, were invited to submit to the leader of the victorious confederation in order to join his forces. Presumably the language of the chief's tribe would become the *lingua franca* for the entire confederacy, at least as long as it lasted.

The Yuezhi were the other nomads with whom the Chinese were in-volved. They lived northwest of China where they were concentrated on the grasslands north of the Tian Shan (literally the Heavenly Mountains) in what is now China's Xinjiang Uighur Autonomous Region. Although today Xinjiang is a part of China, during the Han dynasty it was outside Chinese boundaries and was then thought of as a part of the Western Re-gions, a term that referred to both Central Asia and the Indian subconti-nent, and more vaguely, any place west of them. The Yuezhi were similar to the Xiongnu in many respects. They too were horseback-riding archers and they too were without a written language at this point in time. As in the case of the Xiongnu, much of what is known about them comes from accounts written by Han Chinese. Scholars now believe that they were one of several groups who spoke Tuharan. This language has been classified as an Indo-European language, distantly related to Persian and more closely related to the languages of various Indo-European-speaking tribes who eventually migrated to the more western parts of the steppe. Although, compared to the Xiongnu, they lived relatively distant from China, they had long been known to the Chinese as jade traders.

When steppe cavalries first became a serious threat to northern China in the fifth century BCE, China was in a historical period known as the Warring States. Still using horse-drawn chariots, seven major independent kingdoms in the Yellow and Yangzi River valleys were fighting against each other, each hoping for supremacy over all the others. In addition, whenever there was a breakdown in peaceful trade with the nomads on the northern frontier, the three northernmost states, Qin, Zhao, and Yan, had to contend with raids carried out by steppe cavalries. Long before any Chinese armed forces could arrive on the scene, the nomads could race into a village or town, load stores of silk textiles and food grains onto their horses, and race out again.

In response to these raids each of the three northern states built sturdy walls that climbed up and down through the hills and mountains that divided agricultural China from the pastoral regions. These walls proved to be a useful aid in the Chinese effort to defend their villages from such incursions. Even if the nomads could dismount and climb over the walls, their horses could not, and if the raiders stopped long enough to break holes in the wall for the horses, they made themselves vulnerable to counterattack. Nevertheless, though the walls were useful, they were not sufficient to overcome the larger military problem of trying to fend off steppe cavalries, at a time when China's soldiers were still riding in horse-drawn chariots.

Given this situation, King Wuling (325–299 BCE) of Zhao, one of the rulers who directly faced the Xiongnu across the northern frontier, responded by carrying out a radical reform of his army, transforming his charioteers into a horseback-riding cavalry. In the process of building this expert cavalry, he ordered both his officers and ordinary soldiers to change their style of clothing. The loose, long-sleeved tops and ankle-length skirts that Chinese men wore at that time were unsuitable for horseback riding, so King Wuling ordered his soldiers to abandon their Chinese clothes and put on nomad-style narrow-sleeved, knee-length robes and trousers. In addition he made them practice archery from horseback.

Even though Wuling's reforms improved Zhao's military situation, they caused much unhappiness in the military, and the civilian critics of King Wuling were numerous as well. The principal complaint was that his reforms were "un-Chinese," and thereby undermined Chinese customs by forcing alien ways upon his subjects. By this time the cultural gap between steppe and sown had long since created separate and very different customs and value systems on the two sides of this divide, and each side had developed negative attitudes about the other and its culture. The nomads used their own steppe values of right and wrong to judge the Chinese people they dealt with on the frontier and concluded that they were mercenary and unreliable. On the other side, the Chinese saw themselves as civilized and just, and considered the nomads to be "barbarians" who lacked a high culture (by which they meant a written, classical literature) and were all too ready to resort to brute force to settle disputes. Thus, when King Wuling ordered his armies to wear nomad-style clothes and to develop skills associated only with nomads, many felt that his policies were disgraceful and undermined the values of Chinese culture. Nevertheless, his reforms prevailed and other northern states followed his example out of military necessity.

The walls and the cavalries improved the ability of the three northern states to respond to nomadic raids, but many problems remained, especially with regard to organizing and maintaining Chinese cavalries. Cavalries require large numbers of horses, and the supply of horses in China was limited. In order to remain healthy, horses need large pastures for grazing. Otherwise, maintaining healthy horses requires a very expensive and labor-intensive effort. In China, however, the farmers had long since turned the bulk of the land into fields devoted to the cultivation of food grains and vegetables for humans. In economic terms, the value of the food crops for humans was so great that farmers were unwilling to use land for pastures or hayfields. Consequently the Chinese did not have much knowledge of or experience in raising and training horses, especially military horses. In eastern Eurasia it was only on the steppe, where growing conditions in most places did not favor the production of food grains for humans, that the great grasslands remained, horses were numerous, and human knowledge and experience with horses and their training were extensive. Consequently China was faced with the problem of acquiring horses from nomads with whom they often had hostile relations.

Fortunately for the rulers of these Chinese states there were some pastoral nomads who were not always hostile to them, and one confederation of pastoralists in particular, the Yuezhi, was to become famous as China's trading partner. According to Chinese accounts from the seventh century BCE, that is, even prior to the development of endemic hostilities on the Chinese frontier, the Yuezhi were jade traders as well as pastoralists. Jade has been highly prized by Chinese peoples from the very beginnings of their history, and they treasured it even more than gold. Jade items have been found in abundance in the tombs of China's most ancient rulers, and archaeologists have traced most of the jade in these tombs to sites around Khotan, an oasis town south of the Tian Shan range, on the southern edge of the Takla Makan Desert in what is now China's Xinjiang Uighur Autonomous Region. Chinese texts also indicate that at least by the third century BCE the Yuezhi were already living north of the Tian Shan, between the western end of the mountains and the Turfan Depression. They were thus in an ideal position to serve as middlemen in the trade between the Chinese interior and the Western Regions. Consequently, during the Warring States period, when the northern Chinese desperately needed good horses for their new cavalries, they turned to the Yuezhi for their supply.

In 221 BCE the state of Qin (one of the states on China's northern frontier) brought an end to the Warring States period by defeating the other contending states and creating a single Chinese empire. The conqueror who accomplished this feat is known as Qin Shihuangdi (literally Qin's First Emperor). During the time that he was establishing the new imperial dynasty, China was in constant conflict with the Xiongnu. They had formed a powerful confederacy, and after the unification of China they became the foremost threat to the new emperor's power. In order to deal with frequent Xiongnu raids he embarked on an extraordinary project, to link together into one Great Wall all the walls along the northern frontier that had been built previously by the contending Chinese kingdoms of the Warring States period. Thus, the Great Wall was first and foremost a military defense system. Even so, it also had a significant impact on peaceful trade between nomads and sedentary people. Trade that had once been distributed all along the frontier suddenly became concentrated only at those places where there were gates in the Great Wall. It was only at these gates that peoples from both sides could easily make contact, and it was there that markets formed where farmers and herders could trade their products. (In subsequent centuries the walls along this frontier were rebuilt many times. The last time was during the Ming dynasty [1368–1644 CE].)

Qin Shihuangdi wanted more and more horses in order to build up his cavalries. One Yuezhi chief named Luo made a fortune by trading steppe horses for Chinese silks, which he then traded to other chiefs on the steppe for some of their horses, which he could then sell to the Chinese. According to the historian Sima Qian (ca. 145–86 BCE), Luo's profits from his horse-trading business were ten times the money that he had invested. This wealth made him not only rich but also powerful among the nomads, and Qin Shihuangdi showed his appreciation by granting Luo a position in the Qin court at the same rank as his highest ministers. The Yuezhi people thus became the great ally of the Qin Empire against the Xiongnu. The Qin dynasty, however, did not last long (221–207 BCE), and was soon overthrown from within and replaced by the Han dynasty (206 BCE–221 CE).

Since a devastating civil war had marked the end of the Qin, the new Han dynasty began its rule in a totally defensive position, especially with regard to the Xiongnu on the northern frontier. The situation was so bad that in one battle the Xiongnu surrounded the Han's founding emperor, Gaozong, and almost took him prisoner. The new dynasty also had severe financial problems, and was so impoverished that even the emperor could not afford a full team of four horses to pull his chariot, and his ministers had to ride in carts pulled by oxen. (Although the empire's fate by this time depended upon its cavalries, chariots were still used for the rulers' transportation and for ceremonial purposes.) Thus, Gaozong and the next few emperors had no choice but to try to appease the Xiongnu.

One way of appeasing the nomads was to send princesses from the Han court, some genuine and some not, to the Xiongnu chiefs to become their brides. Although sending Chinese princesses to nomad chiefs under these circumstances was considered to be a national humiliation, the emperors did this to avoid hostilities. They also had the hope that a son of one of the princesses would become the next nomad chief and establish more friendly relations with the Han. The Chinese brides brought with them a large dowry, mostly silks and food grains, and the Xiongnu chiefs in return presented horses as gifts to their fathers-in-law. It is not known whether or not the son of a Han princess ever became a Xiongnu chief during this early period, but even if one of them did, it is highly unlikely that he would have been able to change the attitude of the Xiongnu. The weddings and gift-exchanges, however, did provide some intervals of peace and trade around the gates of the Great Wall.

After more than sixty years of recovery, the Han Empire was strong enough to stop sending royal princesses to the nomads. When the very capable Emperor Wudi (140–87 BCE) assumed the throne, the Han went onto the offensive against the Xiongnu confederacy, who by this time could claim about 300,000 horseback-riding archers. Wudi sent Chinese cavalry expeditions out onto the steppe where they fought like traditional nomads, capturing herds of horses and sheep, and pushing their enemies further away. However, the Xiongnu, never considered retreat to be a defeat, just as they never intended to conquer and rule agricultural lands. Thus, in the absence of any real alliances, once the Chinese armies had returned home, the nomads resumed their raids on villages and towns in the border regions.

Emperor Wudi desperately needed military allies on the steppe in order to impose order along the border. Early in his reign, when news of conflict between the Xiongnu and the Yuezhi first reached the Han court, he decided to send an envoy to the Yuezhi to secure an alliance with this steppe power against the Xiongnu. Because the various officials under Emperor Wudi knew that whoever undertook the role of envoy would face an extremely dangerous journey into a nomadic region still unknown to the Chinese, no high-ranking dignitary was willing to accept this assignment. Thus, it happened that a man named Zhang Qian, a petty official, volunteered and was accepted for this fateful mission. Some time around 139 BCE he, along with a party of a hundred people, set off to find the Yuezhi court. One of the most important people in his party was Ganfu, a native of the steppe, who served Zhang Qian as an expert advisor on nomads.

The journey did not go well. Because it was the only route to the west that the Chinese knew, Zhang set off through territory controlled by the Xiongnu, and before he got very far, they had taken him prisoner. For ten years they would not allow him to leave their camp, apparently hoping that eventually he would join them. Consequently during the time that the Xiongnu were warring with the Yuezhi he was moved along with the Xiongnu camp as they traveled from place to place, and he took a Xiongnu wife and raised a family with her. Nevertheless, Zhang's loyalties remained with his homeland and he secretly kept his Chinese ambassadorial credential (most likely a rod) with him until finally, in 129 BCE he was able to escape with it.

Unfortunately from the point of view of his mission, Zhang's escape came one year too late. The Yuezhi had not fared well in their battles against the Xiongnu. The Xiongnu chief had captured and killed the Yuezhi chief and had his skull made into a drinking vessel, a symbol of victory on the steppe. Thus, some time around 130 BCE almost all the Yuezhi people, including some 100,000 to 200,000 horseback-riding archers, defeated and demoralized, had left their home pastures behind and galloped westward. They crossed the pastures north of the Tian Shan range and did not settle down until they had arrived at the north bank of the Amu River, as it is known today, or the Oxus River, as it was called by the ancient Greeks.

By then they were in a land that Zhang Qian referred to as Daxia and the ancient Greeks called Bactria. Located in the mountains and valleys north of the Indian subcontinent, in present-day terms it was in northeastern Afghanistan and in relatively small pieces of the adjacent parts of Uzbekistan and Tajikistan. For the most part, the land south of the Amu River, where the Yuezhi ultimately settled was a sedentary agricultural region with a long and diverse history. It had once been a part of the great Iranian empire of the Achaemenids, after its conquest by King Darius in the late sixth century BCE. Then in the late fourth century BCE, after the expedition of Alexander the Great, it had become part of the Hellenistic Seleucid territories. Later on, this region rebelled against the Seleucids and became an independent kingdom that continued to maintain many of its Hellenistic traditions. The Yuezhi soon became established in this Hellenized locale, a land that offered good pastures for horses and fertile fields for agriculture, as well as cities that had been much influenced by ancient Greek culture.

After Zhang Qian's escape from the Xiongnu, his search for the Yuezhi led him westward first to the region around Ferghana (which during the Han dynasty was located in what is now Uzbekistan along the banks of the Syr River). He got there only to find out that the Yuezhi tribes that he was looking for had left. A local chief gave him refuge and provided him with an escort to a place Zhang Qian called Kangju (Sogdiana, also in present-day Uzbekistan) and from there he made his way south to the banks of the Amu River and finally found the Yuezhi in 129 BCE. Zhang spent over a year at the Yuezhi court trying to persuade the new chief, a son of the chief killed by the Xiongnu, to make a military alliance with the Han dynasty and return to the Chinese frontier to fight the Xiongnu. Despite Zhang's best efforts, the new king remained unwilling to return to the Chinese frontier. Finally, Zhang gave up and decided to return home to China.

On his way home he was yet again captured by the Xiongnu, but managed to escape from them, this time after only one year. It was a civil war, following the death of the leader of the Xiongnu Confederacy, that afforded him an opportunity to get away, and he hastily returned home to the Han court, together with his Xiongnu wife and children and the loyal Ganfu, some thirteen years after his departure. Upon his arrival he made a report to the emperor and wrote an account of all that he had seen and heard during his long and perilous journey to the Western Regions.

Although Zhang had failed to forge a military alliance with the Yuezhi, the goal of his journey, he did manage to reestablish contacts with them despite the distances involved and the difficulties of traveling through these regions, and these contacts led directly to the resumption of Yuezhi trade with China. In addition, the information that he brought back had a significant impact on Chinese policy and the Chinese government's vision of the outside world. Having spent eleven years moving along with a nomad camp, he had become familiar with the geographic features of the steppe and also had learned much about the customs, values, and political structure of the Xiongnu and other nomadic peoples. Since the nomads at that time had no writing system and no written records, virtually all of our historical knowledge about them during this early time comes from his report.

In addition, Zhang wrote about places that he had only heard about such as Iran, the Indian subcontinent, and the eastern shores of the Mediterranean. Most of his information about India and places west of present-day Afghanistan probably came from merchants in Tuhara-Bactria's markets, who had themselves traveled to these lands. His account of India, for example, is brief, but fairly accurate. What historians now know is that Iran at that time was controlled by the Parthians. Like the Kushan, they too had been steppe nomads. Their original home had been near the southeastern shores of the Caspian Sea, but they had later migrated further south to northeastern Iran. In the middle of the third century they rebelled against the hegemony of the Hellenistic Seleucids,

Alexander's successors who at one point controlled most of the lands between India and the Mediterranean Sea. Due to this rebellion they were able to establish an independent kingdom in northeastern Iran. Taking advantage of the gradual erosion of Seleucid power in the second century BCE, they first gained control over almost all of Iran, and then, at about the same time that the Yuezhi consolidated their power in northern Afghanistan, they established themselves on the Tigris River in present-day Iraq. Once the Yuezhi silk trade began, the Parthians would be one of their most important trading partners.

It was also in these Yuezhi-controlled markets that Zhang Qian noticed a particular kind of bamboo and various textiles that he was sure were from the Shu region of China (present-day Sichuan Province). When he had asked where these products came from, the merchants told him that they were from India, which suggested to Zhang Qian that there were trade routes that linked India with the southwestern part of China where Shu was located. Thus, after his return, he proposed to Emperor Wudi that the court send an expedition to southwestern China to look for any routes that went through the mountains that lay between southern China and India. He suggested that if such routes did exist, and if the Chinese could use them, then China could get access to all the exotic goods and wealth in the Western Regions, without risking the dangerous journey through Xiongnu territory.

Wudi took his advice and sent out several expeditions to search for these southwestern routes to India, but to no avail. The most likely route turned out to be south of Shu, in what is now Yunnan Province. During Zhang Qian's time this area was outside the boundaries of China, and the non-Han people living there had no desire to facilitate someone else's trade with India at their own expense. They simply repelled or killed any intruders, including Emperor Wudi's expedition. As a result, dangerous though they might be, the routes to the Western Regions that went across the steppe and the more northern mountains were the only ones available to China for many centuries thereafter. In spite of these disappointments, Emperor Wudi still thought that he had been well served by Zhang Qian, and Zhang went on to serve as China's ambassador to other steppe peoples in his later career.

By the time that Zhang Qian had returned to China, Xiongnu raids on farming villages along the northern frontier were no longer a serious threat. Emperor Wudi thus had turned his attention to securing the Hexi Corridor (literally, Corridor West of the Yellow River), a long strip of land that lies between the Tibetan plateau and the Mongolian deserts. This strategic corridor connected what was then northwestern China with Xinjiang and the rest of the Western Regions. (Today this corridor is located in China's Gansu Province.) To do this, he extended the Great Wall northwestward through the corridor's arid lands, all the way to the Jade Gate at the western end of the corridor, and set up a military garrison system along this new section of the Wall. (Jade Gate is an English translation of the Chinese word Yumen. There is also a modern city in Gansu that is called Yumen, but it is not at the site where the Jade Gate was located during the Han dynasty. During the Han it was located west of Dunhuang, near Gansu's present-day border with the Xinjiang Uighur Autonomous Region.) A town called Anxi (Peaceful West) became the location of the headquarters for this long and narrow region, and military forces stationed there introduced agriculture to its sparsely populated oases, thereby becoming soldiers and farmers at the same time.

This corridor, protected by the Wall and the military garrisons, provided foreign travelers a relatively safe passage into China's agricultural heartland, and it soon began to attract merchants from far-off lands. Consequently more and more exotic goods such as Roman glassware, Indian cottons, various spices and aromatics, gemstones, and woolen textiles of various origins began passing through the Jade Gate on their way to the capital city of Chang'an (in the vicinity of modern Xi'an). The merchants who brought these goods to the capital also brought information about foreign lands, and from this point on, Chinese historians began to include in their writings much more detailed information about countries as far away as the Indian subcontinent and the eastern Mediterranean.

Although threats to China's northern frontier never faded away, the Han dynasty's relationship with the Xiongnu did become more complex. During the reign of Emperor Yuandi (48–33 BCE) a steppe leader called Huhanxie, the chief of the southern Xiongnu, became an ally of the Chinese in a confrontation between the Han and other steppe nomads. In order to display his important connection to the Han, Huhanxie went on a tribute mission to the court of Emperor Yuandi where he was honored for his loyalty and richly rewarded. Furthermore, in contrast to the early Han emperors who sent princesses to nomad leaders out of weakness, Yuandi decided to bestow upon Huhanxie a royal wife from his own harem in order to demonstrate the significance of this alliance.

In order to find a suitable woman, the emperor's courtiers went to his outer-harem, the residence of the many beautiful women sent to the court from the various parts of the Han Empire. This was where the women waited for their chance to be with the emperor. However, because there were so many of them, the majority of the women spent their entire lives there without so much as seeing the emperor. Even so, the courtiers knew that the prospect of leaving a lonely, but luxurious life in China in order to live with strangers in a nomadic land would have little appeal to the women, and thus they did not expect to find any volunteers. However, they were fortunate, for one of the women, the beautiful and accomplished Wang Zhaojun, came forward to volunteer for the mission.

Emperor Yuandi saw Wang for the first time on the day of the ceremony during which she was to be formally presented to Huhanxie. Shocked by her stunning beauty, he suddenly wanted to have her in his own inner-harem. This could not be, however, for the alliance was too important to be jeopardized by his sudden change of mind. The ceremony took place as planned and Wang left with the Xiongnu leader. The marriage and the alliance were successful. She gave birth to several princes and princesses who were interested in friendship with the Han, and her presence in the Xiongnu court ensured frequent exchanges of gifts and greetings between these steppe rulers and the Han Empire. In spite of difficulties caused by local problems on both sides, an intimate and peaceful relationship between the two powers lasted for several decades.

Because of her sacrifice (leaving her homeland and the luxury of the Han court for the nomadic life of a Xiongnu wife), and her success on what was essentially a diplomatic mission, Wang Zhaojun became the most famous of the many royal women married to nomad chiefs in Chinese history. Villagers remembered this envoy to the steppe and, in order to mark her route, gave the name Zhaojun to several places through which she had passed on her journey to the steppe. Over the many centuries since then, her beauty, musical talent, sorrow upon leaving her homeland, and loneliness in a foreign land have all become part of the Chinese image of her depicted many times in folklore, paintings, songs, and theater.

THE YUEZHI-KUSHAN IN TUHARA (FORMERLY BACTRIA)

After fleeing from the Xiongnu across much of Central Asia, the Yuezhi had moved their court south of the Amu River (into what is now northeastern Afghanistan) some time around 130 BCE. At roughly the same time as this migration the leader of one of the Yuezhi tribes, the Kushan, unified five of these tribes into a single kingdom that ruled over what had recently been Bactria. The Kushan Kingdom quickly became well established in this land of cities, croplands, and pastures, bringing yet another culture to a region that had been both a part of the Iranian Achaemenid Empire and the Hellenistic Seleucid territories. When the Yuezhi-Kushan first established a powerful regime in northern Afghanistan, they were a proud, affluent horseback-riding people, skillful in both fighting and trading. Their numbers included 100,000 horseback-riding archers among a population of 400,000 people, which suggests that every male adult in the tribe who was in good health was a soldier. Nevertheless, the land that they had just taken over had a much larger population and a long-standing cosmopolitan civilization.

In many ways the Hellenistic empire in Asia had reflected the attitudes and traditions of the ancient Greek polity. Accordingly, there had been no highly centralized imperial structure. Instead, the political system was for the most part a network of city-states, within which each city retained a high degree of autonomy. This seems to have been especially true in Bactria, which had fought and won complete independence from the Seleucids. Sima Qian wrote a description of Bactria in the Han dynasty *Shiji* (*The History*) in which he portrayed this region as a remarkably decentralized collection of walled cities. What he and other Chinese found so puzzling was that, unlike China, there was no single great sovereign who ruled over the entire country. Instead, cities still had their own chiefs and were largely autonomous.

The best example of such a city is the archaeological site of Ai-Khanoum on the southern bank of the Amu River, at its confluence with the Kokcha River. Excavated by the French scholar Paul Bernard, it provides an almost comprehensive picture of ancient Greek life in the polis, including a theater, a gymnasium, temples, and a palace. The finest buildings were supported by huge Corinthian style columns with a motif of acanthus leaves on the capital, a clear reflection of Mediterranean ecology and culture. Mosaics, made from local pebbles, covered the floor of the palace bathing area. Sima Qian also wrote that the population of the region was very large, perhaps even more than one million people. His rather detailed knowledge of Bactria and other Kushan held territories came mostly from Zhang Qian, the Han government envoy who had visited the Yuezhi court around 129 BCE, shortly after the Yuezhi-Kushan had become established there.

Unfortunately, there are no descriptions, from any side, of how the Kushan established their rule in Bactria. Nevertheless, both the archaeological record and Zhang Qian's report make it clear that the Yuezhi-Kushan's position in Bactria was not the result of a stereotypical steppe conquest, a warlike invasion carried out by marauding nomads descending on a venerable agricultural society. Instead, it appears to have been more like a meeting and mingling of two substantial populations possessing two extraordinarily different, highly sophisticated cultures.

Apparently, Bactria had already been overrun by other nomadic forces before the Yuezhi-Kushan fled to this region. The city of Ai-Khanoum, for example, had been sacked around 145 BCE, about fifteen years before the Yuezhi-Kushan entered the area. Historical records do not indicate who the perpetrators were, but this date is marked by the last issue of local coins. The palace suffered serious damage, and the rule of Bactrian kings there had also come to an end. By the time that Zhang Qian arrived in this land, shortly after the Yuezhi had arrived, it was no longer known to the Indians as Bactria, but as Tuhara. As mentioned previously, linguistic scholars believe that the Yuezhi spoke an Indo-European language called Tuharan, and the fact that the area was already known in India by this new name so soon after the Yuezhi arrival has suggested to some scholars that the Yuezhi were not the first Tuharan speakers to arrive there. Since other Tuharan speakers would also have been pastoral people from the steppe, this suggests that the Yuezhi had moved into an area already controlled by a pastoral people linguistically related to them and not by a Hellenistic people. In any case the new name for this land has persisted. Even today, this region of northern Afghanistan is still referred to as Tukharistan.

Ordinary life does not seem to have changed much during these troubled times, and even after the emergence of the Yuezhi-Kushan Kingdom the walled cities of Tuhara still chose their own chiefs who continued to manage the cities' domestic affairs. The Hellenistic style of life seems to have persisted for quite some time, with elements of the nomadic culture, namely the equestrian culture, becoming mixed in with it. A Tang dynasty (618–906 CE) Chinese scholar, who updated Sima Qian's *Shiji* (*The History*), added a comment on the section that concerned "the Great Yuezhi" in which he summarized a culture that clearly had interwoven elements from both the Hellenistic and the steppe traditions.

> Great Yuezhi is located about seven thousand *li* north of India. Their land is at a high altitude; the climate is dry; the region is remote. The king of the state calls himself the "son of the heaven." Riding horses in that country are always as numerous as several hundred thousand. The layout of the cities and the palaces are quite similar to those of the Romans (Da Qin, a term for the Roman Empire, including the Greeks). The skin color of people there is reddish white. People are skillful at archery from horseback. Local products, rare goods, treasures, clothing and upholstery are very good, even India cannot compare with it. (*Shiji*, 123/3162)

Although this update of Sima Qian clearly was not up-to-date during the Tang dynasty when it was published, since the Kushan Kingdom fell long before the Tang dynasty ruled China, it probably does reflect conditions in Tuhara some time after Zhang Qian's visit of 129 BCE. Also, the reference to the high altitude and the dry climate suggests that the location is northern Afghanistan, rather than the later Kushan capitals on the Indian subcontinent. This update thus suggests a formerly Hellenistic land ruled by horseback-riding Kushans. It also suggests that the Kushans continued to bring numerous good horses to this land and maintained their nomadic skills and culture. The reference to the reddish-white skin color of its inhabitants suggests that there was still an identifiable population of Greeks and other immigrants from the Mediterranean who had lighter complexions than most of the populations in this part of Asia. In addition, the Hellenistic style was still noticeable in the layout of the cities and the architecture. Thus, it seems that the establishment of Yuezhi-Kushan power in northern Afghanistan was not a destructive phenomenon, but a process that took place over several decades. Clearly these nomads did not come to destroy the cities and change all the lands into pastures (the stereotypical vision of nomad conquests), but came to reside there as rulers and citizens, while still keeping their horses and practicing their riding skills.

Once they had arrived in Tuhara, the Kushans became familiar with the local culture, especially with the well-rooted material culture of the Mediterranean world they found there. They soon learned to enjoy and trade in grape wine, for example. Their rulers also continued to correspond with the Han court, and their traders continued to travel to China. From Zhang Qian's report it is clear that markets had long flourished there, and that among the many merchants trading in Tuhara were people familiar with India, Iran, and the eastern Mediterranean. The Han Chinese court as well as its successors were always willing to admit traders from the Yuezhi-Kushan territories, and to issue passports to them so that they could cross the border and travel inside China wherever their business took them.

Official Chinese documents from that time gave all the travelers from the Kushan Kingdom and later the Kushan Empire the surname "Zhi" (as in Yuezhi), regardless of what their name or ethnicity actually was, or which part of the Kushan-ruled territories they came from. It didn't matter to the Chinese if their ethnicity was Indian, Central Asian, or Western Asian, or whether they were dark-skinned or light-skinned, they all were given the surname "Zhi" to use while they were in China. This was because the Chinese continued to think of the people who ruled the Kushan territories as the Yuezhi nomads, who had once been concentrated on their northwestern frontier. Since the Chinese do not use a phonetic writing system that lends itself to spelling out the sounds of a foreign name, Chinese officials at that time frequently assigned foreigners a Chinese character for their surname, and often chose the character more for its meaning than its sound. Thus, when they had to pick a character to write down a Kushan surname on their forms, they always gave them the surname "*Zhi*" to indicate that they came from the realm of the Yuezhi-Kushan, which by this time was known as Tuhara. The people from Tuhara probably did not mind being called Yuezhi or being surnamed "*Zhi*" as long as they could continue to be the world's most important dealers in Chinese silks.

THE POLITICAL, CULTURAL, AND SYMBOLIC SIGNIFICANCE OF HORSES, CHARIOTS, AND SILK

Not long after 1750 BCE when the horse-drawn chariot's military importance became well established in sedentary areas, this military vehicle became not just a means of transport, but also a symbol of power. In China when the importance of chariots on the battlefield was at a peak, Shang rulers (sixteenth to eleventh centuries BCE) considered themselves so closely linked to their vehicles and the horses that pulled them that they ensured that both would be entombed beside their own burial places when they died. Many centuries after the Shang had fallen, when the military significance of chariots had declined due to the increasing use of cavalries, the symbolic value of the chariot did not decline, but became even greater. Long after chariot warfare had ended, throughout much of Eurasia the horse-drawn chariot became the mobile throne of rulers, and the use of a chariot became a common means of displaying both royalty and divinity in almost all established sedentary cultures in Eurasia. Eventually, in the cultural representations of the powerful in Greece, Iran, India, and China, it was not soldiers, but only kings and gods who rode in chariots while hunting or warring against their foes.

Due to a lack of sources historians know relatively little about the cultural changes that the transition to chariot warfare brought to ancient societies. Much more, however, is known about the turmoil caused by the transition from chariots to cavalry. The vociferous opposition to King Wuling of Zhao's fourth century BCE reforms ordering officers and soldiers to wear nomad-style clothing indicates that both the cultural and social changes required by this transition were substantial. Eventually, even in many fundamentally sedentary societies, horseback riding and horseback-riding regalia were incorporated into the rituals of state. Although their actual reliance on cavalries did not displace the chariot from ceremonial processions, sedentary societies like China did add new equestrian features to their displays of power and prestige. And for the first time rulers and elites in sedentary societies began to think of this new equestrian culture as a part of their own high culture, in spite of its alien, nomadic roots.

In the new equestrian culture, the quality of the horse became even more important to the rider's status than it had been in the days of the horse-drawn chariot. After Zhang Qian's return from his long journey to the western regions, the most prized mounts in China became the "heavenly horses" of Ferghana, one of the locales that he had visited during his search for the Yuezhi. Legends about these horses were numerous, and some even claimed that the horses really were from the skies. The heavenly horses were also known as "blood-sweating horses," for reasons that remain unclear. Taller and sleeker with well-muscled contours, they were faster and had greater endurance than the breeds that were more common on China's northern frontier. Furthermore, horses raised in Ferghana had other advantages. In this more western area of the steppe, the climate was milder, there was somewhat more rainfall, and the grass grew higher than on the Mongolian steppe directly north of China. In addition, the pastoralists in Ferghana fed their horses alfalfa, a local domesticate that they knew to be a very nutritious grass.

Emperor Wudi was determined to have more of these heavenly horses and sent out an envoy, well supplied with gold and silk, to the Ferghana area to buy them. Unfortunately, the local chief there was unwilling to sell any of his horses and further insulted the emperor by killing the Han envoy. Thus, Wudi in 104 BCE sent General Li Guangli out to conquer the offending chiefdom. Li's expedition, however, met with grave difficulties in the desert, lost many men in battles, and finally retreated back toward the Great Wall, only to find that the Jade Gate was locked and that they could not get inside the Wall. Emperor Wudi was determined that the expedition should try again and had given the Jade Gate garrison orders not to let any soldiers from General Li's expedition come through the gate, and to kill any soldier who disobeyed the order and tried to get through it. General Li thus had no choice but to turn his army around and go back. Eventually he succeeded in having the offending chief killed and returned with 3,000 heavenly horses.

On the Chinese side, the initial purpose of trading silks to some of the nomads for horses was to build cavalries, all the better to fight with other nomads who were not so friendly, so that China could protect the villagers and the cultivated fields of its agricultural society. Once the military value of good riding horses became obvious to the sedentary society, the possession of these rare and expensive animals became identified with power and prestigious connections. The "heavenly horses," in particular, became a symbol of imperial power and royalty, and the demand for beautiful imported horses persisted as equestrian culture became an integral part of Chinese high culture. Even now in the vicinity of the city of Xi'an, next to the monumental tomb of Wudi, there still stands a large stone sculpture of a powerful horse triumphantly trampling on a defeated Xiongnu warrior.

The arrival of the horses from Ferghana led to more cultural exchange, since along with the horses came two Central Asian domesticates, alfalfa and grape vines. Emperor Wudi issued an order that both these plants, which were new to China, be grown near the capital on good cropland. Clearly the alfalfa was for the horses, but it is unclear exactly why the grapes had so much royal appeal. Given the proximity of Ferghana to Hellenized kingdoms such as Bactria, it appears that the Greek talent for grape-growing and wine-making had spread to peoples in the region of Ferghana, and from there the plant made its way to China along with the alfalfa. However, there is no evidence that the Chinese made grape wine at this time, and they clearly remained committed only to their own rice wines. Thus, the grape vines grown in China must have been appreciated just for their visual appeal, the shade they provided when they were grown over some wooden support, for their fresh fruit, and perhaps as a treat for the horses as well. For whatever reason, grape vines (but not grape wines) became widespread in Han China, and could be found gracing various palaces and public places.

Around the same time that the horses were acquiring a new symbolic meaning in sedentary societies, Chinese silk was also taking on new meanings among the nomads on the grasslands. During the Qin and Han dynasties the Chinese had supplied large quantities of silk to powerful nomad chiefs on their northern frontiers. The chiefs, in turn, bestowed silk upon their most important subordinates and steppe allies. They were obligated by steppe values and protocols to redistribute their wealth, including silk, to valued members of their retinue so that they too could share in the chief's display of power and prestige. Only by liberally sharing silk and other rare goods with those that were most important to him could the chief maintain their loyalty. The possession of fine silks on the steppe thus became a symbol of powerful and prestigious connections as much or more than a symbol of wealth, and, ironically, Chinese silks thus became an important part of the glue that held the nomad confederacies together.

In summary, on the Chinese frontier, the migrations of nomadic peoples on the Eurasian steppe and their interactions with a sedentary society significantly increased the demand for nomad-raised horses and Chinese-made silks and attached to these trade goods new symbolic meanings and a different kind of value. The early development and expansion of the silk roads was thus due in large part to the ongoing desire of both the nomads and the sedentary rulers to acquire foreign goods that would enhance their power and prestige at home.

It is also clear that the origin of the silk roads was directly related to the conflicts fought and the alliances forged among peoples from two different ecological zones, the Yuezhi and the Xiongnu on the steppe, and China's Han Empire. During this time, when China was still the world's sole producer of silk, this textile played an important role in a wide variety of events. It was directly related to China's military power, since it could be traded to the nomads in order to acquire horses for Chinese cavalries. In addition, both the Qin and the early Han emperors sent large quantities of silk textiles and floss to appease the nomads and keep them from raiding Chinese settlements. Some of the silks were government-made brocades, tapestries, and embroidered materials for the nobles of the tribe, but many more were plain silk textiles and floss produced by Chinese farm women, some of which were traded westward by the nomads. Silk was also crucial in diplomacy as the gift that sealed diplomatic agreements on the steppe. Such transactions between the Chinese and steppe nomads spread the fame of Chinese silk throughout the steppe and beyond. Also, within China this textile acquired an international economic significance since it was used to purchase the exotic luxuries that traders from the Western Regions and beyond were bringing to China. It is also clear that the far-reaching interactions among these very diverse peoples increased their knowledge about peoples of other cultures and led to cultural changes within each of the areas involved. Some of the changes were obvious to all, especially when they were new, but as time passed, their origins were forgotten, and later generations were oblivious to their origins and never thought about whence they had come.

In addition, after the migration of the Yuezhi to Afghanistan, these skillful traders of jade, horses, and silk had found an ideal place from which traders could carry Chinese silks to the Indian subcontinent and Iran, both of which were nearby. As a result, the desire for silks spread even further west, all the way to the Mediterranean Sea. The growing demand for silk within the Roman Empire would send its traders to Egyptian shores from which they could cross the Arabian Sea to ports on the

Indian subcontinent's western coast. In the first century CE, at approximately the same time that traders from the Roman Empire started sailing eastward to India, the Kushan Kingdom expanded its boundaries southward into what is now Pakistan and India. The two would meet in the ports of India, and for the first time a silk road, part overland and part overseas, would be carrying large quantities of Chinese silks all the way from China to various Mediterranean Sea ports, a development discussed in the next chapter.

FOR FURTHER READING

Barfield, Thomas. "The Hsiung-nu [Xiongnu] Imperial Confederacy: Organization and Foreign Policy."*The Journal of Asian Studies*, 41 (Nov. 1981), 45–61.

Barfield, Thomas. "Steppe Empire: China and the Silk Road Nomads as a Force in International Trade and Politics." In *Nomads in the Sedentary World*, ed. Anatoly Khazanov and Andre Wink. London: Curzon Press, 2001.

Liu, Xinru. "Migrations and Settlement of the Yuezhi-Kushan: Interaction and Interdependence of Nomadic and Sedentary Societies,"*Journal of World History* 12 (Fall 2001).

Sima Qian. *Records of the Grand Historian: Han Dynasty*. Edited and translated by Burton Watson. Hong Kong and New York: Renditions—Columbia University Press, Rev. Ed., 1993.

Yu, Yingshi. *Trade and Expansion in Han China*. Berkeley: University of California Press, 1967.

TIMELINE

Middle of first century CE	Yuezhi-Kushan cross Hindu Kush and take control of what is now Pakistan and northeastern India.
	Hippalus (a Greek pilot) learns the patterns of the monsoon winds in the Indian Ocean.
	Roman Empire traders begin making overseas voyages from Egypt's Red Sea coast to India in the same manner that Arab sailors had previously pioneered.
	Yuezhi-Kushan and Roman Empire merchants meet in ports on northwest coast of Indian subcontinent (in present-day Pakistan and India).
	Periplus of the Erythraean Sea describes routes, navigation, ports, and products all around the Arabian Sea.
69–79 CE	Reign of Roman emperor Vespasian. His advisor, Pliny the Elder, complains about the drain of Roman bullion to India.
Middle to late first century CE (?)	Kushan king Kanishka is a devotee of Buddhism.
	Ashvaghosha, a comtemporary of King Kanishka, moves to Kushan realm and writes a history of the Buddha's life.
Middle of first century CE to second century CE	Roman Empire sailors at Poduca on India's southeast coast.
	The use of Sanskrit place-names in Funan (in present-day Cambodia and southern Vietnam) indicates cultural and commercial exchanges between India and Southeast Asia.

97 CE	Gan Ying is sent on a mission to the west to find the seaports where Parthian and Roman Empire traders meet, so that he can visit the Roman Empire. He reaches a Parthian seaport, but becomes discouraged and returns to China.
166 CE	Traders claiming to be envoys from the Roman emperor arrive in Luoyang, Chinese capital of the Later Han dynasty. The Chinese do not believe them. These traders most likely came from India's east coast to China via Southeast Asia.
Second century CE	Carving of Buddhist sculptures on boulders at Kongwangshan in northern Jiangsu Province in China provides an early indication of Chinese converts to Buddhism. In the portrayal of the Buddha's passing away both the Buddha and the mourners are wearing Kushan-style clothing.

AN OVERSEAS SILK ROAD: ROMAN EMPIRE TRADERS IN INDIA, THE YUEZHI-KUSHAN KINGDOM, AND THE DEVELOPMENT OF MAHAYANA BUDDHISM

GETTING STARTED ON CHAPTER TWO What events led to the establishment of a maritime silk road between Indian ports on the Arabian Sea and Egyptian ports on the Red Sea? What cultural traditions contributed to the remarkably cosmopolitan society that characterized the Kushan Empire? In what directions did Mahayana Buddhism develop once it became established in the northwestern part of the Indian subcontinent? How did these developments contribute to its spread to China?

CHAPTER OUTLINE

The Roman Empire Traders

The Arabian Peninsula and the Early Trade in Aromatic Wood Resins

Gan Ying and a Chinese Attempt To Find the Sea Markets

The Cosmopolitan Kushan Empire

Mahayana Buddhism and Its Spread to China

Around the middle of the first century CE there were two separate but simultaneous expansions of peoples known for their interest in trade. One movement involved the Yuezhi-Kushan nomads. Almost two centuries earlier they had moved from east to west, from the steppe on China's northwest frontier to a region that was northwest of the Indian subcontinent in present-day Afghanistan. Then in the middle of the first century CE they crossed the Hindu Kush mountains and expanded toward the southeast, extending their rule over a large part of the Indian subcontinent. The other expansion, which was solely commercial in nature, was carried out by maritime traders from the eastern end of the Mediterranean whose homelands had been conquered during the eastward expansion of the Roman Empire. In the middle of the first century CE they went eastward from Egypt to India by sea. The people involved in these two expansions met in the Arabian Sea ports on the Indian subcontinent's western coast, in present-day Pakistan and northwestern India.

The markets in these ports brought together two very different peoples, horseback-riding nomads with a long history of overland trade, and eastern Mediterranean traders who had a long history of maritime exchange. The result was a direct linkage of the steppe pastoralists, who controlled the overland silk roads from China to India, with sailors who supplied the Mediterranean basin, soon to be one of the largest markets for silk. Thus, the Yuezhi-Kushan pastoralists and the Mediterranean sailors together created a new, maritime branch of the silk roads. Thereafter, the Kushan Empire became the primary distributor of Chinese silks, not only to the Parthians in Iran, but also to the Roman Empire traders in India. Subsequently, the extraordinarily cosmopolitan Kushan Empire flourished and became the setting for the growth of Mahayana Buddhism, a school of Buddhism that would eventually spread east and become the predominant form of Buddhism in China, Japan, Korea, Vietnam, and Indonesia. (In what is now Indonesia, Hinduism was also widespread, and ultimately Islam became the predominant religion.)

After the Yuezhi-Kushan crossed the Hindu Kush mountain ranges and took control of lands all the way south to the valleys of the Yamuna River and the upper Ganges River in present-day India, their history would become an integral part of the history of the Indian subcontinent. Although the lands that they took had once been a part of India's Mauryan Empire (321–184 BCE), which had unified almost the entire subcontinent in the wake of Alexander's invasion of northwestern India, more than two centuries had passed since the demise of Mauryan power. By the time that the Kushans took over what is now Pakistan and northwestern India, political power had long been fragmented and there had already been a number of foreign invasions in these areas. By taking control of Indian ports on the Arabian Sea coast, the Kushan rulers gained access to ancient maritime routes that led from India to the Persian Gulf, the southern shores of the Arabian Peninsula, and the Red Sea. All of these locations were connected to overland trade routes that led to Mediterranean shores and could thus deliver Asian products, including Chinese silks, to the Roman Empire. This was especially true in both southern Arabia, where there had long been camel caravans that carried goods north to the Mediterranean, and on the Egyptian shores of the Red Sea, where goods were unloaded and portaged across the desert to the Nile River, which delivered them to Alexandria on the southeastern coast of the Mediterranean.

THE ROMAN EMPIRE TRADERS

Like the traders on the Arabian Sea, the Persian Gulf, and the Red Sea, the Mediterranean traders also came from a maritime tradition that was ancient. As early as the second millennium BCE the ships of Phoenicians, Greeks, and Egyptians had carried substantial quantities of wine, food grains, and metals from port to port. However, for close to 2,000 years, the narrow strip of land between the Mediterranean Sea and the Red Sea had prevented these sailors from entering the Red Sea and thereby gaining access to the southern oceans and seas that were south of Asia. It was only after the overland conquests of Alexander the Great (which took place between 334 and 326 BCE), and the Hellenistic Ptolemies rule over Egypt, that a small number of Greek sailors began to establish themselves in the ports on Egypt's Red Sea coast. Nevertheless, even though Alexander and his successors had established Greek colonies as far east as present-day Afghanistan, very few of these Egyptian-based Greek traders ventured out onto the maritime routes that led to the east. It was only after the Roman Empire had established its control over the eastern Mediterranean region in 65 BCE and then made Egypt a Roman province in 30 BCE that the empire's elites began to develop a taste for the eastern goods associated with the luxurious life. Thus, it was not until the first century CE that the incentives for Mediterranean traders to get closer to the sources of Asian goods became irresistible.

The people referred to as Roman Empire traders were mostly Greeks living in Egypt, Hellenized, Greek-speaking Egyptians, or Arabs who were a part of the Roman ruled population due to Rome's takeover of the eastern shores of the Mediterranean. Although historians sometimes refer to them simply as Roman traders, few, if any, were from the city of Rome or even Italy. These traders knew of two competing routes that went from the Mediterranean region to various parts of Asia. In addition to the sea route from the Red Sea to the Indian subcontinent, there was an equally ancient overland route that started in Syria and went eastward to the Iranian plateau. However, because the Parthians in Iran controlled much of the territory through which it passed, and relations between Rome and Parthia were frequently hostile, Roman Empire sailors preferred the maritime route that began on the Egyptian shores of the Red Sea.

Once the Roman Empire sailors became established in Red Sea ports, they were sailing over waters well known to Arab sailors, all the way from southeastern Arabia to India. The Arabs were also familiar with eastern Mediterranean markets, since for many centuries before the establishment of the Roman Empire, they had developed overland routes to supply highly valued goods from the southern part of the Arabian Peninsula and nearby locations, principally frankincense and myrrh, to the eastern Mediterranean markets. These camel caravan routes across Arabia also supplied Mediterranean ports with goods brought from India by sea, including tropical spices, gems, and other varieties of aromatic woods and resins. The familiarity of the Arab sailors with both the Indian ports and the Mediterranean ports provided the key that opened up these routes to sailors from the Roman Empire.

THE ARABIAN PENINSULA AND THE EARLY TRADE IN AROMATIC WOOD RESINS

The Arabian Peninsula had benefited from long-distance trade since ancient times. Its vast desert made agriculture impossible in most places. Oases where palm dates flourished were small and relatively few in number, and camel pastoralism was possible only in limited areas. However, near the peninsula's southern coast, there were two items, frankincense and myrrh, that were much in demand in the Mediterranean basin in ancient times. They were both made from tree resins, and the cultivation of the trees in irrigated fields and the processing of the resins demanded much labor and skill. Early in the first millennium BCE, in the southern part of the peninsula (in present-day Yemen), the Sabaean state was a source of these resins, and was famous throughout the southwestern part of Asia for its great wealth. In the Old Testament, a queen named Sheba visited King Solomon (965–928 BCE) of Israel. This Queen of Sheba may well have been the Queen of Saba. Also, in Yemen, archaeologists have found the ruins of magnificent buildings made with imported alabaster, marble, and limestone, and of even greater significance, a vast irrigation system.

By the time of the Roman Empire, Mediterranean peoples were still interested in frankincense and myrrh since they burned large quantities of incense for their pantheon of gods. These items are also mentioned in the New Testament of the Bible. When Jesus of Nazareth was born, three magi, or sages, from the east went to Bethlehem to pay their respects, carrying gifts of frankincense and myrrh along with gold. Eventually the Himyarite state (115 BCE–525 CE) replaced the Sabaean state in southern Arabia, but it also inherited the latter's language and culture. This was the Arab state that the traders of the Roman Empire encountered when they first entered the Red Sea.

By the time of the Roman Empire, the people living in southern Arabia had long been sailing eastward to the western coast of the Indian subcontinent, and they had discovered an unusual way to get there. Most of the world's sailors at that time stayed relatively close to shore, in order to avoid getting lost at sea. The Arab sailors, however, had discovered how to navigate far from shore, across the open waters between Arabia and India using a wind pattern that was known as the trade monsoon. (The word *monsoon* comes from Arabic and literally means seasonal winds.) In general, between Africa and India the winds on the Arabian Sea blow from southwest to northeast from April to October and from northeast to southwest during the months from October to April. Taking advantage of this wind pattern, in the summer Arab sailors rode the winds across open waters from locations south of Arabia to the northwest coast of the Indian subcontinent, and, after the winds reversed, they returned to the Arabian Peninsula in the winter. Thus, they could make a round trip between the Red Sea and India within one year, which was much faster than the older routes that clung to the coasts between Arabia and India. Due to the quantity of spices such as cinnamon and pepper and the variety of aromatic resins that Arab traders delivered to Mediterranean shores, the peoples of the Mediterranean had long assumed that all of these products were actually grown and harvested somewhere on the Arabian Peninsula and that the spice roads went no further afield. However, by the time of the Roman Empire, they were beginning to realize that many of these items came from much more distant lands in the more eastern parts of Eurasia.

Around the mid-first century CE, a man from the Roman Empire, Hippalus, is said to have discovered, or, more likely, learned from the Arabs, the pattern of the monsoons on the Arabian Sea. From that time Roman Empire traders, based on Egypt's Red Sea coast, ventured out onto open waters to ride the winds that carried them back and forth to the Indian coast, not only to get spices, but also precious stones, minerals, Chinese silk, and other textiles. Within the Mediterranean, Alexandria, at the mouth of the Nile, became the base for this trade in Asian goods, and it was also from Alexandria that the Mediterranean traders sailed their goods south up the Nile River, then portaged them across the desert for a short distance to reach a Red Sea port. There they and their cargos boarded ships sailing to the Indian subcontinent.

Our knowledge of the Arabian Sea trade comes mostly from a manual known as the *Periplus Maris Erythrae (The Circumnavigation of the Red Sea)*. It was written in Greek by an anonymous sailor around the middle of the first century CE, and it provided detailed information about navigation routes, ports, markets, and products all the way from the east coast of Africa to the shores of the Indian subcontinent. It served the Roman Empire traders well. Many of them were Greek or Greek-speaking, and they loaded their ships with one of the most traditional Mediterranean commodities—grape wine in amphorae. An amphora was a ceramic jar specifically designed for shipping wine. It had two ear-shaped handles, one on each side, and a cone-shaped bottom, so that the jar could be anchored upright in sand, either on the beach or in the bottom of a ship. Greeks had long used amphorae to ship olive oil and grape wine, carrying them north in order to trade for tin, copper, and amber, products supplied by the forest and steppe peoples, and south to trade for food grains. The Roman Empire, with large supplies of profitable commodities, especially wine, was thus prepared to trade their wares for eastern luxuries. In addition to wine, the empire's traders also carried linens, red coral, and glassware from the Mediterranean.

The exquisite glassware produced in the eastern Mediterranean would become a welcome commodity wherever Roman ships went, and the red coral, also from the eastern Mediterranean, would become a valued precious stone in South and East Asia. It remains so even to this day, due to its hardness and bright red color. As it turned out, however, the Mediterranean goods they carried were not sufficient to pay for all the exotic goods that the wealthy citizens of the empire desired, so the traders had to use gold and silver coins to pay for some of these goods. Thus, the traders also carried with them large quantities of coins, all solid and sound, that were welcomed in overseas markets, and they also carried some gold plates.

In addition to providing much information about the currents and anchorages in the various ports, the *Periplus* also provided detailed information about the markets. It included information both about the quality and quantity of available goods that would sell in Mediterranean markets and lists of Mediterranean goods that would sell in the Arabian Sea markets. It also reveals that Roman ships stopped at Red Sea ports to pick up topaz, and at ports on the Arabian coasts, especially one called the "Cape of Spice Markets," to buy frankincense and myrrh, which they knew would bring a good price in Indian markets. The Indian port of Barbaricum was the first on the sailors' itinerary that had Chinese silks for sale. It was located at the mouth of the Indus River, and it also offered aromatic woods and resins, spices, gems, and other rare and precious goods from the Indian subcontinent and its numerous trading partners. These included Indian indigo and cotton textiles, aromatic resins such as costus from Kashmir and bdellium from western India, turquoise from Khurasan in central Iran, lapis lazuli from Badakhshan in northeast Afghanistan, and furs from the northern forests brought to India by Central Asians.

Lapis lazuli was a blue stone, treasured in Egypt and southwestern Asia at least since the third millennium BCE. Its stones and the blue pigment made from them were used to decorate the statues of Egyptian pharaohs and kings, but they were mainly used to decorate artworks and weapons. In ancient times the only source of this precious stone was Badakhshan, which, by the time the Roman Empire traders reached India, was ruled by the Yuezhi-Kushan. At this time they were also the sole suppliers of various spices and fragrances made from Himalayan plants such as costus. India had long been famous for its cotton textiles, which were softer and more comfortable than the alternatives, principally linen. Indigo was a blue dye made from a plant extract, and it was especially good for cloth made from plant fibers such as cotton and linen. India's cottons and indigo would maintain their commercial value through the many centuries to modern times.

The Roman Empire traders knew that at Barbaricum all of their cargo would be loaded on boats and taken upstream to the great metropolitan capital of a king. Although the *Periplus* doesn't name it, this metropolis would have been Purushapura, the northern capital of the Kushan Empire, near present-day Peshawar. It was in the region then known as Gandhara in present-day Pakistan and neighboring Afghanistan, and the king they mentioned would have been the Kushan ruler of the time. The list of commodities that the Romans could buy in this port clearly indicates that the sea route of the Roman Empire traders and the Central Asian overland silk road met in this Indian port. Furthermore, by the time that the Roman Empire traders arrived, Kushan hegemony stretched all the way from the frontiers of China, through Central Asia, to the Arabian Sea ports of the Indian continent. Thus, in addition to the Indian products, the Kushans also had access to commodities from eastern Iran and Central Asia. All the commodities that the Roman Empire traders bought there were either from territories controlled by the Kushan Empire or from trade routes that they controlled. Unfortunately, archaeological evidence from this port is not available, since it seems that the site has either disappeared into the sea or been buried by alluvium.

The next stop of the Roman Empire traders was the port of Barygaza, which was located in the Gulf of Cambay, near present-day Bharuch in the Indian province of Gujarat. Barygaza was at the mouth of the Narmada, the river that divides India into what people think of as its north and south. The Narmada runs from east to west all along the southern edge of the Vindhya mountain range for more than 300 miles, and it links many of the ancient Indian trade routes of the north and the south to this west coast port. Thus, the commercial activities of Barygaza were supported by a large hinterland that included many major cities. The city of Ujjain, for example, was about two hundred miles northeast of the port. It was one of the most beautiful and prosperous, so much so that Kalidasa (ca. 400–455 CE), one of India's most famous writers, would later immortalize it in his long poem, *The Cloud Messenger*. In the poem he praised it as a city of heavenly beings who had fallen to earth only because of some celestial transgression.

From Ujjain, the trade routes led further north to the city of Mathura on the Yamuna River. After the Yuezhi-Kushans had established themselves in northern India, they chose Mathura as their southern capital. Thus, again at Barygaza the trade routes linked Roman traders to a Kushan capital. The commodities traded at Barygaza were similar to those at Barbaricum, but the list of exports from Barygaza included additional items such as agate (a striped stone), and carnelian (a translucent red stone), both of which were from the Narmada valley. The *Periplus* also notes that the traders who imported Mediterranean goods at this port were rather particular about the wine that came on Roman Empire ships. Their preference was for Italian wine, but wine from the Syrian coast of the Mediterranean and the Arabian Peninsula was also acceptable.

Even during this early stage of a Mediterranean presence in Indian ports, traders from the Roman Empire did not confine themselves to ports controlled by the Yuezhi-Kushan. They also sailed southward, out of their jurisdiction, and past the southern tip of the Indian peninsula, anchoring in ports on the subcontinent's southeastern coast, far outside the Kushan realm. These sailors were aware that the mouth of the Ganges River was located further north on this coast, but their ships never ventured so far north as present-day Bengal. The *Periplus* declared that it was too difficult to reach there. The most distant port frequented by Roman Empire sailors was Poduca, near present-day Pondicherry on the southeastern coast of India. According to the *Periplus*, Poduca was a source of pearls. When Roman traders landed there, in the first and second centuries CE, India's southeastern coast was not a highly commercialized or urbanized area, and the local, Tamil-speaking people did not keep written records that might shed some light on the Roman presence. However, there were Tamil-speaking bards who wandered from town to town singing songs that praised their heroes and sad ballads about the sorrows of love. Several volumes of these songs, composed in the Tamil language, were collected around the second century CE. Known as the *Shangam*, literally *The Collection*, they offer some evidence of the Roman presence in this area. The poets describe the wealth of the Roman traders and the intoxicating powers of their wine. The *Shangam* also indicates that the Romans came there to purchase pearls and textiles, paying for them with both gold coins and wine. In addition, there is an abundance of archaeological evidence indicating a Roman presence. At the site of Poduca, in the present-day village of Arikamedu, archaeologists have found the remains of a Roman Empire trading depot and port. In the residential areas they found Mediterranean pottery and glassware, and there also were workshops that processed goods for the Mediterranean market.

The spices and fragrances sought by Roman Empire traders were not all products of southern India. Sandalwood, camphor, cinnamon, cassia, and cloves were from further east, either from the mainland or the islands of Southeast Asia. The *Periplus* mentions large ships called *colandia* in the vicinity of Poduca, and indicates that these ships made long voyages to the mouth of the Ganges River as well as to Chryse Island, the ancient Roman name for the Malay Peninsula. It was also around the first and second centuries CE that Southeast Asian rulers began to use Sanskrit words to name important places, an indication that both Hindu and Buddhist traditions were taking root there due to commercial and cultural contacts.

Nevertheless, Roman Empire trade with the southern part of India remained marginal compared to their trade in the ports of northwest India. Although the traders from the Roman Empire did engage in commercial exchanges on India's southeastern coast, these coastal sites proved to be ephemeral, disappearing not long after the Romans departed. Nevertheless, local people still drank the wine, hoarded the gold coins, and remembered this episode in their past.

GAN YING AND A CHINESE ATTEMPT TO FIND THE SEA MARKETS

Both the Roman Empire sailors and the Yuezhi-Kushans were profiting a great deal from their exchanges, and eventually that information made its way back to Luoyang, the capital of the Later Han dynasty (21–221 CE). There were rumors floating around that both the Parthians and the Indians were trading with Roman Empire merchants at "sea markets." At this early date the significance of such markets seemed strange to the Han court. At that time, almost all of China's international trade came in and went out across its inland frontier, and Han Chinese, especially those in the north where the capital was located, rarely had any involvement in overseas commercial activity. Even though the Later Han Empire was a much weaker state than the Han dynasty at the time of Emperor Wudi, the central government still managed to maintain a modest military and administrative presence in the Western Regions (especially in present-day China's Xinjiang Uighur Autonomous Region), and thus most people's attention was focused on the overland routes that went west from China.

In the first century CE, when the Central Asian Silk Road was undergoing further development, people in the Chinese capital were somewhat familiar with Parthians and Indians, but they were not sure who the Romans were. Han military commanders and administrators in the Western Region were even more familiar with Parthian and Kushan traders and issued many passes for them. They had heard about the Romans, and were curious about them, but they had never met anyone from the Roman Empire. Thus, sometime around 97 CE, Ban Chao, the chief administrator and military commander of Chinese stationed in the Western Regions, sent out an envoy named Gan Ying to find the seaports and explore the possibility of direct contact with the Roman Empire, which the Chinese referred to as Da Qin. Since the Chinese knew that the Roman Empire lay on the other side of Parthia, Gan Ying set out for Parthia and, according to the *History of the Later Han*, he succeeded in reaching a seaport called Tiaozhi, the Chinese name for Antioch.

It is difficult to say exactly where this Antioch was located. Before the Parthians ruled over the lands between the Mediterranean and the Indian subcontinent, much of this territory had been ruled by the Hellenistic Seleucids, and one of the Seleucid rulers, Seleucus I Nicator (312–281 BCE), had named a great many cities Antioch in honor of his father. What is clear is that Gan Ying was not in Antioch on the Orontes, which is close to the Mediterranean Sea in present-day Syria. Around 97 CE the Romans had firm control of Antioch on the Orontes, and the *History of the Later Han* makes clear that Gan Ying was in a seaport ruled by a Parthian general. It also says that the city was on a mountain surrounded by sea on three sides, which suggests a location at the head of the Persian Gulf, near modern Basra (in present-day Iraq). Also, the description of the place suggests that it was located closer to Iran than to the Mediterranean since the list of fauna found there included lions, rhinoceroses, zebus, peacocks, and ostriches.

According to the *History of the Later Han*, when Gan Ying inquired about sailing to the Mediterranean from this port, a local sailor told him that "the sea is vast; it takes three months for travelers to cross if the wind is good. If the wind is late, it will take two years for a ship to cross. Thus travelers always carry enough provisions for three years with them on the ship. Traveling on the sea makes people homesick, and more than often people die on the sea." The sailor's words persuaded Gan Ying that he should abandon the effort to make direct contact with either the Roman Empire or its traders. While the sailor in this port may have somewhat exaggerated the difficulties facing a traveler trying to get to the Mediterranean from this Antioch, it would, in fact, have been a long, difficult, and dangerous journey. From a geographical point of view, the shortest route would have been to go back up the Euphrates in order to take a land route from the Euphrates to the eastern Mediterranean coast. This, however, could have proved even more dangerous than any sea route. Warfare and heavy garrisoning on both sides of the Roman-Parthian frontier would have made crossing both difficult and dangerous.

It should also be noted that the Parthian Empire and its traders had no interest in the establishment of a direct linkage between Rome and China. Later the Han Chinese realized that traders from the Parthian Empire profited from selling Han silk to Roman Empire traders, and that a direct linkage between Rome and China could diminish Parthian profits. Furthermore, it is now known that when Roman Empire traders attempted to reach China by traveling across the Parthian Empire, the Parthians stopped them and would not allow them to proceed to China.

Apparently in these early centuries of the silk roads no Chinese envoys attempted to reach the "sea markets" on India's northwestern coast by crossing the deserts and mountains between China and India. Even though relations between the Yuezhi-Kushan, who controlled these routes, and China were generally good, during the Han dynasty even Chinese merchants never ventured across the Pamirs. These routes, too, were dangerous. For example, even after a traveler had crossed the deserts and the highest mountain peaks, some of the highest in the world, there were the equally treacherous vertical slopes and deep gorges along the upper reaches of the Indus River. There was one place in this region where travelers had to cross the river. All along this part of the route the river ran at the bottom of a deep chasm, and the only way to get across was by using a suspension bridge that went from one side of the chasm to the other. This bridge, with a narrow bottom and two sides, was made entirely of knotted ropes, and it simply hung over the chasm, swaying back and forth in the wind. Accounts of this river crossing made it sound so treacherous that Han scholars, truly amazed by this feature of the route, gave this entire region the name *Xuandu*, which translates as "suspended crossing."

It does appear that Roman Empire traders did attempt to reach China from India. Although none of the Indian port cities within Kushan territory had any maritime connection with China, it was possible to reach China by sea from India if one proceeded to ports on India's eastern coast, some of which were frequented by Roman Empire traders. There were a series of interconnected maritime routes that began on India's eastern coast and passed through Southeast Asia, where they linked up with sea routes to China. From the first to the fifth century CE, some travelers who used these routes stayed temporarily in ports controlled by the Southeast Asian kingdom of Funan. (Funan was not the local name for this kingdom. It was the Chinese term for it, and since the only written account of the kingdom is in Chinese, historians refer to it by this name.) Its capital, Vyadhapura, was on the Mekong River, and its territory included parts of what are now the coastlines of Vietnam and Cambodia. Given its location and the size of its abundant rice harvests, it was a convenient place for Southeast Asian ships to stop while they waited for the monsoon winds to shift. (Like the Arab sailors on the Arabian Sea, Southeast Asian sailors took advantage of monsoons that blew toward the Asian landmass during the summer and away from it during the Northern Hemisphere's winter months.)

Apparently, one group of Roman Empire traders did succeed in reaching China by way of a sea route through Southeast Asia. Chinese records indicate that they arrived in the Han capital of Luoyang in 166 CE, claiming to be envoys from the Roman emperor "Andun." The Roman Empire was then under the Antonine dynasty, and it is quite possible that the traders were in fact from the Roman Empire, even if they were not official envoys sent by the emperor. However, because the goods they carried were mostly the same ones that Southeast Asian sailors brought to China—the produce of the southern seas such as turtle shell and ivory—government officials did not believe them when they said they were from the Roman Empire. The Han court saw no evidence that they were from Rome, was unimpressed by their credentials, and refused to conduct any business with them. Thus, neither Han China nor the Roman Empire managed to establish a direct commercial link between the two ends of the Eurasian silk roads. Given the distances involved and the number of competing intermediaries between them, this is not surprising.

While the Han court had no choice but to leave the trade with the Roman Empire traders in the hands of Yuezhi-Kushans and Parthians, much information about the Roman Empire did reach China, some of it true and some mere fantasy. Han scholars recorded in their histories that the Roman Empire was a vast land with many great cities. Unlike China, it did not have a royal family that supplied a hereditary ruler. Instead, the ruler was selected on the basis of merit. The scholars wrote that there was a council of "thirty-six generals" who discussed major issues of state, a comment that is probably a reference to the Roman Senate. More pertinent to trade was the scholars' description of the exotic goods that came from the empire, which they listed as coral, glassware, and amber. They also mentioned the empire's gold and silver coins.

It is also clear from their descriptions of the Roman Empire that the Han Chinese scholars and officials did not realize that China had a world monopoly on silk production. They mention the silk-weaving industries in eastern Mediterranean cities, and in so doing make it clear that they were assuming that these Roman Empire silk weavers also practiced sericulture, the production and harvesting of the filaments from silk worm cocoons. They had no idea that all the raw material used in this eastern Mediterranean industry came from China.

While elites in both places sought to embellish their lives with beautiful things from faraway lands, the Roman demand for Asian products outgrew the Asian demand for Mediterranean products. In Rome, Pliny the Elder (ca. 23–79 CE) complained about an imbalance in the trade and wrote in his *Natural History* that "in no year does India drain off less than 50 million *sestertii* from our empire" (6.26.101). He also complained that the fondness of Roman women for silk clothing was partially responsible for the drain of gold and silver out of the empire. Some modern historians have argued, however, that he put too much blame for this problem on the Asian trade, and that the empire's military campaigns were probably a more significant drain on the empire's store of bullion. In any case, Pliny's words seem to have had little impact on Roman buying habits. The Roman Empire's elites, enjoying the power and splendor of a great empire, felt entitled to luxuries they could not even have imagined in previous centuries.

The Cosmopolitan Kushan Empire

Kushan power lasted roughly 350 years, beginning with the establishment of the Yuezhi-Kushan Kingdom in the vicinity of the Amu River in northern Afghanistan in the second half of the second century BCE (ca. 130 BCE), and ending with its subordination to Iran's new and expanding Sasanid Empire (after 240 CE). For the last two hundred of those years, from its mid-first century CE conquest of present-day Pakistan and northern India and the construction of an empire that embraced a large part of Central Asia as well, the Kushan Empire was one of the world's richest and most strategically placed powers on the globe. Nevertheless, the significance of the Kushan Empire has in large part been missing from the historical traditions of the places they ruled, as well as from world history.

Unfortunately from the perspective of historians, the Yuezhi-Kushans, even after they became literate, did not write down their own historical tradition. When the empire was broken up for all time, fragments of it went to what is now Pakistan, India, Iran, and various Central Asian countries. Within almost all of these countries, the pieces of what had been the Yuezhi-Kushan Empire were just one part of a larger whole and they lost their former identity as a part of the Kushan Empire. It is only when one begins to study cross-cultural exchanges among these places and China that the power, the wealth, and the significance of the Kushan Empire emerges. Due to the key role that it played in material and cultural exchanges, it had a fundamental impact on much of Eurasia, and especially on northern China and northern India.

The sources of the extraordinary cosmopolitanism of the Kushan Empire were many and varied. The foundation for this diversity was the large and highly diverse empire that they had conquered. Especially after they took over the northwestern part of the Indian subcontinent, the Kushan occupied a large territory that included dramatically different ecological zones. They had direct access not only to the commercial products of agricultural India, but also mineral and plant products from the mountains of Central Asia and animal products from the steppe. Last but not least, the Kushans had lived for centuries on the Chinese frontier, and unlike most nomads, had been allies of the Chinese and had had good relations with various Chinese rulers and farmers.

At the same time that elements of their own equestrian culture began to take root in Afghanistan and on the Indian subcontinent, the Yuezhi-Kushans preserved the many different cultures they found in these lands and made substantial contributions to their growth as well. Also, due to all their commercial networks, a wide variety of people from outside the empire came there to trade, and they too contributed to the diversity in the empire's cities. As the Kushan Empire grew even richer, a vibrant cosmopolitan culture grew up within their bounds. Its rulers amassed truly amazing collections of treasures in their palaces, amazing both because of their value, and the diverse origins of their contents. Even ordinary people benefited, since international trade stimulated economic activity to the extent that many new cities sprang up along the trade routes within the empire and its ancient cities expanded due to new construction. For example, for the first time since the demise of the Indus River civilization in the second millennium BCE, palaces and many private residences in the cities and towns on or near the river were once again built with fired bricks. From the northern capital Purushapura to the southern capital Mathura, multistory houses were built with the large red bricks that are now identified with the Kushan period.

Another element contributing to the empire's cosmopolitan nature was its appreciation for the earlier Hellenistic culture in many of the areas that it controlled. Purushapura, the empire's northern capital, was once a Hellenistic city. Under Kushan rule, the city still maintained a number of Hellenistic characteristics and enjoyed a certain degree of Hellenistic style. For example, a city goddess, who maintained her popularity throughout the Kushan period, was represented wearing a crown modeled after the city wall, which was a symbol of the city's autonomy. Traditional Indian culture also flourished during the Kushan Empire. Mathura, the empire's southern capital, is an ancient Indian city on the Yamuna River. There, outside the Hellenized areas, about a hundred miles south of present-day New Delhi, it was Indian culture that flourished. In its long history, it was during the Kushan period that its fortunes were at their greatest.

Because the site of Kushan Mathura is now covered over by modern residences, it cannot be excavated, but during the Kushan period trade routes radiating from the city were dotted with satellite towns, and a team of German archaeologists was able to excavate one of these. Near Mathura they found the small town of Sonka, where their efforts revealed that most of its structures were two-story red brick buildings. There were also red sandstone sculptures of local deities such as *yakshas* and *nagas* that demonstrate the superb artistic talent of Kushan period craftsmen. In the debris of the buildings, archaeologists also found jewelry made from imported materials from the Mediterranean basin such as red coral as well as red pottery goblets.

The most valuable artworks and treasures were most likely in the Kushan palaces located in the capitals at Purushapura and Mathura, but neither of these has been excavated. Nevertheless, there have been spectacular finds in Afghanistan where the cooler temperatures drew the elites during the summers. There, the Kushan rulers maintained a summer palace at the city of Kapisi-Begram, not far from the present-day capital at Kabul. (Also spelled Bagram, it is the site of the military airport guarded by the British during the most recent war, and it remains the main base of the United States in Afghanistan.) At the Kapisi-Begram site the archaeologists found a palace complex, including rooms full of treasures. At the level dated to the most famous Kushan king, Kanishka, who ruled during the first century CE, there was an assemblage of items that had been collected over a period of 150 years.

Unlike the treasures in the early Kushan tombs at Tillya Tepe (also in Afghanistan), where most items were made from gold and had designs inspired by the steppe, the treasures found near Kapisi-Begram reflect the cosmopolitan nature of the Kushan Empire. From the Mediterranean there were numerous outstanding bronze sculptures and pieces of glassware, which the French archaeologist Joseph Hackin has identified as European, meticulously relating them to sculptures in Europe or artifacts that appear in Renaissance paintings. There were also numerous Chinese artifacts at the site. The majority was lacquer ware, which has a stronger resistance to decay than other Chinese goods of the Han period such as silk. There were also many ivory carvings of images of Indian deities in the collection. Apparently, Kushan rulers not only required foreign traders to visit one of the capitals, they also collected a toll from all traders passing through their territory. It would appear from this collection that the traders invariably had to give some of the best items in their inventories to the rulers as tribute gifts. Consequently, the collection as a whole tells us not only about the material wealth of the Kushans, but also that their rulers appreciated and collected all the different styles of art in Eurasia.

Given their enlarged empire, the Yuezhi-Kushan also had to adapt to a new environment. One obvious problem was the matter of communicating with the local population. When the Yuezhi-Kushan established their kingdom in Afghanistan, they spoke Tuharan, which was different from the languages of the local people and was not a written language when they first entered the region. Communication was made even more complicated by the fact that the local people spoke a variety of different languages, written in different scripts. While the Greeks in the northwest spoke Greek and wrote with the Greek alphabet, the Indians there often spoke Prakrit, a vernacular version of Sanskrit, and wrote it in a script called Kharoshthi. Further south, in the region around the Gulf of Cambay and Mathura, the local people spoke a different dialect of Sanskrit and wrote it in a script called Brahmi. Although all these languages were in the Indo-European linguistic family, they were not mutually intelligible.

To function in and rule a literate society, or simply to keep the tax rolls current, the rulers, themselves, needed to acquire elements of the local cultures, especially a written language. Because the administrative documents of the Kushan have not survived, the most obvious source for studying their official language and its script is nonexistent. Fortunately for historians, they did issue a great many gold and silver coins embossed with both figures and writing. These coins, which were the same weight as the Roman *dinari*, were issued under the names of the Kushan kings. Judging from the legends on the coins, the Kushans adopted Prakrit as their official language, but used the Greek alphabet to write this Indian language. For instance, on a typical coin issued by King Kanishka, the figure on one face of the coin is the Buddha and the accompanying legend "Buddha" is written in Sanskrit using the Greek alphabet. The figure on the other side of the coin is an image of Kanishka, and the legend reads "King, Great King, Kanishka." The words used are Prakrit, but once again the script is not Kharoshthi, with which Prakrit is usually written, but the Greek alphabet. Both the gold and silver coins of the Kushan were of good quality, and archaeological finds show that they were widely used in Central and South Asia, even in parts of the Indian subcontinent that the Kushan never controlled, such as its eastern coast.

Governments have long used coins to display their own sense of who they are and what they stand for, using figures and legends that proclaim the sources of their legitimacy. The figures and legends on the Kushan coins were one of the major means that the kings had to portray the messages they wanted to deliver to their subjects. They also impressed their subjects by making donations to a wide variety of religious institutions. As nomads, they probably worshipped heaven, as most Eurasian steppe people did, and that may be the reason why the kings called themselves by the Sanskrit title "devaputra," which can be translated as either "son of heaven" or "son of God." Another possibility for the origin of this appellation is that the Yuezhi-Kushans followed the Chinese way of claiming a heavenly mandate. Wherever they got the idea of their relationship with higher powers or spheres, the Kushan royal lineage also reinforced their claim to legitimacy through ancestor worship.

Due to the diversity of peoples who lived within their empire, the Kushans encountered many different religions. The Greeks, for example, were a polytheistic people and all of their cities had their own city gods. The Hellenistic peoples in Afghanistan and northwest India had also been quite willing to incorporate indigenous and foreign gods and goddesses into their own pantheon. Thus, in the shrines of the Hellenistic cities, one could find gods from ancient Iran and Mesopotamia whose power had been established in these regions when the Achaemenids had ruled over them from the sixth to fourth centuries BCE. In addition, several temples on the site of Ai-Khanoum were fire altars characteristic of Zoroastrianism, which also came from Iran. These fire altars, too, continued to exist under Kushan rule. And there were many Buddhists and Hindus within their empire.

The Kushan regime facilitated the spread and the mingling of various religious sects. The Greek giant Hercules found a parallel deity in the powerful Indian god Krishna, who had originated in the region around Mathura, the site of the Kushan's southern capital. *Yakshas*, spirits of the forests and patrons of trade, also found their way from the north Indian plain to the northwest. Likewise, Siva and Vasudeva, lords of the new Hindu devotional cults, made their way into the Kushan domains at the same time that the older Brahmanical tradition was declining. Institutional centers of Buddhism and Jainism also moved from their homeland on the lower Ganges plain to the northwest to take advantage of the flourishing trade and general prosperity of that region.

Kushan kings patronized all the religions and cults. Kushan coins honored many of them, though every king had his favorites. King Kanishka was well known for his patronage of Buddhism, and it was the image of the Buddha that appeared most frequently on his coins. Kings and officials also made many donations to religious institutions with detailed stipulations for their use and how the merits thereby gained should be distributed. Some of the votive inscriptions on religious shrines were in the Prakrit language, some written in Greek letters, but most in Kharoshthi script.

Kushan kings also built temples devoted to their own family's lineage and had sculptured images of themselves placed there. So far two temples of this kind have been discovered, one in Surkh Kotal in Afghanistan, and another in Mat, near Mathura. The family temple in Surkh Kotal was built by King Kanishka. Inscriptions from his reign, his own statue, and the statues of two other Kushan rulers have all been found at this site. The family temple at Mat contained statues of Kaniska, as well as King Vima Kadphises, who ruled before him and King Huvishka, who ruled some time after him. It appears that these two family temples were built for the two distinct regions of the empire, one in the core region of Tuhara (in Afghanistan), and one near the southern capital of Mathura.

The architecture of the temple at Surkh Kotal was in the Bactrian Hellenistic style, and most of the inscriptions found at the site were written in the Prakrit language, although six of the seven of these Prakrit inscriptions were in Greek letters. The inscriptions found in the Mat family temple were all in the local Prakrit language and written in Kharoshthi script, as were most inscriptions of that period. Nevertheless, in spite of the linguistic differences, the statues of Kanishka from Surkh Kotal and Mat are almost identical. Although both are now headless, they are clearly equestrian in style and posture. The king wore loose trousers with heavy boots, and his feet were pointing outward, which is a familiar stance on the steppe. The knee-length robe is tightened at the waist with a belt strung with ornamental round medallions. Thus, it seems that the Kushan kings' royal attire was still that of the steppe, despite the hot climate in India.

Although the statues in the family shrines of the Kushan kings represented both the royal lineage and its close relationship with the gods, the kings themselves were not necessarily considered to be gods. The inscriptions on another family temple from the same time period, located near Surkh Kotal at a place called Rabatak, suggest that Kushan kings did not claim divinity for themselves. Although the temple has not survived, the inscriptions have, and they are in better condition than most. What they say is that the temple was built for both gods and kings. In this case the divinities were the Zoroastrian gods Sroshard and Narasa and the kings were Kanishka along with three of his ancestors. Clearly the Kushan kings sought to display a special relationship between themselves and their ancestors and the divinities of several religions, but it also appears that there was a clear distinction between gods and kings.

Ordinary subjects of the Kushan Empire also made many donations to temples. Indeed, the largest body of written sources from the Kushan period are votive inscriptions from both royalty and commoners, mostly in local Prakrit dialects written in Kharoshthi scripts. Commoners—traders, artisans, housewives, monks, and nuns of all religious sects and ethnic backgrounds—often gave the reign and title of the rulers in their inscriptions. One may get a glimpse into the structure of the Kushan state from these titles. The kings often called themselves "King, Great King of Kings, the Son of the Heaven." Although such elaborate titles may seem overdone, in fact, they reflect an awareness on the part of the Kushans that their own sovereignty was a sort of umbrella that floated lightly over a great many other authorities and many different peoples, each with their own traditions of sovereignty and their own historical memories. In this sense, it was meant to be inclusive, recognizing and incorporating all of those memories into their own sense of legitimacy.

Powerful as they were, the Kushans never could, and probably never intended to, maintain direct control of the basic structures of the agrarian societies that they ruled. The Kushan rulers, garbed in their steppe hats, robes, and boots, riding their horses, drinking grape wine in Roman-style goblets, and collecting exotic materials and artworks from all over Eurasia, did not interfere with the patterns of daily life, and do not seem to have spent much time or effort collecting agricultural taxes within their domain. It appears that they adopted a version of the satrapy system previously used by the Iranian Achaemenid Empire. Inscriptions indicate that the official title of Kushan regional officials was *Ksatrapas*, the Sanskrit version of the Persian word *satrap*, meaning governor. The central government of the vast Achaemenid Empire could not and did not set up local administrative offices in every corner of its empire. Instead, satraps or governors were sent to remote regions to collect taxes or tribute and maintain social order, but otherwise they left local administration in the hands of already existing local institutions. The satrapy system suited the Kushans just fine. They made no effort to interfere with local civic and religious institutions. As a result, castes, guilds of artisans and traders, Buddhist and Jain monasteries, and other religious institutions all flourished and maintained customary laws within their own communities.

Representatives of the various social groups also made donations to Buddhist monasteries and other religious establishments. The inscriptions that recorded these gifts reveal an intricate financial network that was often connected with the Roman Empire trade. Everyone and every institution appears to have been involved in the trade. Foreign traders, regardless of their own religion, made donations to the Buddhist monasteries in order to establish personal relationships with local people. Trade guilds made donations, asking for prosperity and safety during their travels on land and sea. Some Buddhist monasteries went so far as to store amphorae of wine for the local traders. Even more surprising was a find made by archaeologist F. R. Allchin. He discovered whole sets of distillation apparatus for the production of strong alcohol in a Buddhist shrine at the

Shaikhan Dheri site, which is located in a city called Pushkalavati in present-day Pakistan.

The Kushan Empire thus ushered in an era of cosmopolitism and created a large region where cross-cultural exchanges were part of everyday life. People from many different places carried out their religious practices freely, and whoever had some means was engaged in trade. This atmosphere provided the background for one of the most important cross-transmissions in Eurasian history, the spread to Central Asia and China of a particular form of Mahyana Buddhism that had flourished within the Kushan Empire.

MAHAYANA BUDDHISM AND ITS SPREAD TO CHINA

Both the cosmopolitan atmosphere and commercialism in the Kushan domain contributed to the success of Mahayana Buddhism, the school of Buddhism that spread most widely from India to various other parts of Asia. In particular, it was this variety that took root in China and eventually became the Buddhism of the Chinese people. Even though it is only one of several schools of Buddhism, when people think of Buddhism today, what they usually have in mind is this Mahayana school that developed during the Kushan age. To understand what is different about this school, in contrast to the older Theravada Buddhism, one has to look back in Indian history to a time before the coming of the Kushans, that is, before the mutual interactions that took place between the international traders and the Buddhists in the first two centuries of the Common Era.

When the Kushans arrived in India, Buddhism was already many centuries old. It originated in the mid and lower ranges of the Ganges River plain in the sixth century BCE. The founder of Buddhism, Shakyamuni (literally, the sage of the Shakya people), grew up in a small republic in the foothills of the Himalayas, on the border of present-day Nepal. At that time numerous states, monarchies, and republics were emerging on the Ganges plain. The tiny republic of the Shakya and the more powerful Confederation of Vajji Republics to its south were struggling to survive among several monarchies, especially Magadha on the lower Ganges and Koshala north of the mid-Ganges. This was also a time when the previously established tribal structure was losing some of its power. Cities had grown up along the banks of the Ganges, attracting people of different status from different localities, and rural-based hierarchies were breaking down in these urban settings.

As in many times of drastic change in history, some people began to question the fairness of the social system, and they also looked back in history trying to find the origins of social evils and injustices, and even the origin of human society and the universe. In short, it was a time for thinking about how things got this way and what could be done about it. Many new schools of thought appeared to challenge the orthodoxy of the traditional religion, Brahmanism, and its social practices, including the caste system. In this environment, the Shakya people gave birth to one of the greatest thinkers in world history, Buddha, while the Confederacy of Vajji Republics produced Mahavira, who founded the Jain religion.

The message of the Buddha's teaching was the Four Truths: Life is full of suffering; suffering is caused by desires; the only way to get rid of suffering is to suppress desires; and it is only by following the eight right ways, or disciplines, that one may get rid of desires and reach the state of *nirvana*. In Sanskrit *nir* means zero or none, while *vana* means existence. Thus, *nirvana* is a state of nonexistence. To understand why one would want to reach a state of nonexistence, one has to know that in India life was not thought of as a passage from birth to death, but as eternal cycles of birth and death. According to Buddhism and many other Indian systems of thought, after a person dies, his or her soul is reborn into another life. The status of one's next life depends on the merits and demerits that one accumulated in the previous life. In other words, a virtuous person will be reborn to a life that is better.

A woman might be reborn as a man, or a peasant might be reborn as a noble. However, no matter what form of life one has, it is still full of suffering. It is only when one gets to the state of nonexistence that he or she can break out of the vicious cycles of suffering. All the eight right ways, such as the right way of thinking, the right way of making a living, and the right way of speaking, are self-disciplinary approaches to virtuous behavior. Whether one gets closer to *nirvana* or further away from it in one's next life depends completely on one's own conduct in his or her present life. In this early form of Buddhism, no one could help you reach the goal of *nirvana* or even a better status of living in the next life.

The Buddha soon attracted many followers. Some became his disciples, following him on foot from one city to another to preach. Eventually these disciples took on the role of monks, the *sangha* in Sanskrit, while other believers remained in their homes going about their ordinary business, in order to support the monks by providing them with temporary lodging and food. Most supporters of the Buddha were urban-based merchants. In Buddhist and Jain thought agriculture was not the ideal way of making a living since tilling the land kills insects, and taking any life, re-gardless of its status, counts against one at rebirth. The Buddha engaged in many conversations with "householders," a respectful term used to refer to merchant-entrepreneurs, and guided them through the problems of or-dinary life in return for their material support of the monks. For instance, when asked by a householder about how to manage one's money, the Bud-dha advised him that one should spend only one-fourth of one's income for living expenses, save another fourth in preparation for hard times, and use the remaining half to invest in business.

The teachings of the Buddha survived his death and over the next sev-eral centuries continued to flourish in India. Around the first century BCE, when a prosperous trade began to emerge in the northwestern part of the Indian subcontinent, Buddhist merchants moved there, as did the Bud-dhist monks, and this region became a significant center of their activities. It is not surprising that the monks followed the merchants, but it is inter-esting to note how this geographical shift of commercial activity influ-enced religious geography. For one thing, many relics of the Buddha began to appear in the northwest, where the Buddha in his lifetime had never been. Also legends about the Buddha's historical life as well as his previ-ous lives began to emerge linking him to this region.

In one legend the Kushan king, Kanishka, fought a war with one of the kings on the mid-Ganges plain in order to obtain the begging bowl of the Buddha and to bring back a famous Buddhist sage called Ashvaghosha. For the next several hundred years this sacred bowl rested in a shrine in the northwestern city of Nagrahara and brought many pilgrims there. Ash-vaghosha, one of the most important writers of Mahayana Buddhism, did move to the northwest where he wrote several dramas in the Sanskrit language, the more scholarly, elite version of the vernacular Prakrit, that the Buddha had used when teaching. He also wrote a Sanskrit biography of the Buddha, in which the setting resembled much more the urban life of the Kushan cities where he was living than the more simple life of Kapilavastu, where the Buddha had actually lived, in the foothills of the Hi-malayas. He was a master of the Sanskrit language and a powerful writer, so it is not surprising that it is his biography of the Buddha that has become the major source of most publications about the sage in our own time.

In Ashvaghosha's version of the Buddha's life story, the sage was a prince living a luxurious life in a king's palace. However, his sudden ex-posure to some of the realities of life, such as poverty, sickness, aging, and death, so appalled him that he decided to bring an end to his idyllic, shel-tered life in the palace. He left home to teach the four noble truths and the eight ways toward the liberation of humankind from suffering. In this text, Ashvaghosha provides a detailed description of the local setting, with its neatly laid out streets, multistoried buildings, beautifully clothed and ornamented people, horses, and horse-drawn vehicles. In so doing, he was taking his readers not to the foothills of the Himalayas, but to the Kushan cities of Taxila, Purushapura, and Mathura.

Also, due to the patronage of Kushan rulers and rich traders, the Buddhist monks, as a community, became extraordinarily rich and built many stupas and monasteries. By this time the stupa had long been a part of the landscape along the middle and lower plains of the Ganges River. Long before Buddhism emerged there, these dome-like structures were tombs built over the graves of outstanding members of society. When in the fifth century BCE the Buddha made his passage to *nirvana*, according to one of the earliest texts, he told his followers to build stupas to mark the places where his ashes were being kept. He did not name a successor to be the leader of his disciples but asked them all to follow his teachings. Thus, the stupas, which held his remains, became symbols of his person, and also gathering places for his followers. The early Buddhist stupas were domes built with bricks or stones. Later, during India's Mauryan Empire (ca. 321–184 BCE), stupas became larger, taller, and more elaborate under royal patronage. In northern India exquisite sculptures of trees, animals, and young women covered the stone railings that appeared around important stupas.

In northwest India under the Kushans the importance of the stupa as a religious center grew rapidly, and monasteries were built around the stupas in order to house Buddhist monks. Monks no longer wandered from city to city, as they had when the Buddha lived, but settled in the monasteries. Also in the Kushan period the stupas and monasteries were constructed with beautiful stone and decorated with finely carved sculptures. Many of the latter were scenes about the life or former lives of the Buddha, and many of these were drawn from Ashvaghosha's description of the Buddha's life, as were many other artworks of the Kushan period. Indeed, some of this artwork portrays themes such as drinking and dancing that no one now can explain in terms of their relevance to Buddhist theology.

The style that developed in the Kushan's southern capital is known as Mathuran Buddhist art (in present-day northern India), while the one that developed in the northwest region (in present-day Pakistan and Afghanistan) is called Gandharan art. While there are many differences in the two styles, both forms exhibit the urban flavor of Ashvaghosha's writings. Mathuran artists had developed their skills and traditions from working on statues of folk deities such as *yakshas*, the spirits of the forest, and *nagas*, the snake gods. Sculptures on the sandstone railings of stupas in northern India show young women playing flutes, practicing acrobatics, or drinking wine on the street, under the stares of people watching from the balconies above them.

Located in a region where Hellenistic influence had been strong, the Gandharan style is distinguished by its Greek and Roman elements, as well as images drawn from nomadic steppe culture. For example, the dome of one of the earliest stupas (located in the cosmopolitan city of Taxila in present-day northern Pakistan) is covered with sculptured upside-down acanthus leaves. Acanthus is a Mediterranean plant, and the sculptors of ancient Greece frequently used it to adorn the monumental buildings of their cities. After Alexander of Macedonia had led his armies east and Greek settlements were established all the way to what is now Afghanistan, these leaves became one of the most typical design elements in Hellenistic art in Asia. Also, in the northwest region, the sculptures carved on the granite railings and panels of monasteries and stupas include figures of men and women dressed in Roman, Greek, or steppe styles, engaging in sports and music, or drinking from high-footed goblets filled with wine from large Greek-style jars or wine serving bowls.

In this Gandharan art, even the representations of the Buddha recall Mediterranean styles. The Buddha's robes look remarkably like Mediterranean togas, complete with the meticulously carved draping of the material that is characteristic of Greek and Roman sculpture. However, the Buddha's stance is more like that of the Kushan kings, with the feet pointing outward. Equally interesting is that in this artwork the Buddha is closely associated with horses. He rides a horse when leaving home to begin his quest for the spiritual life, and the image of a horse returning to the city with an empty saddle became the very symbol of the Buddha's denunciation of secular life. In short, the Buddhist art of both the Mathuran and Gandharan schools demonstrates not only the elegance of urban culture, but also the tenacity of steppe life in that cosmopolitan age.

In this commercial environment, Buddhist theology developed in a more abstract and abstruse direction. The Mahayana theologian Nagajuna emphasized the meaninglessness or emptiness of both matter and material life. Not only the objects observed were empty, even the observers were empty. For most followers, including the merchants, such concepts made Buddhist theology difficult to understand. However, a series of Mahayana Buddhist texts composed in this period offered a solution. A text called the *Lotus Sutra*, for example, states that the truth of the Buddha is very difficult to comprehend, indeed, almost impossible for commoners to

STŪPA IN BLOCK E, SIRKAP.

ILLUSTRATION 2-1   SKETCH OF BUDDHIST STUPA

First century BCE. This stupa is one of the the earliest found in the region where Gandaran styles flourished. It is located in the cosmopolitian city of Taxila, east of Peshawar, Pakistan, near the site of the northern capital of the Kushan Empire. The acanthus leaves, although upside-down, are reminiscent of the Corinthian columns of ancient Greece and demonstrate the Hellenistic influence on Gandaran Buddhist art and architecture. Acanthus is a Mediterranean plant, and its leaves are the most typical Greek design element found throughout the Hellenistic world. This sketch was included in John Marshall, *Taxila*, Vol. III, Cambridge University Press, 1951, Plate 125. *(Source: Reprinted with the permission of Cambridge University Press.)*

understand. Therefore, one should get in the *Mahayana* (literally, the great vehicle) of the Buddhas and bodhisattvas to cross the ocean of suffering. Mahayana, the great vehicle, was so great that it could carry all believers to heavens and lands filled with numerous Buddhas, not just Buddha the sage who had founded the religion, but many deified Buddhas and bodhisattvas. The bodhisattvas were a multitude of gods who had once been holy men who could have crossed the threshold to *nirvana*, but decided not to in order to stay in this world to help others to cross the ocean of sufferings. Avalokiteshvara was the bodhisattava endorsed by the *Lotus Sutra*.

The existence of these Buddhas and bodhisattvas created a new universe for devotees of Buddhism, one in which material donations to monasteries could bring religious merit to the donors. By making a donation to a monastery in the name of a Buddha or bodhisattva, lay devotees could gain sufficient merit to get into the great vehicle, which would bring salvation in the afterlife, or even happiness in this life. Mahayana theology thus blended the commercial value of exchanges into its basic doctrine and thereafter tremendous wealth flowed into the monasteries.

It also endorsed many of the items of international trade that originated in or passed through Kushan territory. The *Lotus Sutra* and other Sanskrit Mahayana texts designate seven treasures, in addition to silks, as the best gifts for Buddhas and bodhisattvas. The treasures were gold, silver, lapis lazuli, crystal, coral, carnelian or agate, and pearls, and according to the texts, the Buddha lands and heavens were decorated with these seven. All of them, along with silk, were commodities in high demand in the Central Asian silk road trade and in the seaborne Mediterranean-Indian trade. Apparently Buddhist devotees followed these instructions precisely, since the remains of these seven treasures and silks are ubiquitous in the archaeological sites along these routes and have been found among the ruins of Buddhist institutions in India, Central Asia, and China.

By this time the monasteries were rich and they were willing to host devoted travelers. The bodhisattva doctrine of helping others to cross the ocean of suffering had become evangelical in spirit, and it would not be long before Buddhist missionaries began traveling along with merchants from India to China. By the end of the first century CE, there were small communities of Buddhist merchants and monks in Luoyang and other major cities of the Later Han dynasty. Most of these early Buddhist missionaries possessed a Chinese surname, either An, indicating Parthian ethnicity, or Zhi, which indicated that they had come from the Kushan realm. Nevertheless, during the Later Han period, roughly the first two centuries CE, Buddhism in China would remain almost exclusively an organized religion only within the diaspora communities of foreign traders, most of whom were from the Kushan Empire. Meanwhile, Buddhist artifacts and symbols of the Buddha spread rapidly across China, and have been found all the way from Mongolia to the Sichuan basin in southwestern China. These finds are numerous, but the context within which they have been found suggests that people were not actually becoming

Buddhists. Apparently they were incorporating isolated elements of Buddhism into their folk religions and did not understand that Buddhism was a separate religious system.

There is, however, one exception to this generalization, a group of sculptures (dated to the second century CE) on China's eastern coast that is a clear sign of Buddhism being practiced among Chinese. On a small hill called Kongwangshan, near the port city of Lianyungang in northern Jiangsu Province near the Shandong border, many Buddhist figures are carved on the side of large boulders, and apparently Chinese people did go there to worship during the Later Han dynasty. Although the sculptures also portray standing Buddhas, the most impressive scene is a prostrate Buddha surrounded by lines of standing mourners, the scene of Buddha's passing away. These carvings are roughly done, which suggests that they were not carved by professional artists, and the most striking thing about them is that all of the figures, whether those of the Buddha or his worshippers, are in the Kushan style. The standing Buddha is almost identical with the Buddha on Kushan coins; and the worshippers of the prostrate Buddha wear pointed hats, high boots, and knee-length robes, very much in the style of the nomadic people in the Kushan domains. This second century site on China's eastern coast marks the high point of the Kushan Empire, and clearly indicates the role of its traders in transmitting Buddhism to China. Given the steppe-style clothing worn by the worshippers, it would appear that the route of transmission to this coastal site was still the overland routes from India to China. In addition, there is no evidence for the existence of a commercial sea route linking Chinese ports to the Indian ports that were located within the Kushan Empire.

At the same time that the trade between China and the Kushan Empire and between the Kushan Empire and the Roman Empire was flourishing, overland routes on the Eurasian steppe were in the process of shifting south off of the grasslands and onto deserts. Like the sea voyages, desert crossings could be treacherous. Nevertheless, merchant caravans made their way through these lands, and the traffic in silk contributed to the prosperity and development of oasis towns and cities within these deserts. In the west, in the deserts between the Euphrates and the Mediterranean, these oasis cities were much older than the silk roads, but in the east, in the Takla Makan Desert (located in present-day China's Xinjiang Uighur Autonomous Region) the Chinese, the Kushans, and the Sogdians (from present-day Uzbekistan) would contribute to the growth of yet another remarkably cosmopolitan culture.

FOR FURTHER READING

Basham, A. L. *The Wonder That Was India*. New York: Grove, 1954. Plate XXXII shows the Hellenistic city goddess at Purushapura with her crown that resembled the city wall.

Begley, Vimala, and Richard Daniel De Puma. *Rome and India, the Ancient Sea Trade*. Oxford: Oxford University Press, 1992.

Bowen, R. L., and F. P. Albright, eds. *Archaeological Discoveries in South Arabia*. Baltimore: Publications of the American Foundation for the Study of Man, 1958.

Liu, Xinru. *Ancient India and Ancient China, Trade and Religious Exchanges AD 1600*. Oxford: Oxford University Press, 1988.

———. "Migration and Settlement of the Yuezhi-Kushan: Interaction and Interdependence of Nomadic and Sedentary Societies."*Journal of World History*, 12, no. 2 (2001), pp. 261–92.

Miller, James Innes. *The Spice Trade of the Roman Empire, 29 BC to AD 641*. Oxford: Clarendon, 1969.

The Periplus of the Erythraean Sea, translated from the Greek and annotated by Wilfred H. Schoff, Longmans. New York: Green and Co., 1912. A more recent publication provides a better English translation: Lionel Casson, *The Periplus Maris Erythraei*. Princeton University Press, 1989.

Ray, Himanshu P. *The Wind of Change, Buddhism and the Maritime Links of Early South Asia*. Oxford: Oxford University Press, 1994.

Srinivasan, Doris, ed. *Mathura, the Cultural Heritage*. New Delhi: American Institute of Indian Studies, 1989.

Wheeler, Mortimer. *Rome beyond the Imperial Frontiers*. London: G. Bell and Sons Ltd., 1954.

Part One: Silk Roads In Eurasia's Eastern Deserts

140–87 BCE	Reign of Emperor Han Wudi.
	Extension of Great Wall to ancient Yumen (Jade Gate).
	Irrigated agriculture established in oases of Hexi Corridor and Takla Makan Desert.
	Passport system begins.
107 BCE	Han general Li Guangli defeats ruler of Ferghana.
	Thereafter, Takla Makan Desert oases look to Han military for protection.
	Chinese establish a military presence on northern rim of Takla Makan Desert.
100 BCE	Beginning of establishment of military and farming settlements in Takla Makan, introduction of irrigation; population in Takla Makan oases grows rapidly; immigration increases; oases residents come to rely on both long-distance trade and local agriculture.
25–221 CE (Later Han)	Takla Makan oases on both northern and southern rims of the desert become well-established stopping places for those going to and from China.
221 CE	Han dynasty falls.
220s CE	Founders of Sasanid dynasty overthrow Parthians in Iran.
ca. 240s	Sasanid army subordinates much of Kushan Empire.
	Many Yuezhi-Kushan and Indians flee to oases on Takla Makan's southern rim, establishing Buddhist institutions. Hellenistic-style viticulture established in these oases.

Third and fourth centuries CE	Local administration in Hexi Corridor keeps traffic flowing; trade networks persist despite political chaos.
	Mahayana Buddhism continues to spread in China, gaining in significance.
	Sogdians emerge as intermediaries between Sasanid Iran and China; Sogdian language becomes principal commercial language in oases of Takla Makan's northern rim, remains so until eighth century.
	Yuezhi-Kushans and Indians migrate to southern rim of Takla Makan, where (Indian) Prakrit language written in Kharoshthi script became preeminent and remained so for centuries.
320–330	Decade of much military turmoil in China; Sogdian letters found at Dunhuang date to this decade.
Fourth and fifth centuries CE	Monumental statues of Buddhas carved on stone cliffs along Central Asian Silk Road from Bamiyan to Yungang.

PART TWO: SILK ROADS IN EURASIA'S WESTERN DESERTS

Early first millennium BCE	Growth of Palmyra, known in the Bible as Tadmor.
At least by fourth century BCE	Petra founded by local Nabataeans to service caravans delivering incense from southern Arabia to eastern Mediterranean ports.
312–281 BCE	Reign of Seleucus I Nicator, who founded Zeugma-Apamea (now in Turkey).
ca. 280 BCE	Founding of Dura in the Syrian Desert. A Hellenistic Seleucid city that began as a Macedonian town.
ca. mid-100s BCE to early 100s CE	Peak of the trade through Petra.

Mid-first century CE	Beginning of Roman Empire sea route from Red Sea to Kushan Empire's Arabian Sea ports.
Early 100s CE	Petra in decline, possibly due to Roman traders using Red Sea ports that portaged goods to the Nile River, which delivered them to cities on the Nile, including Alexandria on the Mediterranean.
165 CE	Romans took over Dura and renamed it Europus. Under Roman control its commercial significance declined, and its significance was largely military. The same was true of Zeugma-Apamea.
Second to third century CE	Tadmor-Palmyra at its peak. Was within the Roman sphere, but was not occupied. Became the most important commercial center bringing goods across the Roman frontier from Iran.
226 CE	Sasanids overthrow Parthians, and rule Iran.
227 CE	Sasanids take southern Mesopotamia from Parthians and establish their capital at Ctesiphon.
260 CE	Roman position so deteriorated that Sasanids capture Roman Emperor Valerian.
267 CE	Palmyreans, with Roman aid, successfully defend the city from a Sasanid attack.
269 CE	Palmyrean Queen Zenobia leads an army against Rome, taking over Egypt and part of Anatolia.
272 CE	Romans capture Queen Zenobia and destroy Palmyra. Thereafter the eastern Eurasian desert routes are no longer a significant part of the silk roads.

THE DESERT ROUTES: SECOND CENTURY BCE TO FIFTH CENTURY CE

GETTING STARTED ON CHAPTER THREE: Compared to the earliest silk roads across the eastern part of the Eurasian steppe, what advantages did routes through the Hexi Corridor and the Takla Makan Desert have? How did these locations change after the silk roads began to pass through them? In what ways were the desert oases near the Mediterranean different from those in the Hexi Corridor and the Takla Makan? What impact did the Seleucids have on the Western desert oases? What was the nature of the desert oases' relationship with traders and armies from the Roman Empire?

CHAPTER OUTLINE

Although the earliest overland silk roads were located on the Eurasian steppe, it was not long before they shifted southward, away from the grasslands and onto routes that passed through desert oases. Indeed, in the early twentieth century, before scholars became aware of the importance of steppe peoples and maritime traders in the formation of the routes, the classic perception of the silk road focused exclusively on these desert routes that passed through cities now buried under desert sands. However, after it became known that the first routes had emerged out of a dynamic of both exchange and conflict between nomads and sedentary peoples on the Chinese frontier, it became clear that nomadic peoples had played the largest part in their creation. Also, from a geographical point of view, the routes that traversed the vast grasslands were easier on travelers and the animals that transported them, especially where the terrain was relatively flat.

Nevertheless, the traffic on these routes gradually shifted southward onto the desert routes, mainly because security was always a problem on the steppe. Although some nomadic peoples were much involved with the trade and protected it, others were not, and the latter could make traveling across the steppe a dangerous proposition. Because nomadic groups sometimes challenged each other for pastures and other resources, and memberships in alliances and confederations often changed, caravan leaders could never be sure that their arrangements for safe passage would be effective. Thus, many silk traders on the overland routes came to prefer the desert crossings that were protected by Chinese armies in the east and by Roman armies in the west.

Traveling across deserts exposed the traders to extremely harsh natural conditions and had its own perils, but at least the caravans were relatively safe from sudden attacks by large numbers of raiders on horseback. Horses are high-maintenance animals in a desert, and people who take them very far into a desert generally have to carry along supplies of both water and food for these animals. Such requirements would have discouraged both raiders, who must travel light in order to make a speedy getaway, and traders, who need the carrying space for their trade goods. Thus, in the deserts it was camels, not horses, that were the most efficient means of transportation both for people and cargo. The camels used in Central Asia, known as Bactrian camels, are large and sturdy two-humped animals. The humps store fat, which enables them to survive long journeys and the harsh conditions of deserts. Also thick pads under their hooves enable them to walk for long distances over sand and other desert soils.

In order to secure the route that carried commercial traffic into and out of China, the Han Empire during the reign of Emperor Wudi (140–87 BCE) had extended the Great Wall westward to the Jade Gate. This extension ran through the Hexi Corridor, a long and arid strip of land that lies between the Qilian Mountains and the Mongolian deserts. To support the garrisons stationed along this extension of the Great Wall, the Han Empire began introducing irrigated agriculture to various locales that were within the Wall. Also due to the Chinese presence, agriculture began to take hold outside the Jade Gate, in the oases around the edges of the Takla Makan Desert. The introduction of irrigated agriculture would lead to profound changes in this area. Agricultural production made it possible for the oases to support larger and larger populations, and ultimately, in the third century CE, to serve as a refuge for Buddhist populations that migrated there from the Kushan Empire. While the Kushan immigrants settled on the desert's southern rim, Sogdians (whose homeland was in present-day Uzbekistan) settled along its northern rim. Thus, it is not surprising that highly cosmopolitan cultures would begin to flourish in this basin.

By the Later Han (the first two centuries CE) the oases on both the northern and southern rims of the Takla Makan Desert had become stopping places on trade routes that led from the Jade Gate to what is now Afghanistan and Uzbekistan. From these locations, the caravan traders could go southeast to the Indian subcontinent to trade with the numerous merchants who frequented the seaports on India's Arabian Sea coast. Another option for the traders was to follow routes from Afghanistan and Uzbekistan that went west to the Iranian plateau, which was under the rule of the Parthians (ca. 250 BCE–226 CE). The Parthians, like the Kushans, had originally been nomads before they took over a sedentary society, and they too remained skilled horseback riders and archers. By this time the Parthian Empire had expanded and controlled not only the Iranian plateau but also Mesopotamia, where it contested with the Romans for the formerly Hellenistic regions of western Asia, including lands near the eastern shores of the Mediterranean.

As the Roman Empire managed to expand its eastern frontier to the Euphrates River (ca. 113–117 CE), the Parthians proved to be a formidable enemy. After several battles, the Romans realized that they could not take all of Mesopotamia from the Parthians and would have to be content with holding the lands west of the Euphrates. This impasse made the Syrian Desert and the Roman-controlled portion of the Arabian Desert the eastern frontier of the Roman Empire. Within these deserts Rome acquired several caravan cities that marked the western ends of the silk roads. When Rome acquired them, they were already prospering from the silk trade, since they were located on long-standing trade routes that carried Chinese silks along with other goods from Iran and southern Arabia to various Mediterranean ports. Although some of these oasis cities had quite diverse populations, they were essentially Arab cities within a Roman-controlled sphere. The four that were most involved in the silk trade were Petra in present-day Jordan, Palmyra in present-day Syria, Zeugma-Apamea on the upper Euphrates in present-day Turkey, and Dura Europus on the middle Euphrates in present-day Syria near its border with Iraq.

Unlike the oasis towns that developed near China, these cities predated the development of any silk roads. Palmyra and Petra predated even the expeditions of Alexander of Macedonia, and both Zeugma-Apamea and Dura-Europus had become important during the Hellenistic period when the Seleucids ruled much of the land between the Mediterranean and India. Palmyra, especially, has a special place in the historiography of the silk roads, for it was within its ruins that twentieth century archaeologists found many eastern luxuries, including silk textiles woven in Han China. These silks, dated to the first and second centuries CE, are the earliest and most important material evidence of commercial links between the Mediterranean world and Han China.

THE HEXI CORRIDOR AND THE GREAT WALL

When Emperor Wudi (r. 140–87 BCE) of the Han dynasty had the Great Wall extended along the Hexi Corridor in order to protect the trade route, there was very little agriculture in this region. Annual precipitation was low, and the limited vegetation was constantly threatened by shifting sand dunes from the Mongolian deserts that lay on its northeastern flank. It was thus necessary to transport food grains from other parts of China to the frontier to feed the garrison troops stationed there, a necessity that caused a severe drain on the treasuries of the empire. There was, however, a possible source of water, if one knew how to tap it. The Qilian Mountains line the corridor's southwestern flank, and every year melted snow from their peaks runs down the mountain side and replenishes underground water reserves at their base. To solve its food supply problem, the Chinese government came up with a program that was called the "garrisoning and farming system." They would use this underground water to irrigate the land, and use soldiers to grow food crops on the irrigated fields.

Because hostilities were only sporadic, soldiers for much of the time were not engaged in military activities and were free to do other things such as build irrigation systems and claim the former wasteland for crop production. Eventually they could produce much of their own food and food for their families as well. Many of the soldiers had been peasants before they became soldiers and were thus familiar with agriculture. In addition they could bring their families there to help cultivate the land and, in the case of their wives and daughters, to also weave silk textiles. Another advantage of this system from the government's perspective was that the presence of the families might encourage the soldiers to become permanent settlers in this frontier region.

Thus, this "garrisoning and farming system" was an important innovation of the Han Empire and it set a pattern for all Chinese governments up until modern times. The extension of the Great Wall and the trade route that it protected succeeded in carrying Chinese agricultural technology westward. Furthermore, once the military-agricultural settlements were established along this section of the Wall, not only did soldiers have a reliable supply of provisions, the villages and towns that resulted provided the first facilities for travelers on this desert route, supplying them accommodations and other essentials.

Official records of the Han Empire do not provide detailed information on the organization of the military-agricultural settlements. However, the soldiers and officials garrisoning the Wall wrote reports, and recorded such things as local commercial transactions and contracts on thin, narrow slips of wood, which were tied together with string and then rolled up for storage. (Paper, which was invented in China during the Han dynasty, was not yet in general use.) Officials collected travelers' passports and identification documents, which were also written on wooden slips, and received government documents containing orders and regulations to be carried out locally. Many of these bundles were stored in the watch towers of the Great Wall, where they have been found by archaeologists. Most of those discovered so far are from a series of watch towers around Juyan, the northernmost extension of the Great Wall into the Mongolian deserts. Another collection was found at Dunhuang, a large garrison town about fifty miles inside the Han dynasty's Jade Gate in present-day Gansu Province.

Although they were written in well-known Chinese characters, reading these wooden slips today is very difficult, in part because the vocabulary is archaic and colloquial. There is, in addition, a much bigger problem. The wooden slips have survived for more than two thousand years, but the strings that tied them together have not, and deciding which ones go together and reconstructing their proper sequence is a formidable job. Nevertheless, due to the efforts of many scholars, historians can now get at least some idea of the soldiers' life along the Wall. The basic working unit appears to have been a watchtower along with an agricultural settlement.

Each watchtower was the base for a military unit, and the site where the soldiers performed their usual military duty. The head of the watchtower held the lowest rank within the category of military commander. There were also officials at the watchtower who were in charge of assigning land to soldiers and keeping production records and other related data. Other officials were in charge of supplying water to the watchtowers, as well as water to irrigate the fields. The agricultural yields in this corridor did not match those from traditional areas of Chinese farming further inside the Great Wall, but due to irrigation, they were relatively reliable. Soldiers received salaries, and the government often paid them not with money, but with rolls of plain silk textiles. The government had warehouses full of this kind of silk because Chinese farming households generally used it to pay their taxes to the government. Many records also reveal that soldiers could use this silk as currency to pay for their local purchases.

The principal mission of the soldiers was to prevent horseback-riding Xiongnu raiders from getting through the Wall and looting villages, towns, and caravans. In addition, they checked the identification documents of travelers. The early passport system, which began during the reign of Emperor Wudi, was rather simple since the documents, issued to both Chinese and foreigners, were for only one leg of a trip. A Chinese traveler obtained the passport from officials in his home county, who noted his name, purpose for traveling, and the contents of his baggage on wooden slips. When he reached the Wall, the passport was surrendered to the soldiers and deposited in the local watchtower while he carried on his business outside the gate. It is not clear whether or not he needed another passport when he passed through the gate on his way home. Foreigners presumably obtained passports when they entered China and surrendered them to county officials when they arrived at their destination. There were times when a foreign traveler needed to have an interior pass that was issued at his destination and used to return to the same watchtower through which he had entered, but much of the time there was no such requirement. In the latter case, when the foreign traveler was leaving China, the officers in the watchtower just located their record of his entry in their files and indicated on it that he was leaving.

By the third century CE, the government had improved the system by supplying a round-trip passport that included a more detailed description of the traveler. Foreigners entering China had to carry this revised passport wherever they went, and then surrender it to the watchtower when they left. Thus, the passports of foreigners accumulated in the watchtowers. Chinese travelers also needed passes to leave through these watchtowers and reenter China, but it seems that they then carried them back home with them, for they are rarely found in the watchtowers. Most of the round-trip passports have been found in the town of Dunhuang, inside the Great Wall, and many of these belonged to foreigners entering and exiting China. (This may be because many foreigners actually lived in Dunhuang for long periods of time, and were able to keep their Chinese passports with them.) These passports include information about the person's place of origin (such as Parthia or the Yuezhi-Kushan Empire), destination (often the capital at Luoyang or another large city), physical appearance (whether the complexion was light or dark and whether the individual's stature was tall or short), and a description of the kind of clothes worn by the traveler. The latter item included information about robes, trousers, jackets, and footwear, which, most likely, would have provided an indication of a traveler's ethnicity. For instance, trousers and boots would indicate that a person was of steppe origin, perhaps Yuezhi-Kushan or Parthian, and was not Han Chinese.

This passport system actually survived the fall of the Han dynasty in 221 CE. By the mid-third century not only had the Han dynasty fallen, but so had the Yuezhi-Kushan Empire and the Parthian Empire, and China proper was torn by civil wars. Nevertheless, passports from the third and fourth centuries CE indicate that local administrators in the Hexi Corridor somehow kept the commercial traffic flowing in and out of China. By this time both food production and sericulture were well established in the corridor, and local agricultural production certainly contributed to its stability. Archaeologists have found painted bricks in a graveyard near the Jiayu Gate, a short distance east of the Jade Gate, that portray various kinds of agricultural work, including scenes of a man plowing the field with a bullock and a woman collecting mulberry leaves for feeding silk worms. Clearly, the typical agricultural pattern of the Chinese household had become established there.

Even with the relatively self-sufficient farming settlements along the corridor, traders during these centuries faced many difficulties since political power in the interior of China was fragmented and frequently changing hands. Commerce was especially precarious during the decade following 310 CE when several nomadic groups invaded northern China causing the Western Jin dynasty (ca. 265–317) to flee to the south. The impact that this instability had on individual traders is revealed by a mailbag full of letters found west of Dunhuang in 1907. British archaeologist Aurel Stein (1862–1943) was excavating at Site T XII when he found the mailbag, which apparently had been left in a watchtower. The letters had been written by Sogdians who resided in Luoyang, the capital city of the Jin, and in the oases towns of the Hexi Corridor. They were written in the Sogdian language on Chinese paper and were inserted into cloth envelopes made either from silk or a coarse textile, and were addressed to people in Sogdiana or to their compatriots living in the oases towns outside the Jade Gate. One letter is particularly informative. The writer was a trader living in the Hexi Corridor and his letter was addressed to his partners in Samarkand, a major city in Sogdiana, in present day Uzbekistan. He told them that conditions in China had deteriorated rapidly after the Xiongnu sacked Luoyang and Ye, another large city in north China, causing the emperor to flee. As a result of the chaos, he had lost contact with his partners who were based in various Chinese cities. He also told them that he was very ill, and did not expect to live long enough to return home. He thus asked his partners to distribute to his heirs the property that he had in Samarkand.

Even though the letters in this mailbag never reached their destinations, they nevertheless suggest that the demand for Chinese goods and the profits from this long-distance trade must have been so great that traders were willing to risk their lives by persisting in their business during this dangerous time. As a result of their efforts, the trading networks survived and commerce continued throughout these centuries. Out of necessity, they maintained their own networks and facilities to ensure the transportation of goods and information, and even though this batch of letters got lost, the networks appear to have been effective and efficient even under such difficult circumstances. It took several centuries for the invaders from the steppe to settle down peacefully as rulers of China and reestablish some sort of stability on this desert route. The commercial networks maintained by the traders also facilitated the spread of Mahayana Buddhism eastward from India to China, and the continuing influx of Buddhism into China contributed significantly to the transition process that turned nomadic rulers into sedentary-style emperors, eventually bringing some stability to China.

OASES AROUND THE TAKLA MAKAN DESERT

After the Chinese style of agriculture had been established in the Hexi Corridor, the Han government made an effort to establish farming in oases west of the Jade Gate, especially those within the Takla Makan Desert. The desert lies within a large oval basin, more than six hundred miles long, and is almost completely surrounded by high mountains. On its northern side the Tian Shan range separates it from the Eurasian steppe, and on its southern side the Kunlun Mountains separate it from the Tibetan high-lands. On its western end, the Pamirs separate it from what is now Tajik-istan, and the Karakorum Mountains separate it from what is now northern Pakistan. The only opening in this ring of mountains is on the basin's eastern side, facing China's Jade Gate. Ecological conditions in the oases were similar to those in the Hexi Corridor, but the political environ-ment was quite different. During the Han dynasty the Chinese govern-ment had firm control over the Hexi Corridor, but the oases of the Takla Makan could not be claimed by any of the large empires, and each of its oasis towns was essentially an independent state.

The floor of the Takla Makan Desert is extraordinarily dry and covered by shifting sand dunes. Neither agriculture nor pastoralism is possible on the basin's floor. The oases cling to the foothills of the mountains where snowmelt rushes down the mountainsides creating short rivers and un-derground water reserves. The northern route passed through a string of oases along the southern side of the Tian Shan range, and the southern route passed through a string of oases on the northern edge of the Kunlun Mountains. These routes constituted much of what became known as the Central Asian Silk Road. The oases on both sides of the desert were con-stantly threatened by sand dunes, and, without irrigation, there could be no agriculture of any significance. Although the towns were small, they had long served as a home for nomads, some of whom lived there year-round tending camels and sheep, and for immigrants from India and China who engaged in limited farming. Many different languages were spoken in these towns, but during the Han period, most of them belonged to the Indo-European linguistic family. There was never a Great Wall in this desert to protect the oases or the caravans from nomadic raiders, but during those centuries of the Han dynasty when the Chinese military pres-ence was strong in the region, China did become involved in protecting the safety and viability of the Takla Makan trade routes, and promoting irri-gation and agriculture in the oases.

After the Han general Li Guangli defeated the king of Ferghana (ca.107 BCE) and brought back the heavenly horses to the court of Wudi, the oases looked to the Han military for protection. For China, keeping a military force in the Western Regions was costly, even more costly than maintaining a military presence in the Hexi Corridor, but the Han dynasty nevertheless set up a military headquarters on the northern route of the Takla Makan. Starting around 100 BCE, it also established military and farming settlements in the oasis towns of Luntai and Quli, near the military headquarters. These settlements not only supplied food for the soldiers, but also introduced agricultural technology such as irrigation. The result was a spectacular increase in population in the oasis towns. According to statistics provided by the *History of the Han* and the *History of the Later Han*, the number of households in nine major oases increased by almost six times during the first century CE. In particular, the population of Khotan, a large oasis on the southern route, increased from 3,300 to 32,000 households. Khotan had always been famous as a source of jade, but this remarkable increase in population transformed it into an important caravan city-state. Clearly such increases were due not only to natural population growth, but also to significant immigration into the region. Whatever the sources of the increased population, the residents came to rely on both local agriculture and the transit trade to ensure their survival.

The trade routes along the edges of the Takla Makan survived the collapse of the Han Empire in the early part of the third century CE and the ensuing chaos in China proper, as can be seen from the collection of Sogdian letters found at Dunhuang. Not all the letters were addressed to recipients in Sogdiana, itself. Many of the ones addressed to other destinations had been sent to their compatriots in the oases of the Takla Makan. After the fall of the Parthians and the establishment of Sasanid power in Iran, the Sogdians served as the intermediaries between Iran and China. The relationship of the Sogdians with the Iranians was of long-standing, and their language, which was Indo-European, was closely related to Persian. After the Chinese military presence in the Western Regions weakened and eventually disappeared altogether, Sogdians migrated to the oases along the northern side of the Takla Makan and established trading outposts there, from which they ran their trading networks in China. These immigrants brought the Sogdian language with them and established it there as the principal commercial language. Sogdian influence persisted in this area for about five centuries, that is, until the eighth century CE when the Muslim Abbasid Caliphate conquered Sogdiana and almost simultaneously Turkic peoples from the eastern steppe directly north of China began migrating westward, settling throughout all of Central Asia.

On the southern route of the Takla Makan, most immigrants were either Yuezhi-Kushans or Indians who had lived within the Kushan Empire. After Iran's Sasanid Empire subjugated the Kushan Empire, many Yuezhi-Kushans and Indians migrated to the oases along the Takla Makan's southern route, all the way east to the Shanshan state at the desert's southeastern end. The caravan city-state of Khotan may well have been the center of their activities since it was home to many Kushan traders and many

Kushan Empire coins have been found there. By far the most numerous coins in Khotan are multilingual coins that have a legend written in Chinese characters on one side, and on the other side a legend written in the Kharoshthi script. The Kharoshthi script came from northwestern India, where it was used to write Prakrit, a vernacular form of Sanskrit. When the Kushans had ruled there, they had adopted it as one of their official languages. Thus, after their immigration to the southern oases of the Takla Makan, this Indian language became the predominant written language of Khotan, for both official and commercial purposes, and remained so for several centuries thereafter.

At least for some of the Central Asian traders who were active on the southern rim of the desert, Chinese was still the language used for passports. In the early twentieth century, within the territory of Shanshan in the oasis of Niya, the archaeologist Aurel Stein found several passports issued between 266 and 274 CE. According to Lin Meicun, a Chinese expert on this silk road, these travelers must have been Yuezhi-Kushans because the surname on the their passports was "Zhi," the Chinese designation for people from the Kushan Empire. Two of them were described as dark complected, and one was described as white. At least one of the passports, the one of the white-faced traveler, was signed by the governor of Dunhuang. Because the governor signed his passport, this trader was most likely a permanent resident of Dunhuang who traveled the southern route of the Takla Makan for business reasons.

BUDDHIST ESTABLISHMENTS ON THE DESERT ROUTES

Increased agricultural production and population growth in the oases made it possible to sustain additional traffic on the routes as well as new cultural institutions. As indicated in Chapter Two, Buddhist institutions began spreading from the Kushan Empire to Han China during the first two centuries CE. However, during these two centuries, there were no Buddhist establishments in either the Takla Makan Desert or the Hexi Corridor, two significant parts of the route that linked the two large empires. This phenomenon puzzled scholars since they assumed that the people who built these institutions would have built them all along the trade routes from the Indian subcontinent to China, including the sections that went through the desert areas.

It now appears that this assumption was wrong. For many decades archaeologists looked, in vain, for traces of Buddhist establishments in these areas that could be dated to the first two centuries CE. This futile search was finally abandoned, however, after E. Zurcher, a famous scholar of Buddhism, pointed out in 1990 a possible answer to the puzzle. During the earliest centuries of the silk roads, the populations in the oases of these areas were too small to support religious institutions of the sort that would leave behind an archaeological record. Brave as they were, the Buddhist missionaries, just like the merchants of that time, only passed through the desert areas, quickening their pace to reach China. Later, however, after the Kushan Empire had fallen and Han military capabilities had weakened, the populations in the oases had reached the point that the establishment of monasteries became feasible.

This population growth would have been impossible without the sophisticated irrigation systems that the Han soldiers had built. The new agricultural foundation established during the Han dynasty made possible a natural increase in the population, as well as a large inflow of immigrants, including many long-distance traders who were seeking a safe haven from political and military conflicts in the surrounding areas. In particular, the fall of the Kushan Empire in the third century CE contributed to the flow of immigrants and the sudden appearance of many Buddhist establishments in the oases, especially along the southern route. With the population growing and large numbers of merchants actually based in the oasis towns and cities, Buddhist priests recognized the need to serve these communities and began establishing the religious institutions of their faith in these desert locales.

It is the construction of stupas that best symbolizes the initial arrival of Buddhist religious establishments in this desert region. Established by Buddhist immigrants from the Kushan Empire, the stupas soon became centers for spreading Buddhism as well as other elements of the culture of the Kushan Empire, including the Prakrit language and the Kharoshthi script with which it was written. Such a stupa appeared at Niya, an archaeological site on the southern route. (In the official histories of the Han, completed during that dynasty and shortly after its demise, the town is referred to as Jingjue. Today it is located in Minfeng County, in China's Xinjiang Uighur Autonomous Region.) The site at Niya is one of the best places to study everyday life in an oasis town that developed into a Buddhist center. Prior to the arrival of Buddhist institutions, it had been one of the locales that benefited from the Han dynasty's introduction of irrigated agriculture. In fact, archaeologists working near Niya even found a Han dynasty mold that had been used to make seals for the personnel in the Chinese Office for Propagating Agriculture. It was also here that the third century CE Chinese language passports of the three Yuezhi-Kushan were found.

Niya is a relatively well-preserved site, revealing town life and commerce on the southern route of the Takla Makan soon after Buddhism was established there. When the site was first discovered, it was almost totally buried in sand, but excavations revealed that it had once spread along both banks of the Niya River, which disappeared in later centuries. Its central landmark was a Buddhist monastery and a stupa. The larger part of the town spread lengthwise in an east-west direction for about ten kilometers, and was about two kilometers wide in the north-south direction. South of this section there was an additional cluster of several dozen houses.

The houses had wooden frames, but the walls were made of sun-baked bricks or clay. Often, both the interiors and the exteriors of the houses were beautifully painted. Fireplaces inside the houses kept people warm in the winter; and outside the houses there were animal stables and fruit trees. Inside the homes archaeologists have found wooden furniture, wooden and clay containers for storing food grains such as wheat, oats, and millet, domestic animal bones, bronze mirrors, and beautiful textiles made from silk and wool. The cemetery was located about 2 km to the north, further into the desert, where similar artifacts were buried in the graves. About 2 km south of the monastery, there was an ironworks, where ore was smelted and poured into casts.

The excavation indicated that by the second century CE Niya had become a securely established agricultural settlement and an attractive station for the transit trade. Then, in the third century, it became the meeting place of Indian and Chinese cultures, as well as a center of Buddhism. Hundreds of documents have been found there, many in the Kharoshthi script, and some written in Chinese characters. Apparently both writing systems were common. The coins, mentioned earlier, with a Kharoshthi legend on one side and a Chinese legend on the other, were also plentiful. In addition, Chinese documents, such as passports and orders from the governor of Dunhuang were found. The latter were dated according to the official dating system of China's Jin dynasty, which suggests that some sort of distant Chinese authority was recognized in this oasis. Nevertheless, numerous administrative documents written in the local Prakrit language indicate that the local government operated mainly in the political style of the Kushan Empire, and that the local rulers called themselves Great King or Son of Heaven, like the Kushan kings had before them.

The documents frequently refer to Chinese residents, giving their surname as *Cina* (meaning Chinese), followed by a given name in the local Prakrit language. Many of the documents record commercial transactions and disputes involving various people and property such as camels, slaves, land, vineyards, clothing, and textiles. Although many copper coins have been found there, the documents rarely mention them, perhaps because they were used only for ordinary, daily transactions that did not involve large sums. Instead, there are many references to rolls of silk textiles being used as currency. Textiles were also a major form of property. This is suggested by documents that include lists of peoples' possessions such as numerous items of clothing made from silk, wool, and linen, as well as by the number of textiles recovered at this site. Obviously, the people of Niya were much involved in the silk trade and benefited from it both materially and culturally.

One of the documents, No. 324, which dates to the mid-third century CE, describes a legal case that reveals the multicultural aspects of life in this oasis. A group of people called Supis, probably a nomadic tribe, had raided the kingdom and carried away a slave. Since the oases were places where nomads and agriculturists came into contact, and relations between them were not always good, both sides looted and enslaved people of the other side. Also small-scale slave trading was common in such border regions. The slave that the Supis had stolen had belonged to a respected local resident called Yonu. Since Yonu was a common Indian term for Greeks, his name suggests that he was of Greek origin. The Supis had later sold the slave to a Chinese named Sgasi for two gold staters and two drachmas. Sgasi thought that he had thereby become the lawful owner of the slave. However, Yonu recognized his former slave and wanted the slave returned to him. The case went to court and the judge ruled against Yonu. He explained that Sgasi's purchase of the slave had been legal and thus he did not have to simply return the slave to Yonu. However, the judge went on to say that Sgasi did have to put the slave up for sale.

The judge's reasoning was that since the purchase of the slave by the Chinese had been a legal transaction, he should be able to recover his investment, even if he could not keep the slave. (The judge's ruling that Sgasi could not keep the slave may have been intended to provide an opportunity for Yonu to buy him back.) Whether one agrees with the final decision on the case or not, it is certainly interesting to see the variety of cultural traditions that were involved. The document is in an Indian language and script that Kushan immigrants brought to the oasis. The original owner appears to have been of Greek origin, and when the Chinese bought the slave from the Supi nomad, he paid for him in staters and drachmas, which were either Greek coins or copies of Greek coins. The use of this Greek currency is just one indication that the Kushans had brought along with them many elements of the Hellenistic culture of Bactria, which they had once ruled. It is also interesting to note that the Chinese immigrants in Niya do not appear to have had any problem using foreign languages and currencies.

The Kushans are also the most likely candidate for the establishment of Hellenistic-style viticulture in this region. Document No. 419 records the purchase of a vineyard, a large transaction that was held at the monastery, with several monks witnessing the purchase and sale. The two sellers, Budhila and Budhaya, two sons of a monk, were selling the vineyard to a certain Ananda, a person with an Indian name, for one gold stater and 2 *muli*, supplemented by another 12 *muli*. Historians still have not discovered what a *muli* was, but the stater was certainly the Greek currency unit. Viticulture became an essential part of the oasis economy, as well as the subject of textile design. A piece of cotton batik cloth found in Niya exemplifies the appeal of viticulture in the region. On the remaining corner of the textile, a Hellenistic-style Bactrian goddess is holding a grape-filled cornucopia.

That monasteries functioned as centers of local and interregional economic activities is not surprising. These institutions had performed the same functions within the Kushan Empire. Having enthusiastically incorporated elements of Indian and Hellenized Bactrian culture into their own, the Kushans, when they migrated to the oases of the Takla Makan, brought their highly cosmopolitan culture along with them. Nor is it surprising that the monks acted as witnesses to contracts and purchase and sale agreements, since in India they had long since provided a wide variety of services to travelers, both pilgrims and traders. Although all monks may not have been virtuous all the time, the traders came to trust them as reliable witnesses and judicious arbiters. Thus, after the arrival of numerous Kushan immigrants with their highly diverse cultural traditions, the oasis of Niya became a small but cosmopolitan kingdom where Chinese residents as well as their language became an integral part of the mix.

Niya was only one of many oases around the Takla Makan Desert, and in the centuries to come many more Buddhist monasteries would be established along the silk roads, providing a variety of services to local residents and travelers. The monasteries were also home to various styles of architecture, painting, and sculpture. While Buddhist establishments on the southern route, like those at Niya, demonstrate a close relationship with the art and architecture of the formerly Kushan areas on the Indian subcontinent, those on the northern routes, where Sogdian merchants were numerous, demonstrate a relationship with the Iranian-influenced styles of Sogdiana. In addition, once Buddhist institutions had become part of the local landscape, they began to reflect local Takla Makan styles that pre-dated the influx of immigrants, and the art and architecture of the oases thus developed its own unique style. Thus, one could say that much of the Buddhist art and architecture, including stupas, monasteries, cave paint-ings, and sculptures, that had marked the trade routes of the Buddhist homeland in India in the first century CE, were successfully transplanted to the Central Asian desert routes about two or three centuries later.

By the fourth and fifth centuries CE, huge statues of the Buddha be-gan to emerge on the faces of high stone cliffs along the silk road. These carvings were so large that they could be seen from a great distance and they thus served as landmarks for weary travelers, Buddhist or not, for many centuries. At the western end of the desert route, at Bamiyan in the Hindu Kush Mountains in present-day Afghanistan, two statues, one thirty-seven and the other fifty-five meters in height, were carved on the face of a cliff. At roughly the same time, that is, beginning in the fourth century, Buddhist cave sites began to emerge on the northern edge of the Takla Makan Desert at Kezil, near Kucha, in the Hexi Corridor at Dun-huang, and at Yungang on the northern edge of China's Shanxi Province, where there also were several exceedingly large statues of the Buddha carved on the face of a cliff. Although, individually, the Yungang Buddhas are not as impressive as those at Bamiyan, they dominate the entrances to a whole series of caves that run along the foothills for more than one kilo-meter. At the time it was built, this Buddhist landmark at Yungang marked the eastern end of the silk road. Thus, one could say that from Bamiyan to Yungang, Buddhist monuments marked the entire length of what was traditionally known as the Central Asian Silk Road. Since the Buddhist monasteries at these sites provided the basic facilities for trav-elers, they made a significant contribution to the stability and viability of the silk roads' desert routes.

DESERT ROUTES ON THE ROMAN FRONTIER

Once the caravans leaving China loaded with silks, furs, and other goods reached the gigantic statues of the Buddha at Bamiyan in present day Afghanistan, they had reached the western end of the Central Asian silk road. From Bamiyan traders could either go southward to the Indus River Valley to supply the Arabian Sea ports, or they could go westward to the Iranian plateau. Greek, Roman, and Chinese sources make it obvious that the Iranians played a significant role in this trade and that Iranian culture was omnipresent on these silk roads. However, there is almost no data, literary or archaeological, regarding how the Iranians, either the Parthians prior to 227 CE or the Sasanid thereafter, managed the long-distance trade. Even more remarkable is that no silk textiles from these centuries have ever been found in Iran.

To the west of Iran, however, inside the eastern frontier of the Roman Empire, in the deserts of present-day Turkey, Syria, and Jordan, the ruins of several caravan cities have survived for almost two millennia. In large part this was due to the dry climate of the deserts and, in some cases, to the shifting sands that covered the ruins. These caravan cities, including Petra in Jordan, Palmyra and Dura Europus in Syria, and Zeugma-Apamea in Turkey, prospered during the early stages of the silk road trade. Petra had long-standing connections to the seaports of southern Arabia, but the others were supplied mainly by Iran. They all supplied the Mediterranean market with silks, resins, spices, and other rare and valuable products that came from the eastern and southern parts of Asia. Even though these cities were under Roman protection, their merchants were able to trade with the Iranians, the archenemy of the Romans, in order to obtain these goods. Frequent warfare characterized these centuries of rivalry between the two empires, and the fortunes of the cities as well as the trade went up and down due mainly to political conflicts and hostilities.

The problems that the Romans faced when extending their power and their trade to the caravan cities were quite different from those that the Han Empire had faced when extending its power westward. The Han government, to ensure the survival of the trade routes in the Western Regions, had promoted agriculture and thus introduced irrigation technology to the desert oases enabling them to support substantial populations for the first time. In contrast, the trade routes across the deserts of southwestern Asia were already well established when the Romans took over Syria, a region that had been under the rule of the Hellenistic Seleucids for about three hundred years. The Nabataeans, a Semitic people based in northern Arabia, also had had, for several centuries, a well-established trading position, moving goods back and forth between the Mediterranean markets and the coastal markets of southern Arabia where rare Asian goods came in. East of Syria the Romans were up against the Parthians, whose powerful cavalries controlled a strategic section of the land routes that came from China through Central Asia. The Romans strengthened their garrisons along the Euphrates River, which became the virtual border of the two empires. Their military camps were a conspicuous presence in the cities along this frontier, and very little is said about trade in the Roman sources. Likewise, historical references to the cities on the Euphrates, such as Zeugma-Apamea and Dura-Europus, are mostly about military campaigns and the movement of troops.

Nevertheless, the military conflicts in these deserts did not stop the movement of trade goods. First, Petra in the rock-strewn mountains of Jordan, and then Palmyra in the Syrian Desert transformed themselves into splendid caravan cities, flourishing as a result of their commercial contacts with both the Roman Empire and cities in the Parthian Empire. Numerous pieces of Han Chinese silk textiles have been excavated from Palmyra, providing the first material evidence of Chinese goods on this westernmost extension of the silk road. To understand the dynamics of war and trade in the deserts of southwestern Asia, one has to first go back in time in order to examine political, economic, and social conditions in the Nabataean cities prior to the Roman conquests.

HELLENISTIC CITIES UNDER THE SELEUCIDS

Alexander of Macedonia set out to conquer lands to the east of the Mediterranean in 334 BCE and by 326 BCE he had reached the Punjab in India. He had many garrison towns built along the way and named them all Alexandria. After his untimely death in 323 BCE, Seleucus I Nicator (312–281 BCE), his successor in the eastern part of the conquered territory, followed his example and had many more cities built. According to a contemporary writer known as Appian, Seleucus named sixteen of the sites Antioch after his father, five Laodicea after his mother, nine Seleucia after himself, three Apamea after one of his wives, and one after another wife, which is called Stratonicea.

Not all of the cities have been located by archaeologists, especially those in Iran. These newly created cities had a fundamental impact on the amount of communication and interaction among the various parts of Eurasia, and the impact of Greek culture was felt all the way to Central Asia and India. During the Seleucid Empire Antioch on the Orontes River (in present-day Syria) and Seleucia on the Tigris River (in present-day Iraq) developed into major metropolitan areas, as well as centers of culture and trade. Greek-speaking soldiers in the many garrison towns married local women and started families there. These Hellenistic cities were in many ways quite like those in their Greek homeland, except that they were ethnically and especially linguistically diverse. Surrounded by totally different language groups, Greek residents in these cities, soldiers, their family members, and traders often spoke two or even more languages. Greek, however, persisted as the official language, and Greek letters were carried by coins and other official inscriptions all over Eurasia.

Although initially all the Hellenistic cities in Eurasia were under the reign of the Seleucid monarchs, every city had a remarkably complete set of institutions characteristic of an independent Greek polis, and each controlled a small territory surrounding it. In other words, during the Seleucid period the Greek city-state structure somehow survived intact under an overall monarchical umbrella. Every city had a theater to perform Greek drama, a gymnasium, temples housing Greek deities or local deities, a palace for the ruler, and often a mint to issue coins. The famous Greek colonnades were a distinguishing landmark in these cities, and paintings and mosaics decorated the walls and floors inside the buildings. The Greeks also established olive gardens and vineyards in the new territories. In all the cities, Dionysus, the god for wine and art, and especially drama, was one of the most popular deities. The Greeks continued the agricultural and trading patterns of their homeland, producing and selling olive oil and wine in exchange for other goods.

Although the Greeks only ruled one part of the Punjab (in present-day Pakistan and India), and eventually lost political control over it to the Mauryan Empire (ca. 321–184 BCE), they maintained their Greek culture under Mauryan rule and thus elements of the Hellenistic polis persisted as far east as the Punjab. Seleucus I Nicator signed a treaty with the Mauryan Empire, which ruled over much of the Indian subcontinent, and even gave a Greek princess as a bride to the Mauryan king Chandragupta. The Seleucid ruler was very interested in elephants and obtained many from India through treaty and trade. However, at this point in time there was no silk to be had in India and thus there was no silk trade. As we have seen, before the migration of the Yuezhi nomads to what had been Bactria around the year 130 BCE, there was no silk trade beyond the frontiers of China. It was only after the Yuezhi-Kushan migration to what had been Bactria that the trade routes would be extended all the way from the Chinese frontier to the Mediterranean, moving in the opposite direction of the expeditions of Alexander.

THE SILK TRADE IN EURASIA'S WESTERN DESERTS

The eastern overland trade of people from the Roman Empire was based on the infrastructure built by Alexander and the Seleucids. Their eastern overland trade was thus constructed upon a Hellenistic foundation. The reader may recall that, as discussed in Chapter Two, Hellenistic culture had remained strong as far east as Afghanistan and the northwestern part of the Indian subcontinent, and that both of these areas became a part of the Kushan Empire, the principal supplier of silk. Thus, in the first century CE, when traders from the Roman Empire began to make a serious effort to obtain silks and other Asian luxuries, the Greek language and scripts, Greek currency, the all-inclusive Greek religious practices and cultural values, as well as viticulture, gymnasiums, and theaters, could be found all across Syria, Mesopotamia, Iran, and Afghanistan.

The only major obstacle to Roman overland trade with the east was the power of the Parthians in Iran. By origin, the Parthians were nomads who did not have a tradition of recording their own or others' histories. This is probably the reason why theirs is the least known of all the ancient Iranian dynasties. Nevertheless, the neighbors of the Parthians seemed to know them well as shrewd traders. To their east the Han Chinese people were familiar with them through trade, and to their west, the Romans fought with them for control of the lands through which major trade routes passed. After several futile attempts to cross the Euphrates, by 117 CE the Roman emperors finally realized they could not defeat the Parthians east of the river. The Parthians also understood that the Romans would not give up Syria with its rich coastal cities and commercial enterprises. For the Romans, holding the line at the Euphrates served to protect the empire's commercial interests west of that line. The city of Zeugma-Apamea, on the upper reaches of the Euphrates, appears to have been the premier garrison post for holding this frontier, and Antioch on the Orontes acted as its supplier and supporter.

The city of Zeugma, in present-day Turkey, was located at the site where Seleucus I Nicator had built a Seleucia on the west bank of the Euphrates and an Apamea on its eastern bank. A bridge over the river joined the two cities. (Zeugma in Greek means a joint, a place where two things connect.) It was from here that many of the Roman campaigns against the Parthians began by crossing the bridge over the Euphrates. When the Parthians had the upper hand in Mesopotamia, the strategic position of Zeugma was even more significant to the Romans, since losing Zeugma would have meant the loss of Antioch and the whole of Syria. As a result, in Roman times Zeugma was more of a garrison city than a trading center, which it had been during the Hellenistic period. Even in the Roman period, Greek continued to be the language used there. Most inscriptions were written in Greek, along with a few in Latin, and none have been found in the local languages.

At the present time, the site of Zeugma is under water since the Turkish government built a dam across the Euphrates a short distance below the town. In the early 1990s when the dam was under construction, archaeologists from various countries rushed to the site in an attempt to learn as much as possible and salvage whatever they could. The excavations of 1992–1994 revealed a Roman villa and many exquisite artifacts. Among the findings was a mosaic that covered the entire floor of one room. The scene, which included ten figures, depicted the wedding of Dionysus and Ariadne, and was most likely based on an earlier Greek painting. That Dionysus, the Greek god of wine and art, appeared in this location was no accident. Whether the master of the villa was a Roman military general or a local magnate, he certainly identified with the Greek way of life. Many Greek cultural elements, including language, religion, art, and viticulture, remained strong in Zeugma in spite of the overwhelming presence of the Roman military and the constant threat of attacks from Iran. These cultural elements kept the city linked with other Hellenistic cities on both sides of the Euphrates, and these links no doubt contributed to the persistence of the city's Hellenistic culture.

Roman garrisons in Zeugma communicated with other garrison posts up and down the river, including Dura-Europus, on the Euphrates downstream from Zeugma, in present-day Syria not far from the Iraqi border. Today it is one of the most systematically excavated garrison towns. It began as a Macedonian garrison around 280 BCE, and many of the Greek soldiers who settled there married the local Semitic women. During the centuries of confrontations, first between the Romans and the Parthians, and later between the Romans and the Sasanid, Dura changed hands several times. Thus, both the Romans and the Parthians left their legacies in the city. The Parthians had conquered the city in the mid-second century BCE when it was ruled by the Seleucids, and later they used it as a garrison town against the Romans. As a result, many Iranians came there with their own material culture, including their own clothing styles, and blended in with the local Semitic peoples and the Greeks. Even today lively images of Parthian aristocrats and cavalries on galloping horses remain on its walls.

The Romans took over Dura in 165 CE, and renamed the city Europus. At that time Dura-Europus became their easternmost garrison station, protecting the routes to Palmyra and the Mediterranean coast. Here, too, within the limits of the city itself, defense was more important than trade during the Roman period. Roman soldiers ruled over it and an elaborate Roman-style bath was built to make the soldiers feel at home. As late as

250 CE, a troupe of entertainers that included some eighty to ninety individuals was sent from Zeugma to Dura-Europus to entertain the soldiers. By that time, the Sasanids had already replaced the Parthians as the lords of Iran and Mesopotamia, and the Romans' days there were limited. Shapur I of the Sasanid dynasty crossed the Euphrates in the late 250s CE at Dura-Europus, and perhaps also at Zeugma-Apamea, and the Romans were pushed back all the way to Antioch on the Orontes. Thereafter, the Romans lost Dura-Europus and never recovered it.

The Roman garrison towns such as Zeugma-Apamea and Dura-Europa had originally been Macedonian garrison towns, which then transformed themselves into centers of culture and trade during several centuries of Seleucid rule. As frontier posts of the Roman Empire, they gained in strategic importance but lost most of their commercial significance. Their very existence, however, was important because they protected the eastern frontier of Rome's commercial position and contributed to the protection of caravan routes and related commercial networks. The traders who delivered the silks, spices, fragrances, and other luxuries were Arabs, whose camel caravans crossed the deserts between the garrison stations and Palmyra and between the southern Arabian seaports and Petra. The camels on these routes were Arabian camels (also known as dromedary camels), which have only one hump. They are leaner and have thinner coats (useful in warmer climates) than the Central Asian (Bactrian) camels, but they have equal endurance and are just as tough as the latter. Only those Arab traders, who had the husbandry skills required to manage the camels and the linguistic skills to converse with their counterparts in cities beyond the Roman Empire's borders could carry out this long-distance trade in luxuries that crossed the deserts.

Unlike Zeugma and Dura-Europas, Petra and Palmyra remained truly commercial caravan cities even after the Roman armies came to southwestern Asia. Judging just from the visual appearance of their architectural remains, these cities looked more Greek than either Dura or Zeugma. Nevertheless, from their founding until their abandonment, most of the residents were Semitic peoples. The Arabs in this region had been engaged in the long-distance trade long before the Greeks arrived on the scene, but under the suzerainty of the Seleucids, they had learned the Greek language and had become familiar with elements of Greek culture in order to further their commercial interests. During the several centuries that these cities flourished, their residents created a unique commercial culture that drew from many sources, including the Hellenistic, Iranian, and Arab worlds.

Originally the growth of Petra had resulted from the trade in aromatic wood resins, mostly frankincense and myrrh, which were harvested in southern Arabia, and from the trade in South and Southeast Asian spices that could be acquired in the seaports located on the peninsula's southern coast. As discussed in Chapter Two, by the first century CE the Roman Empire traders' quest to reach the source of these commodities had prompted their interest in sailing on the Red Sea and the Arabian Sea. At that time, an Arab people called Nabataeans, who lived in the northern part of the peninsula, controlled the overland routes between the Mediterranean ports and the southern Arabian sources of frankincense and myrrh. Nabataean history actually goes back at least to the fourth century BCE, when they were sheep herders in the rocky ravines of Jordan. These ravines were in the red sandstone mountains that stretch from the Gulf of Aqaba in the Red Sea to the Dead Sea. They had learned to survive in this harsh desert land by digging cisterns in solid rock to preserve rainwater and by seeking shelter in the caves. In one of the valleys the Nabataeans supplied water and food to caravans, which passed through these mountains on their way from southern Arabia to the Mediterranean, initially carrying frankincense and myrrh. To accommodate the caravans, they began carving into the rock in order to build cave rooms for the travelers. The valley then developed from a caravan camp into a caravan city that eventually become known as Petra. Both the Ptolemies in Egypt and the Seleucids in Syria and Iran tried to take over Petra, but neither succeeded. Even though it absorbed much of the Greek cultural heritage, Petra managed to maintain its independence from these Hellenistic kingdoms.

Petra is a Greek word meaning rock, and that is the very material from which it was built. At the center of the city was a 300-yard-long colonnade made from the local red sandstone. The royal palace, marketplaces, and major temples, all of the same sandstone, flanked the main street. A nymphaeum, a curved wall embracing a fountain and a statue, marked the entrance to the colonnade, and a huge gate with bas-relief sculpture was at the end of the main street. Between the monumental buildings, colonnaded porticos of shops and hotels lined the street. Behind them, residential houses stretched all the way to the foothills, and many of these were essentially caves, cut right into the mountain side, with a façade of colonnaded halls carved on the front wall.

Several major structures were located outside the "downtown" area. An amphitheater with forty-five rows of seats, divided into three horizontal sectors probably dates to the first century CE. There were numerous temples, altars, and sacrificial grounds around the city, housing Greek,

Arabian, and Iranian gods and goddesses. A necropolis housed the dead, both the rich and the poor, in cave tombs with Greek façades. All these rose-colored rock structures are quite well preserved in the dry climate, still glowing under the dazzling desert sun.

Although the traders and residents of Petra spoke a local version of the Nabataean language, its military commanders and governors had Greek titles, since Greek remained the lingua franca of Hellenistic western Asia. The fortunes of Petra went up and down with the volume of trade passing through. Its peak came when Seleucid power was waning, and Roman power had not yet arrived. For about 250 years, from the mid-second century BCE to the early second century CE, the merchant-rulers of Petra controlled the main "spice road," supplying Mediterranean ports with spices, aromatic resins, and other rare goods from Arabia, eastern Africa, and South and Southeast Asia. Petra's trading networks reached as far north as Phoenicia, on the Mediterranean Sea, where the presence of their trading communities was marked by their temples. Petra's fortunes began to dwindle, however, after the development of the first maritime silk road. After the Kushan Empire, the primary dealer in Chinese silks, expanded from Afghanistan into northeastern and northern India and traders from the Roman Empire, based in Egypt, found their way to the Red Sea and began sailing to ports in southern Arabia as well as to Arabian Sea ports within the Kushan domain in India, the glory of this commercial kingdom seems to have settled upon another caravan city, Palmyra.

Palmyra, a marble city that arose in the midst of the Syrian Desert, became the greatest caravan city of the Roman east. Its colonnade, theater, senate building, agora (market area), and temples were all larger and grander than those of Petra or any other Hellenistic city in western Asia. The original settlement at the site had been known as Tadmor, a town that is mentioned in the Bible and apparently dated back at least to the time of King Solomon. It was the Romans who renamed the city Palmyra, which means "palm trees" in Latin. The Greek architectural style covered the city with a strong Hellenistic veneer, but the masters of the city were neither Greeks nor Romans. The Arab-speaking princes from local tribes formed a kind of oligarchy that managed the affairs of the city-state. While most people spoke the local language Palmyraean, Greek was the official language for conducting most business. Its people worshipped many deities, old and new, of both local and foreign origins, and some of the local deities took on Greek names.

Palmyra was at its peak from the second to the third centuries CE, when the Romans and the Iranians fought all along the Euphrates. While the Ro-

mans sent legions to garrison the towns on the Euphrates, they did not oc-
cupy Palmyra and allowed it to manage its own affairs, including its trade,
without any interference from them. Even though battles might rage on the
frontier, the Roman market still demanded silks, incense, and other luxuries
from the east. Under such conditions, only the Palmyraeans managed to
continue the trade across this contested frontier, due to their linguistic and
business skills and a large commercial network that spanned the embattled
front in many locales. Archaeologists have found a famous stone tablet
known as "The Tariff of Palmyra," which records the tariffs imposed on arriving caravans. It is a long text of more than 400 lines, written in both Greek
and Palmyraean. The tablet's title, two lines long, is given in Greek letters,
and its date is given in the Roman style indicating that it was published on
April 18, 137 CE. This tablet established a newly revised tariff schedule on
various sorts of merchandise, including such things as purple dye, dry
goods, balm oil, and olive oil, as well as slaves. However, it did not give specific instructions regarding the tariffs on textiles, presumably because there
were so many different kinds, and each could vary in its quality.

The Palmyraeans dealt in a great many different textiles. Excavations
at the city's necropolis have uncovered more than 500 different pieces of
cloth, woven from linen, wool, cotton, and silk. Most of the linen textiles
were probably produced locally. The cottons were from Mesopotamia or
India. Among the woolen textiles, there were a few pieces of cashmere,
which must have come from Kashmir or nearby highlands in Central Asia.
Most of the silk cloth had been woven in Han China, although some of it
could have been woven in Central Asia using imported Chinese yarns. At
this point in time it was only the Chinese who knew the secret of sericulture, the production and harvesting of silk filaments from silkworm cocoons, so any production elsewhere depended on Chinese materials,
which could be in the form of yarn, floss, or fabrics. Since there were silk
yarns and dyes at Palmyra, it is possible that the Mediterranean cities or
even Palmyra itself were already weaving their own silk textiles using
these imported materials.

The necropolis, literally, the city of the dead, was a marble replica of
the city of the living and their activities, or at least the activities of its
wealthier inhabitants, and it covered an area almost as large as Palmyra itself. It was probably because the Palmyraeans believed in an afterlife that
closely resembled life on earth that they built such elaborate tombs and
carved their surfaces with life-like representations of the dead enjoying the
same pleasures as the living. The deceased were shown reclining on
Greek-style couches, often holding goblets in their hands. Although the

couches, drinking vessels, and hairstyles are Hellenistic, the long robes depicted are similar to those of the Parthians. The hems on these robes are often portrayed with strips of cloth decorated with exquisite designs similar to the elaborately decorated textiles that Parthians actually wore. Clearly wealthy Palmyraeans enjoyed the best of the material cultures all around them, and especially the luxurious clothing made from a variety of fine textiles. In addition, it is quite clear that many were enthusiastic wine drinkers, given the number of drinking scenes and the frequency that grapes and grape leaves appear as motifs on these works of art.

Numerous sculptures also depict camel caravans and an occasional horse on the grand tombs. Goods that came from Iran came by horse caravans, and camel caravans delivered the goods from the Arabian Peninsula. Apparently the deceased traders had imagined themselves carrying on trade in the afterlife. It is also possible that the carvings sought to portray the lives that they had actually led and perpetuate people's memories of them. In real life, the commercial enterprises of Palmyra extended far beyond the oases. The city provided financial services to caravans and sent merchants to faraway countries where they set up trading communities called "Funduk." These outposts usually included a caravanserai, a hostel that provided facilities for the caravan traders and their animals, as well as warehouses, offices, and often a temple. Many of the Palmyraean outposts were in cities under Parthian rule, such as Babylon and Vologesia, which was located near the place where the waters of the Euphrates and Tigris rivers flow into the Persian Gulf. Apparently it was because of the usefulness of these networks, which extended well into Iranian territory, that the Romans let an independent Palmyra grow into an even more powerful commercial empire.

The Iranian threat to the Roman frontier increased after the Sasanid dynasty replaced the Parthians. It was originally based in southern Iran near the eastern shores of the Persian Gulf, and in 227 CE it took over southern Mesopotamia from the Parthians. By 260 the Roman position in the east had deteriorated to the point that the emperor Valerian was captured by the Sasanids at the battle at Edessa, a short distance east of Zeugma, and soon Palmyra itself was threatened. The Palmyraeans then rose up, with the support of the Romans, to defend their independence from the Sasanids and in 267 successfully pushed back the Iranian invasion. Then in 269, an emboldened Palmyraean army, under the queen Zenobia, overreached itself and challenged the Romans by occupying Egypt and a large part of Anatolia. The emperor Aurelian subsequently defeated the Palmyraeans, seized the city, and captured Zenobia in 272.

They then destroyed the city, ending the glory of the trading empire of Palmyra.

The story of these western desert routes ended with the Roman defeat of Palmyra. The silk roads in other parts of Eurasia, however, did not come to an end, but adjusted to the new circumstances. In spite of political turmoil in China, beginning in the third century CE, the desert routes and oasis cities in Central Asia flourished and silk continued to reach Iran and India's Arabian Sea ports. In the 330s CE, about fifty years after the defeat of the Palmyraeans, two new power centers would emerge. In India, the Gupta Empire, based on the Ganges River, got direct or indirect control over much of the Indian subcontinent, and almost simultaneously the Roman emperor Constantine moved the capital of the empire from Rome to Byzantium, a small town on the Bosporus (in what is now Turkey). Thereafter, the Byzantine Empire would gradually develop into both a large market for and an important producer of silk textiles, thus assuming a major role in the Eurasian trade. Under Byzantine rule, Christianity became more closely linked to state power, and the same was true of the Zoroastrian religion in Iran under the Sasanids and Hinduism in India under the Guptas. In China, after the fall of the Han dynasty, Chinese political unity disintegrated, and among the large number of regional powers that rose and fell in China, many would become closely associated with Buddhism. Thus, the next chapter examines the curious relationships that developed between the silk trade and the religions of Zoroastrianism, Christianity, and Buddhism.

FOR FURTHER READING

Burrow, T. *A Translation of the Kharoshthi Documents from Chinese Turkestan*. London: The Royal Asiatic Society, 1940.

Juliano, Annette, and Judith Lerner. *Monks and Merchants: Silk Road Treasures from Northwest China*. New York: Abrams Books, 2002.

Kennedy, David. "The Twin Towns of Zeugma on the Euphrates."*Journal of Roman Archaeology*. Portsmouth, RI, July, 1998.

Lin, Meicun. *The Serindian Civilization*. Beijing: Dongfang Publisher, 1995.

Rostovtzeff, M. *Caravan Cities*, English translation by D. and T. Talbot Rice. Paris: Presses Universitaries de France, 1932.

Schmidt-Clinet, Andreas, Annemarie Stauffer, and Khaled Al-As'ad. *Die Textilien aus Palmyra*. Mainz Am Rhein: Verlag Philipp von Zabern, 2000.

TIMELINE

Iran

ca. 224–661 CE	Sasanid dynasty rules Iran, after overthrowing the Parthians.

Sasanids set out to reestablish ancient Iranian religion of Zoroastrianism (founded sixth century BCE during Achaemenid rule) and ancient traditions, and to diminish the influence of Hellenistic culture that had prospered in Iran during Parthian rule.

Zoroastrianism spread from Iran to Central Asia, especially to Sogdiana. Sogdian traders who had been Buddhists from the second to fourth centuries CE become Zoroastrians.

Silk-weaving industry in Iran flourished from time of wars with Rome. Sasanid kings begin to wear silk robes.

The *simurgh* became the most frequently used symbol for royalty and divinity. Iranian silks and textile designs made their way to Byzantium. Iranian silks are very popular in China. Silks and designs from Zoroastrian converts in Central Asia are also popular in China.

Iranian silks woven with gold threads can be found in both Byzantium and China.

661 CE Muslim Arab cavalries conquer Iran.

Europe

311 CE Constantine, emperor of the Roman Empire, legalizes Christianity.

330 CE Constantine moves Roman Empire capital from Rome eastward to Byzantium, a town on the Bosporus (renamed Constantinople, now Istanbul, Turkey).

Fourth Century	Chistians become interested in relics of saints to put in church altars. Rome is a major source of relics, which are kept in silk wrappings. A bishop is buried in silk garments.
Fifth Century	All Christian bishops are buried in silk liturgical robes and stoles. Silk textiles are used to adorn churches.
481–511 CE	Clovis unifies the Franks in Western Europe. His queen Clotilda, a Christian, uses silks to decorate the church for the baptism of their child.
Sixth Century	Silk textiles become a marker of sainthood. The very presence of silk cloth on a tomb was evidence that the remains were those of a canonized saint.
527–565 CE	Reign of Emperor Justinian, who published a law code that contained sumptuary laws limiting the wearing of purple silks to the royal family and highest ranks of Christian clergy.
	Justinian makes silk production in Byzantium a royal monopoly. He also makes the distribution of government-produced silks to foreign diplomats and church officials a royal monopoly.
	Justinian monopolizes all silk raw materials coming into Byzantium.
	Justinian forms an alliance with Ethiopia to break the control of the Himyarites in Yemen over supplies of Chinese-made silk yarns coming by sea from India.
	Sericulture begins in the Byzantine Empire. Justinian most likely was a promoter of this development. This eventually leads to Byzantium becoming a major producer of silk.

Seventh Century	Sericulture is well established in Byzantium, the first place outside China and its frontiers to engage in sericulture. This monopoly in the western part of Eurasian does not last long. By the end of the century sericulture can be found all the way from China to Byzantium.
648 CE	Bishops of Rome begin to gather up relics of many martyrs outside the city of Rome and safeguard them inside the city. The skulls of St. Peter and St. Paul are enshrined within the cathedral church of the Bishop of Rome, contributing to the Roman Church becoming the symbolic center for the entire Christian community in Western Europe.

China

ca. 220–581 CE	China fragmented, ruled by numerous regional powers. Many of those in the north had steppe origins. Buddhism becomes firmly established in China during these centuries.
399–414 CE	Faxian's pilgrimage to India.
439–534 CE	Tuoba lineage of Xianbei (originally from Mongolia) establish the Northern Wei dynasty, ruling over northern China. Sponsored the carving of monumental Buddhas at Yungang and Luoyang. Rulers of Northern Wei claim to be reincarnations of the Buddha. By 477 CE in Pingcheng, the first capital, there are more than 100 monasteries. Later the Xianbei move the capital to Luoyang, where more than 1,000 monasteries are built.

581–618 CE	Sui dynasty reunites China, reestablishes oral exams on Confucian classics for aspiring officials. Introduces written examinations for some government offices.
	Buddhism still flourishes in China and remains close to the centers of political power.
618–906 CE	Tang dynasty rules China. Furthered the written examination system based on Confucian classics.
	Established a color-coded bureaucracy, in which certain colors of silk could only be worn by certain ranks of officialdom. As in Byzantium, purple was the highest-ranked color. By the end of the dynasty these rules were rarely enforced, in large part because nongovernmental, expensive, finely made, and decorated silks, often imported from Iran and other locations, were so abundant.

India

ca. 320–550 CE	Gupta dynasty rules much of India, directly or indirectly. Although Buddhist monasteries in India continue to flourish, the Gupta rulers were Hindus who saw themselves as inheritors and restorers of ancient Indian religious and cultural foundations that were rooted in Brahmanism.
Sixth Century	In India Buddhist artwork had changed from emphasis on sculpture to an emphasis on murals. The best examples are at the Ajanta caves. This style spreads along silk roads to China.

ZOROASTRIANISM, CHRISTIANITY, AND BUDDHISM: POLITICAL TURMOIL AND A NEW RELATIONSHIP BETWEEN EMPIRE AND RELIGION

GETTING STARTED ON CHAPTER FOUR: How did the silk trade survive and prosper during and after the political upheavals of the third and fourth centuries CE? How did the beliefs and customs of religious organizations contribute to the demand for silks? What explains the increasing importance of Zoroastrian traders, especially the Sogdians, in the silk trade? What policies did the Byzantine emperor Justinian pursue in order to solve the problem of shortages of silk raw materials? For what purposes did governments in Tang China and Byzantium use silk? How did the trade in silk contribute to cultural exchanges?

CHAPTER OUTLINE

Upheavals

Religions, Institutions, and Values

Buddhist Networks

Zoroastrian Networks

Christian Networks

The Byzantine Empire's Government Silk Monopoly

The Tang Empire and Government Restrictions on Some Varieties of Silk

UPHEAVALS

Early in the third century CE a series of major political upheavals began all along the silk roads. They would continue into the fourth century, and in some places longer, bringing about not only dynastic changes, but also major cultural transformations all across Eurasia, from China to the Mediterranean. In spite of these hostilities and the disruptions they caused, trade along the silk roads continued, often sustained by nongovernmental trading communities and religious institutions. In the years following these upheavals, the relationship between new or transformed political powers and religions would become unusually close. This chapter will examine Zoroastrianism in Iran, Christianity in Byzantium, and Buddhism in China with special attention to their use of silk textiles.

Between 224 and 226 CE the Sasanid dynasty came to power in Iran. The founders of this new dynasty were Iranians who had been under the rule of the formerly nomadic Parthians for about four centuries. They overthrew the Parthians, and took direct control over both Iran and Mesopotamia. They also expanded eastward in an attempt to reestablish the borders of Iran's ancient Achaemenid Empire. In their domestic policies they sought to reestablish the ancient Iranian religion of Zoroastrianism and to diminish the impact that Hellenistic culture had had on Iran under Parthian rule.

Iran was not alone in such endeavors. A century later the Gupta dynasty (ca. 320–550 CE) came to power in India. They were based in northeastern India along the Ganges River, in the same locale from which the Mauryan Empire had once ruled most of the subcontinent. This locale had remained well outside the bounds of what had been Kushan-controlled territory. The Guptas eventually controlled much of India, directly or indirectly. Like the Sasanids in Iran, once in power the Gupta kings sought to restore the traditions of India's ancient past, especially the glories of the Mauryan Empire. However, unlike the later Mauryan rulers they were not Buddhists, but Hindus. Hinduism had its roots in ancient Indian Brahminism, and thus the Guptas, in a manner reminiscent of the Sassanians, saw themselves as the inheritors and restorers of the most ancient religious and cultural foundations of their land. They, however, did not attempt to suppress Buddhism. Buddhist institutions, including monasteries, continued to flourish under their rule.

By 220 CE, just a few years before the Sasanid victory over the Parthians, the Han dynasty had reached a state of total collapse, the empire had begun to fragment, and thereafter nomadic peoples overran much of northern China. From 220 until 581 CE there was no central government that ruled all of China. The political unity that the Qin and Han had created disappeared and a variety of regional powers, many of them ruled by invaders, controlled what had been Han China. There was much political instability even at the regional level and many of these powers were short-lived. Such upheavals began to undermine the foundations of the Confucian world, and Buddhism gradually grew deep roots in China, and at the same time became closely associated with many of the rulers of the regional powers within China. When China was reunified in the sixth century CE by the short-lived Sui dynasty, and then in the seventh century by the long-lived Tang, the close relationship between Buddhism and the state continued to flourish, at least until the eighth century CE.

Although the Roman Empire did not completely collapse, it was also in a state of crisis, and it underwent a transition that changed it fundamentally. In 330 CE, the Roman emperor Constantine moved the imperial capital from Rome to Byzantium. Byzantium was then a small town on the Bosporus in the eastern, Greek-speaking part of the empire. The town grew into a great metropolis, and although its name was changed to Constantinople, the empire that it ruled became known as Byzantium. (The same city is now in Turkey, and has been known as Istanbul since the fifteenth century CE.) Prior to this momentous move toward the east, Roman control over the provinces was already being challenged, especially by various European peoples on its northern frontiers. After the capital was moved from Latin-speaking Rome to Greek-speaking Byzantium, the disintegration of imperial power in the western part of the empire accelerated.

However, as we have seen in Chapter Three, trade and communications between various parts of Eurasia continued on both the sea routes and the overland routes. During these upheavals, the only places along the established trade routes that truly disappeared from history were some of the desert caravan cities that were near the eastern Roman frontier, such as Petra and Palmyra. All the other major trading routes and the infrastructure that had grown up along them remained intact, sustained by both long-established private trading communities and religious institutions. At first it was only the Sasanid government that was actively enlarging its position in both territory and trade, but by the fifth century, the Byzantine Empire also was becoming a great trading power. Within another century, the latter had consolidated its power, and was monopolizing the production and trading of various luxuries, especially silk textiles, over a large territory.

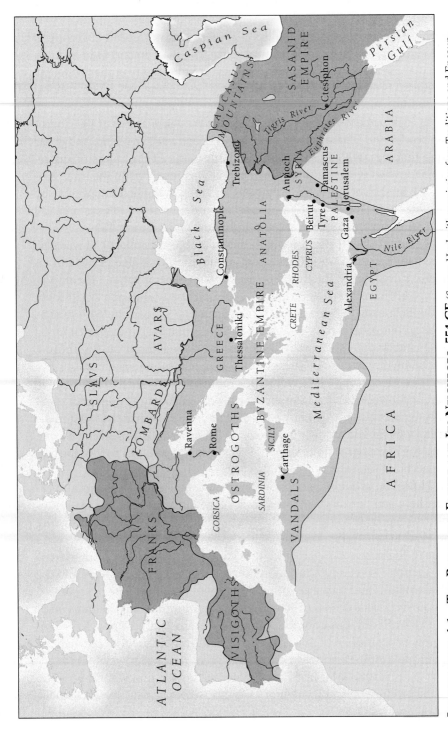

ILLUSTRATION 4-1 THE BYZANTINE EMPIRE AND ITS NEIGHBORS, 554 CE *(Source: Used with premission from Traditions and Encounters (2nd ed.), by Jerry H. Bentely and Herbert F. Ziegler. Copyright 2003 by McGraw-Hill.)*

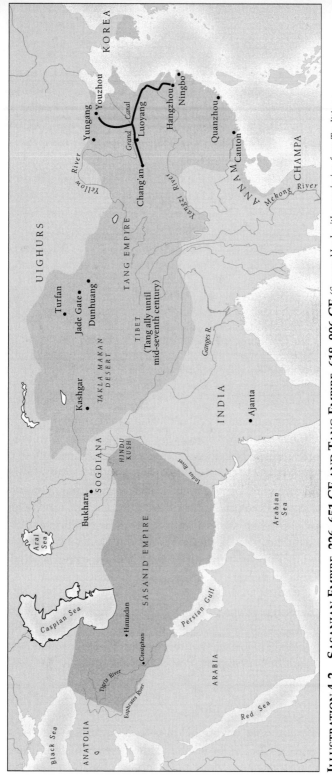

ILLUSTRATION 4-2 SASANIAN EMPIRE, 226–651 CE AND TANG EMPIRE, 618–906 CE (*Source: Used with permission from Traditions and Encounters (2nd ed.), by Jerry H. Bentley and Herbert F. Ziegler. Copyright 2003 by McGraw-Hill.*)

After China was reunified in the late sixth century, the Sui and Tang empires, like Byzantium, issued sumptuary laws to monopolize fine silks and other fine textiles in an effort to strengthen the imperial structure. Thus, in the early middle ages, namely from the fifth through the early tenth centuries, a new pattern of trade and communications would emerge and prosper. By the seventh century the Byzantine Empire had mastered the techniques of sericulture and the harvesting of filaments from the silk-worms' cocoons. Thus, for a time the Byzantine Empire and the Tang Empire, at opposite ends of Eurasia, would share the domination of the silk trade due to their shared monopoly of the production of silk threads and yarns, and consequently, their significant role in the distribution of silk products.

RELIGIONS, INSTITUTIONS, AND VALUES

In those empires where Christianity and Buddhism flourished, their historical inheritance included not only the trade networks of the previous period, but the religious value systems as well. In the early middle ages, in spite of the fact that some religions in Eurasia expressed serious doubts about the religious consequences of pursuing commercial profits, trade nevertheless flourished right along with the religious institutions. In particular, Christianity and Buddhism condemned the untrammeled pursuit of material wealth, and identified religious sanctity with a withdrawal from the mundane world and a focus upon the spiritual. Nevertheless, it was the customs and the practices of the religious institutions themselves that played one of the most significant roles in the creation and the sustenance of the demand for luxuries from faraway lands, especially silks. In addition, the imperial governments of Byzantium and China sought to use specially made silks to mark the distinguished positions of their members within society. They also desired these restricted silks so that they could make grand demonstrations of their religious devotion by donating large quantities of these textiles to religious institutions. Accordingly, to ensure their own supplies, government administrators were intimately involved with the importation and exportation of these goods.

BUDDHIST NETWORKS

As discussed in previous chapters, Mahayana Buddhism arrived in China in the first century CE. Under Kushan rule this school of Buddhism had flourished in northwestern India and Afghanistan, and most of the early believers and promoters in China were traders from the Kushan Empire, the Parthian Empire, and Sogdiana in Central Asia. Nevertheless, even at this early time, various elements of Buddhism had been blended into local folk religions, wherein the Buddha and the bodhisattvas had been added to their collection of local deities by Chinese villagers and townspeople. It was also in the first century CE that the spread of Buddhism suffered a serious setback in China. During the reign of Emperor Mingdi (58–75 CE), Liu Ying, a prince of the Han dynasty, was patronizing both Buddhism and Daoism and performing elaborate public rituals in the name of Buddhism. The emperor suspected the prince of hiding behind these religions, when what he actually intended to do was to seize the throne for himself with the aid of a "foreign cult." The emperor succeeded in suppressing the movement, and the prince eventually committed suicide. In addition, about 2,000 people in his entourage, including Buddhist priests, were implicated in the "conspiracy." It was a catastrophe for Buddhism in China, and almost a century went by before it began to recover. In short, Buddhism never won the hearts and souls of the ruling elite during the Han Empire.

The opportunity for Buddhism came after the demise of the Han Empire. Once the central government had weakened, civil wars broke out. The battles between the warlords caused severe disruptions, resulting in large-scale and long-distance migrations of populations. Such disruptions weakened the basic unit of China's social fabric, the Confucian patriarchal family, and the destruction of the empire weakened the Confucian justification for imperial power. During the early Han dynasty, Emperor Wudi, famous for expanding China's imperial presence into the Western Regions, had also established Confucianism as the social and political orthodoxy throughout the empire. In Confucian thought, the centralized authority of the imperial state was legitimized by the movement of heavenly bodies in the sky. In the same way that planets and stars move in an orderly way around a central, stable point in the sky—the North Star, the Chinese political realm should be centered upon a central point, the imperial person. Thus, the Confucians envisioned a continuous hierarchy of centralized power beginning in the sky above, and radiating down to the imperial center on earth, through the state structure to local authorities.

At the local level, authority radiated from the deceased ancestors of the local community to the living patriarchal heads of families. The relationships between the celestial realm and the emperor, referred to as the son of heaven, and between the ruler and his subjects were both spoken of as father-son relationships. Or, starting from the smallest unit, the one closest to the earth, one could say that the real-life familial relationship between father and son became the quintessential metaphor of the relationship between ruler and subject, as well as the relationship between the celestial realm and the emperor. The use of a familial relationship as the metaphor that permeated and legitimized hierarchical politics clearly is an indication of the significance of the family unit, which organized everyone in the society into the patriarchal system.

In the fourth century when large numbers of nomads came into north China, many local families and individuals fled south of the Yangzi River. Under such trying circumstances, the Confucian family structure, along with its patriarchal ceremonies, often could not be sustained, and in the north the nomads and their descendants had their own quite different social structures and value systems. The nomads built many small states in north China, most of which lasted only a few decades. In Chinese historical records, this time was referred to as "the Sixteen States built by Five Barbarians" (ca. 317–420). It was during this time of fundamental disorientation that Buddhism spread not only among the common people who looked for some anchor amidst the chaos, but also appealed to many rulers, both Chinese and foreign.

When rulers from a nomadic background were faced with the problems of administering sedentary societies, they often sought ideological guidance from holy men. Thus, Buddhist priests were able to convert some of the new rulers, thereby reducing political violence against the population and military violence during the changing of regimes. The nomadic rulers who patronized Buddhism also supported the long-distance trade with regions west of China. This was especially true after the Tuoba family of the Xianbei, a nomadic people from the steppe, unified northern China and established the Northern Wei dynasty (ca. 439–534). Indeed, it was the emperors of the Northern Wei who sponsored the carving of the giant statues of the Buddhas at Yungang and the town of Longmen near Luoyang, in order to proclaim their faith in Buddhism and to substantiate the legitimacy of their rule in China as reincarnations of the Buddha. The desert routes in what is now Chinese Central Asia actually flourished in this period when the nomads ruled northern China. Oasis towns around the Takla Makan Desert and in the Hexi Corridor built Buddhist monasteries and profited from the passing trade. In part, their prosperity was due to earlier Han dynasty agricultural developments that enabled the arable land around the oases to support a substantial population and trade. In addition, it could also be attributed to the economic demand for luxuries from the east and the west of these drylands that kept the commodities flowing along the desert routes. It might also be noted that one of the most important sources of this demand was the religious institutions of the time.

By the fifth century, the rulers of China had become devout Buddhists, accepting its cosmology and concepts of life and death. They also relied on Buddhist institutions to promote the well-being of their realms, making extensive investments in institutional construction and donating grand sums and valuable items to them. In the city of Pingcheng, the early capital of the Northern Wei, more than one hundred monasteries had been built by the year 477, including a state monastery. (The Yungang monuments are near this early capital.) After the Northern Wei moved its capital to Luoyang, it built another state monastery within that city, which was an explicit copy of the one at Pingcheng. In both places it was named Yongning, which translates into English as "Ever-lasting Peace." In addition, several huge statues of the Buddha were carved on the cliffs at Longmen, near the new capital, in the same way that they had been carved on the cliffs at Yungang. Within the next 40 years, in the city of Luoyang alone, more than 1,000 Buddhist monasteries appeared.

Following the examples of the rulers and nobles, commoners in northern China vied with each other in contributing to the construction of cave temples and the carving of statues of Buddhist figures. Those who could not afford to sponsor the carving of a statue or a cave with their own individual resources organized themselves into lay believers' societies, combining their resources and affiliating themselves to a monastery so that they too could gain merit from these projects. From the votive inscriptions on the statues and in the cave temples, one learns that many of these donors had come to Buddhism to find meaning in their lives and some sense of security after losing their families. They also wished for benefits, either to help their deceased loved ones to be reborn into one of the heavens of Mahayana Buddhism or to bring a sense of well-being to those who had survived.

The numerous Buddhist monasteries were major consumers of food, clothing, and luxuries. When decorating the stupas with the Seven Treasures, the emperors, ministers, nobles, monks, and nuns, and even the members of the lay societies, were all following the instructions and models provided by Mahayana Buddhist texts such as the *Lotus Sutra* and the *Western Pure Land Sutra*. The Seven Treasures, as discussed in Chapter Two, were a collection of precious metals and stones frequently traded on the silk roads. Gold and silver, for example, were the materials from which Roman and Persian coins were made. Lapis lazuli was a precious stone that in ancient times could only be found in Badakhshan in northeastern Afghanistan. Crystal was an export of India; red coral was a product of the eastern Mediterranean; carnelian (or agate) was either from the Vindaya Mountains of western India or from Central Asia; and pearls were from the Persian Gulf or the strait between India's southern tip and Sri Lanka. When decorating the stupas, Buddhist devotees again followed the instructions of Mahayana Buddhist texts literally. Some 1,500 years after the stupa in the Yongning Monastery of the Northern Wei capital Luoyang had burned down, modern archaeologists still found pieces of these precious stones and metals in the ruins.

The most conspicuous of the Seven Treasures in the ruins of Yongning was lapis lazuli. In the ancient world, this dark blue stone had already been a highly valued commodity for 2,000 years. Since one of the Mahayana Buddhist texts had described the hair of the Buddha as the color of lapis lazuli, Buddhist artists used a pigment made by grinding the lapis lazuli stone into a powder, from which they made blue pigments in order to paint the hair of the Buddha and, in some places, even that of the bodhisattvas and other heavenly beings. From the cave murals in Central Asia to the cave sculptures in China, the hair of the Buddha was consistently painted in this lapis lazuli blue. From the time of the Kushan Empire, this shade of blue became the most notable color in all Buddhist art.

In addition to the jewels, incense, made from imported resins such as frankincense and myrrh, was essential for Buddhist rituals and ceremony. There is little doubt that these particular varieties of incense must have come from the Arabian Peninsula. This was a time when the integrity of the western part of the Roman Empire was declining, and the demand for incense to burn before its gods was diminishing. However, in Asia the Buddhist demand for these products was growing. Thus, Arab and Indian sailors continued to ship the aromatic resins from the Arabian Peninsula to the seaports on the western coast of India, whence they were carried overland to Central Asia and China.

In addition to the Seven Treasures, Mahayana Buddhist texts also proclaimed silk to be one of the most appropriate gifts for the Buddha or bodhisattvas. Accordingly, Chinese silk textiles were widely used in monasteries and religious ceremonies in Central and South Asia. One of the most notable uses of silk cloth was to make banners. These were not ordinary banners of the sort that might be carried in parades today, but religious works of art. Donors bought these large embroidered or painted silk cloths from the monastery, often added their own signatures to them, and then donated them back to the monasteries. The monks then displayed

ILLUSTRATION 4-3   HEAD OF A BUDDHA, FIFTH TO SIXTH CENTURY CE.
The hair on this wooden sculpture is painted with a pigment made from lapis lazuli, the
sacred color of Buddhism. One of the seven treasures of Mahayana Buddhism, this dark
blue stone was ground into a powder and mixed with other ingredients to make the paint.
In ancient times its only source was Badakhshan in present-day Afghanistan. This sculpture
was found in Central Asia at Tumshuk (in present-day China's Xinjiang Uighur
Autonomous Region), and it is now located at the Museum fuer Indische Kunst, Staatliche
Museum zu Berlin. *(Photo: Iris Papadopoulos. Museum fuer Indische Kunst, Staatliche Museum
zu Berlin, Berlin, Germany. Photo credit: Bildarchiv Preussischer Kulturbesitz/Art Resource, NY.)*

these pieces around the stupas. When there was a festival, they would
choose the best ones to carry in the procession.

In 399 CE when the Buddhist monk Faxian was on his way from
China to India, he passed through some of the oases towns that line the
edges of the Takla Makan Desert. He noticed that the monasteries in these
towns had many such banners and that they were used in the festivals. In
an account of his pilgrimage, he mentioned this monastic use of silk, and

in particular mentioned one of the festivals in a town that he called Jiecha, most likely the city known today as Kashgar. After his arrival in India he noticed that there Buddhists also used these silk banners in rituals and ceremonies. Many subsequent pilgrims had read Faxian's account and thus when they made their own journeys to India, they carried along with them many of these silk banners as well as silk incense bags to bestow as gifts along the way.

Although the rulers of nomadic origin in northern China gave large quantities of their imported and domestic valuables to Buddhist monasteries, they did not give them all away. They personally enjoyed these luxuries and, when possible, they controlled their manufacture and production. However, the association of these valuables with Buddhist monasteries and the rulers' faith in Buddhist doctrine made them appreciate the value of such goods all the more. Commoners, such as traders, however, were not supposed to possess and enjoy these luxuries even if they could afford them. Nevertheless, once these goods became associated with Buddhist devotion, commoners had a good pretext for purchasing them since they could claim that they were not for their own use, but for religious donations. Buddhism thus created both the demand and the facilities for the long-distance trade in luxuries, even at a time when there was no large and powerful empire in China or along its frontiers to supervise and protect the trade.

During this time it was the Hindu Gupta dynasty that controlled the original Buddhist homeland on the Gangetic Plain. Buddhist monasteries continued to flourish under these Hindu rulers, and the monasteries that had been established along the major trade routes in Kushan times also continued to function without royal patronage after both the Kushan and the Han empires had fallen. Buddhist cave complexes located along the mountainous routes that led both northward and southward from the seaports on India's Arabian Sea coast gained additional patronage from traders. By the sixth century, the artwork in these caves had changed from sculpture to mural paintings. The most famous are the Ajanta caves, which were located outside the Gupta realm, on the southern edge of the Vindhya Mountains that divide northern from southern India. Murals on the caves' walls illustrate the *Jataka* stories, the stories of the former lives of the Buddha before he was born as Shakyamuni. He appears in these stories as kings, princes, deer, and elephants, among other things. Curiously, there is no lapis lazuli pigment used on any of the paintings of the hair. Apparently in India this precious color was reserved only for the hair of the post-enlightenment Buddha and was not used on the hair of the Buddha's previous incarnations. Nevertheless, the pigment does appear once, on the neck of a peacock. The murals in these Indian caves had a significant impact on illustrations of the sutras and on cave paintings done along the overland route between India and China. The themes, artistic styles, and motifs became models for much of the Buddhist art in Chinese Central Asia, including the famous cave paintings at Dunhuang, just inside the Jade Gate at the western end of the Hexi Corridor.

ZOROASTRIAN NETWORKS

In Iran and Mesopotamia, the Sasanid dynasty promoted itself as the true inheritor of the ancient Persian civilization that had flourished during the Achaemenid period (533–330 BCE), and rejected the Hellenistic culture that had flourished under the Parthians, whom they had overthrown. Indeed, one of the rationales for overthrowing the Parthians was that the former nomads had gone too far in promoting un-Iranian, international, Hellenistic culture. After the Sasanids had replaced the Parthians as the masters of Iran, they attempted to rid the empire of obvious reminders of Hellenistic power. Its rulers, for example, removed Greek letters from Iranian coins, and gave pride of place to the Zoroastrian religion. It had been the religion of Iran since the Achaemenid Empire in the sixth century BCE, and even though the Parthian Empire had supported Zoroastrian institutions, they also supported other religions and did not seek to promote a culture that was Zoroastrian. However, because the Sasanids identified this religion with ancient Persian civilization, the culture of the region became much more explicitly Zoroastrian under their rule. The Sasanids also returned to ancient Achaemenid traditions of monumental art, sponsoring the carving of regal rock reliefs on the sides of mountains. In addition, they promoted more portable artwork, such as silver vessels and silk textiles that depicted Zoroastrian religious symbols.

When Iranian traders carried such items to other parts of Eurasia, the Zoroastrian art motifs traveled westward and eastward, eventually influencing artistic styles in Christian Byzantium and in Tang China where Buddhism prevailed. The religion of the Iranian empire's traders also underwent a transformation. Traders from the Parthian Empire who had traveled the silk roads in previous centuries were often Buddhists and they, like the Kushans, had propagated Buddhism when trading in China. Iranian traders from the Sasanid period, however, were Zoroastrian, and they built Zoroastrian temples wherever they established trading posts. These temples not only served as centers for their religious activities, but also as warehouses where traders could store their trade goods.

The linkage of Zoroastrian culture with long-distance trade was obvious to all involved. Iranian traders were well known for their fabulous wealth, and their silver vessels and silk textiles were much admired and enjoyed a strong demand in markets throughout Eurasia. The Zoroastrian art motifs on these Sasanid wares were eagerly copied in other parts of Eurasia. Yet the world outside ancient Iran had understood very little about Zoroastrianism, and the same was true during Sasanid times, in spite of the profusion of information about the religion coming out of Iran along with its trade wares.

The modern world still knows little about this once-influential religion. One reason is that people outside Iran knew little about it even in Sasanid times, and another reason is that the religion has largely disappeared from its Iranian homeland. The seventh-century Muslim Arab conquest of the Sasanid Empire led to widespread Islamic conversions in the lands that had long been Zoroastrian, and eventually, over a period of centuries, the number of believers in the religion's homeland became insignificant. In fact, today the best-known Zoroastrian communities are located outside Iran in cities on India's western coast, where believers fled, probably following their ancient trade routes, and where they still maintain this ancient religion to this day. Parsees, as the Zoroastrians living in India are now called, also preserved the archaic Zoroastrian text called the *Avesta*, as well as translations and digests of this text in a later Persian language called Pahlavi or Parthian.

The cosmological universe of Zoroastrianism was divided into two mutually repulsive and attractive opposites, the bright half (the good) and the dark half (evil). Prior to the Achaemenid Empire, they prayed and worshiped before a fire out under the open sky. Burning wood and incense, they were not worshipping the fire, but what it symbolized—fire, sun, and light, which all symbolized the energy of the creator. By the time of the Achaemenid Empire, the fire was placed inside a temple, and it was this fire temple and the priests that tended the fires that migrated along the silk roads wherever the Zoroastrians traders went. In the Zoroastrian universe, there were many creatures, some sacred and some evil. It was thus a religion full of deities and demons. Zoroastrian priests, known as magi, performed magic during some religious rituals, in order to demonstrate its cosmological concepts. The religion not only had a significant impact on Iran and Central Asia, but also on several regions west of Iran. Zoroaster, the founder of the religion, is portrayed as a sage in classical Greek sources, and early Christians also viewed the three magi as sages who brought gifts to the newborn Jesus. In addition early Christians sometimes studied Zoroastrianism for religious inspiration.

The repertoire of Zoroastrian animal motifs was quite large, drawing upon animals from both the real world and the imagined, and Iranian artists and artisans often incorporated them into their works. The *simurgh* stands out as the most frequently used motif for royalty and divinity. It had a mammal's head, often a dog head, the body of a winged bird, and a peacock's tail. It appears on many gilded silver vessels, a specialty of Sasanid Iran. When silk weaving developed in Iran during the Sasanid period, aided by war prisoners from cities on the Roman frontier such as Antioch in Syria, Sasanid rulers began wearing silk robes with intricately woven patterns and designs, the *simurgh* among them. An example can be found on the rock relief of Taq-i-Bustan (near modern Hamadan, Iran) where the figures of the Sasanian kings are carved. Some two dozen different textile patterns are displayed on their costumes, including the *simurgh*, which appears on the robe of King Khusraw (590–628). Also several Iranian silk textiles with the *simurgh* design have been found in various archaeological sites, although, surprisingly, none of these sites is located in Iran.

In Persian art the *simurgh* and other animal motifs are often surrounded by frames in the shape of a lozenge (which resembles a four-sided diamond), an oval, or, quite often, roundels (circles). On silk textiles the animal images are often surrounded by what art historians call "pearl roundels," meaning a large circle formed by smaller circles or "pearls." The animal's postures are rigid, and the colors on the silk textiles are often somber, such as dark blue or green. The way that Iranian artists portrayed the *simurgh* suggests that it was a sacred object. In the *Avesta* there is a bird called "Saena," which perches on the tree of all seeds. Zoroastrians believe that this bird is the spreader of life and even his feathers have great healing value. Apparently, by the Sasanid period, this sacred bird had developed into the *simurgh*, representing great wisdom.

Whatever the religious connotation, the *simurgh*, as a motif, caught the imagination of consumers in markets throughout much of Eurasia, and weavers in a variety of locales, inside and outside Iran, wove its image into their silks. The motif even entered the repertoire of Byzantine producers of silk textiles, who belonged to a very strictly monopolized industry. One piece of Byzantine silk, with patterns of *simurghs* and flying horses framed by pearl roundels on a violet background, was clearly an imitation of Persian silks. Thus, even after the seventh-century demise

ILLUSTRATION 4-4   SILVER EWER WITH *SIMURGH*, FIFTH TO SIXTH CENTURY CE.
Gilded silver vessels like this one were a specialty of Sasanid Iran. Part of the repertoire of
Zoroastrian animal motifs, the *Simurgh*, with a mammal's head, the wings of a bird, and the
tail of a peacock, was the most frequently used motif for royalty and divinity. When silk
weaving developed in Iran during the Sasanid period, rulers began wearing silk robes with
intricately woven patterns and designs, the *simurgh* among them. *(Source: Courtesy of The
State Hermitage Museum, St. Petersburg.)*

of the Sasanid Empire and the gradual disappearance of Zoroastrianism
within Iranian borders, *simurgh*-patterned silk textiles were still produced outside Iran.

Another bird motif was used on many samples of pearl roundel silks
found in Iran, Central Asia, and China. The majestic style of this bird also
suggests royalty and divinity. It differed from the *simurgh* in that it did not
have any mammalian parts, but it had ribbons flowing from the back of the
bird's head to the back of its neck (perhaps reminiscent of a horse's mane),
and a string of pearls hanging from its beak. This motif, which prevailed

in regions east of Iran from the sixth to the eighth centuries, may also have been an artistic representation of Saena, the sacred bird of the *Avesta*.

It was during the Sasanid period that Iranian traders spread Zoroastrianism to Central Asia. For example, the Sogdian traders (from present-day Uzbekistan), many of whom had been Buddhists during the second to the fourth centuries, became Zoroastrians in the following centuries. In the sixth century, after the Turks had created a powerful nomad confederacy on the steppe, they too converted to Zoroastrianism. By the fourth century, the Sogdians had become the most visible trading community in the eastern part of Eurasia, and once the Turkish confederacy formed, the Sogdians represented the Turkish chiefs in trade negotiations with the courts of both Sasanid Iran and Byzantium. Zoroastrianism also spread to the Sogdian trading posts in the Hexi Corridor in China.

In the Sogdian language, the leaders of these trading communities were called *sartapao*, a word that was derived from the Sanskrit word *sarthavaha*, meaning "leader" or "caravan leader." From the time of the Northern Wei (386–534), the Sogdians were so prominent among the traders in China that when the rulers of the Northern Wei established an office to supervise foreign traders they called it the "Sabao," the Chinese rendering of *sartapao*. During the Northern Qi (550–577), the Sabao was placed under the Department of Foreign Affairs, and one Sabao officer was in charge of foreign trade in the capital, and another one administered the affairs of foreign traders in prefectures outside the capital. The Sabao office for foreign trade continued to exist during the Sui and Tang dynasties, and the Tang officials also added an office that dealt specifically with Zoroastrian affairs.

Thus, the name of the office that dealt with all foreign traders in China, from the time of the Northern dynasties (ca. 431–581 CE) through the Tang dynasty (618–906 CE) was actually the Chinese version of the Sanskrit-derived Sogdian word for caravan leader. This was in large part because the office was mainly dealing with Sogdians. These traders carried a wide variety of commodities that included goods from Iran, the Turks on the steppe, India, and even Byzantium. Iranian goods, however, were the largest part of their inventory. They also were largely responsible for spreading Iranian silver coins all along the silk roads. More than 1,000 such coins have been found in the section of the route that lies within the modern boundaries of China.

During this time, Iranian-style silk textiles and silver vessels were precious commodities, much appreciated by Chinese royalty. Art historians, for example, have pondered the origins of a silver ewer found in the tomb of Li Xian, a prince of the Northern Zhou (557–581). Its shape and technical qualities are in the style of Sasanid Iran, but the human figures are in the Hellenistic style of Bactria. Also, the scene on the ewer shows soldiers bidding farewell to their wives before departing for war, a common theme in Greek and Hellenistic art. The art historians concluded that this ewer was made somewhere in Sogdiana or in the Hellenized part of Afghanistan where both Hellenistic traditions and Sasanid culture had influenced local artistic traditions. Thus, it appears that these Central Asian artisans were combining Iranian-style artifacts with Hellenistic images and that such pieces were desired by the royal elites of China, where they were delivered by Zoroastrian traders.

In the seventh century, after the Muslim Arab conquest of Iran, the Zoroastrian community in Sogdiana grew even larger. After many Iranians took refuge in the western parts of Central Asia, such as Sogdiana and various places that had been part of the Kushan Empire, Iranian culture developed even stronger roots in Central Asia. One place in particular stands out. In the homeland of the Sogdians, a Persian-Sogdian style of silk textile developed around the town of Zandan, near the city of Bukhara. Weavers there used Chinese silk yarn and dyestuff to make silk textiles with Iranian motifs. *Zandani*, as the silk textiles were called, soon became much sought after and sold all over Eurasia. They even found their way westward to many churches and cathedrals in Europe where they were used to wrap the relics of Christian saints, and eastward to Dunhuang, where they were used to make the covers on Buddhist texts.

In China, Zoroastrian traders, both Iranians and Sogdians, still carried out their commercial activities under the supervision of the Sabao (the Office of Foreign Trade) and the *Xianzheng* (the Office of Zoroastrian Affairs). Also there were Zoroastrian priests who accompanied and aided Iranian and Sogdian merchants whenever they traveled to foreign countries, and they established temples and performed rituals wherever the traders' communities were located. Many Sogdian traders visited Chang'an and even died there, taking with them to their graves figurines of grooms, musicians, and traders, all in Sogdian style, and all associated with camel and horse caravans. In major centers such as Liangzhou in the Hexi Corridor and Luoyang in the central part of northern China, Zoroastrian temples held public festivals on an annual basis. During these events a priest would perform feats of magic such as cutting open his own belly, stirring his intestines, and then healing the wound, all in a matter of minutes. Or, he would seem to travel a couple of miles in a few moments. Such performances certainly stunned their Chinese audiences and scholars recorded these events with great amazement. Nevertheless, it appears that the local people who appreciated the beauty of Iranian artworks and enjoyed the performances of Zoroastrian rituals did not understand or even perceive the religious implications of either.

CHRISTIAN NETWORKS

The early Christians of the Roman Empire had practiced a frugal way of life, and had been critical of the extravagant lifestyle of wealthy Romans. During the first few centuries CE, they were a persecuted minority, and had no part in the long-distance trade in luxuries. In 311, when the capital was still in Rome, this situation began to change when the Emperor Constantine legalized Christianity, thereby allowing Christians to freely preach their religion. The legalization of Christianity came about during a period of imperial decline. At the same time Christianity began to spread into the forested areas of western and northern Europe, as well as to various parts of Asia and North Africa. Given the weakness of the Roman Empire, the hierarchy of the Christian church became increasingly significant, and as it did so, it also became closely connected to the Eurasian luxury trade. Although the hierarchy never explicitly acknowledged this fact, Christian institutions became important consumers and distributors of products, including silks, which the long-distance trade routes delivered.

The elites of the Roman Empire had not only enjoyed many luxuries in their lives and burned expensive incense for their gods, they had also buried valuables in their tombs and held festivals for their dead. Funerals, especially, were showcases of family wealth and status. Early Christians were very critical of this practice and most ordinary believers, faithful to the teachings about living simply, went to face their heavenly Lord without such worldly possessions. However, as early as the fourth century, when a bishop was buried wearing silk garments, this began to change, at least for the church hierarchy. By the next century, all bishops appear to have been buried with luxurious liturgical vestments. One should keep in mind that by this time the glory of the Roman Empire was gone, material life throughout the Mediterranean region was much less affluent, and the less-developed areas of western and northern Europe were even poorer. In short, there is no doubt that the liturgical robes and stoles in these graves had come from the east by way of the long-distance trade routes.

In the western part of Europe the Roman civil structure was also collapsing at this time. The cities, the roads, and the currency system of the empire were disappearing. Even after Clovis unified the Franks (481–511), de-urbanization continued in the northwestern part of what had been the Roman Empire. Christian churches, like their contemporary Buddhist monasteries in the eastern part of Eurasia, assumed the role of maintaining various threads of secular civilization. In the absence of other authority, churches tended to become the center of community activity. The clergy provided alms to lessen the misery of the poor, and the church also sustained some modicum of justice in the society by protecting the weak. Literacy in many places was limited to the clergy and the monks, so they also served by drafting and notarizing contracts and other documents. In addition, the church's use of grape wine and bread as sacraments in the communion service sustained agricultural traditions that dated from the earlier material culture of the Greeks and Romans. The beauty of the silk liturgical vestments, dyed in royal purple or woven with sophisticated patterns, provided the faithful in the poorer parts of Europe with a visual taste of the rewards to come in a heavenly paradise. While the western part of Europe sank deeper and deeper into what some historians have called the Dark Ages, the Christian churches clung to some elements of the classical civilization and went about Christianizing the polytheists of this region.

Within the European context, Christianity mainly spread from the eastern Mediterranean region to the west and north. At the end of the sixth century, there were five patriarchal sees where bishops were installed, none of which was west of Rome. Four were on or near the shores of the eastern Mediterranean. Thus, the church's hierarchy was concentrated in the east and Rome's centrality within the Mediterranean world persisted only in a geographical sense. The bishop at Constantinople, which had become the empire's political capital by 324, was at the political center of the empire and enjoyed the patronage of the emperors. The other sees in the east, at Antioch, Jerusalem and Alexandria, maintained their urban amenities, and from a religious perspective, could claim proximity to the original homeland of Christianity.

Rome was increasingly at a disadvantage. It was no longer the capital of a powerful empire, and it was distant from the birthplace of the religion. Furthermore, when it had been the imperial center of a polytheistic empire, it had been infamous as a site where many Christians had been persecuted and martyred. Nevertheless, when the major centers in the east began to send out monks and clergy to proselytize in the west and north, establishing monastic communities and churches and reviving viticulture and wineries, Rome, too, was an active participant. In what became Western Europe it had a certain advantage due to proximity and due to its reputation of past imperial glories among the various polytheistic peoples of the region. Thus, eventually the patriarchal see of Rome became the primary center from which Western Europe was Christianized, sending out one bishop after another armed with a Bible, relics of a saint, and a set of liturgical vestments made from fine silk cloth.

Church authorities in Constantinople eventually were disturbed by Rome's ambitions in the west, and feared that it was undermining the proper balance of power among the various holy sees. The emperors at Byzantium believed that they should have a preeminent position in the church leadership because they were in Constantine's capital and he was the first Roman emperor who had permitted Christians to freely preach and had subsequently converted to Christianity himself. They also pointed out that most of the emperors at Byzantium up until their own time had been enthusiastic patrons of Christianity, unlike those at Rome before Constantine. On the Italian peninsula there was no such correspondence between political power and church authority, and, in general, political power on the peninsula was fragmented and unstable.

The church hierarchy at Rome, however, had a different perspective. In their view, Rome had been the see of Saint Peter, whom they thought of as the foremost apostle of Christ. Furthermore, since Saint Peter was believed to hold the key to the gate of heaven, the faithful who wanted to go to heaven when they died had to please Saint Peter. Perhaps even more significant to Rome's position was its access to the bones of saints, which were treated as sacred holy relics. When the Roman emperors had persecuted Christians, they had made many martyrs. The martyrs often became saints, and while their souls went to heaven, their remains were buried near Rome. Thus, when the bones, or even small fragments of them, became highly desired items in the Christian world, Rome was able to supply them.

Each of the newly established churches and shrines in Europe needed relics of their patron saint in order to demonstrate their special relationship with him or her. Also, the faithful wanted to be buried close to the relics of a saint because only then could they be assured that the saint would stand behind them and help them when they stood before St. Peter at the gate of heaven. During the fourth century, Christians thus started digging up the corpses of saints to get relics to put in church altars. Since many of the saints had been martyred in Rome, the patriarchal see of Rome became the major source for these relics.

This new religious enthusiasm for relics even caused the Roman church to modify its customs. Previously, they had buried their dead in cemeteries or catacombs outside the city, where the martyrs shared their resting places with others, both Christian and polytheistic. In order to worship the relics of the martyrs, the bishops of Rome had to leave the city and go out into the countryside to the catacombs. However, because the relics of martyrs became so valuable, illegal digging, thefts, smuggling, and illegal trading in relics all became serious problems. In response, in 648, the church in Rome gathered up the relics of many martyrs, including those of St. Peter and St. Paul, and brought them into the city. Their skulls were then enshrined in the Lateran, the cathedral church of the pope, that is, the Bishop of Rome. Thereafter, this Roman church became the symbolic center for the entire Christian community in the western part of Europe.

When Christians reburied or enshrined the relics of saints, they wrapped them in the finest of silk textiles. In addition, the cathedrals and churches that housed the relics were hung with many beautifully decorated silk tapestries, which were intended to convey the beauty of the heavenly paradise where the faithful would go after their deaths. Also when popes entrusted a saint's relics to bishops being sent to found new churches, they placed the relics in pouches made from the most exquisite of silk cloths. Silk textiles thus became a marker of sainthood, so much so that by the sixth century the very presence of silk cloth laid over the top of a tomb was ample evidence that the remains inside were those of a canonized saint. New converts in the western part of Europe also wanted their churches to portray the heavenly paradise, and thus the bishops and their patrons desired to adorn their churches with the same kinds of beautiful silk tapestries as those that could be seen in Rome. Clotilda, the Christian queen of the originally polytheistic Frankish King Clovis, had the local church decorated with silk tapestries and curtains for the baptism of their son. The liturgical robes worn by the bishops at the ceremony also had to be made of the best silk textiles available. She wanted to impress her husband with the splendor of the setting and the solemnity of the ceremony, hoping that it would give her husband a favorable impression of Christianity.

The irony of Rome's situation was that all the raw material for the silk textiles, so intricately related to its prestige and power, had to be imported from distant lands in the eastern part of Asia. It was not until sometime around the sixth century that weavers in the Byzantine Empire began to acquire the technique of sericulture, that is, actually producing silk thread from the filaments that came from the cocoons of silk worms. This knowledge made it possible for Byzantium to become a major producer of silk thread, and thereafter, most of the raw materials used in the silk cloth that decorated the churches of western Europe came from the eastern Mediterranean. Indeed, the Roman church would remain dependent upon silk producers in other lands for six more centuries.

THE BYZANTINE EMPIRE'S GOVERNMENT SILK MONOPOLY

During the early years of the silk roads a silk-weaving industry had developed in several cities on the eastern Mediterranean coast, including Gaza, Beirut, and Tyre (both of the latter two in present-day Lebanon). Prior to the introduction of silk, these cities had long been textile centers, with a history of weaving woolen cloth. Once the silk road developed, they began to weave with silk yarns, using the same techniques and equipment that they used when weaving woolens. However, without any local sericulture to supply the industry with threads, weavers sometimes were short of silk yarn, and even resorted to unraveling imported plain silk textiles to get the threads for their own creations. Due to their skills these weavers were highly prized war captives throughout the centuries that the Roman Empire contested with Iranian powers, first the Parthians and then the Sasanids, for control over the lands east of the Mediterranean. Whichever side had the upper hand in the contest carried out forays into the other's territory and seized the weavers, forcibly settling them in cities on its own side. The weavers in these areas thus drew from both Hellenistic and Persian art traditions, and using silk materials from China, created beautiful silk textiles. After Constantine moved the capital of the Roman Empire from Rome to Byzantium in the fourth century, Byzantium had control of these cities and took full advantage of their silk-weaving industries.

The eastern Mediterranean was also the source of a rare purple dye. The dyestuff was made from an extract that came from a particular kind of shellfish found in the shallow water along this coast. Whole shiploads of the shellfish could produce only a small amount of dye, and thus it was exceedingly rare and expensive. Nevertheless, it was much sought after because of its beautiful color and stability. In particular, the city of Tyre was famous for its production. Dyers in this region knew that when it was applied to wool, a protein fiber, that it did not begin to fade for many years. And since silk was also a protein fiber, the dye worked equally well on it. Thus, when the weavers started using silk yarns, dyers successfully applied this purple dye to both silk yarns and textiles. Subsequently purple-dyed silks became highly desirable, indeed, coveted items in both the Roman and Iranian areas. In monarchial Iran, only the kings and the royal family were allowed to wear purple clothes, but initially in the Roman Empire whoever could afford them could wear them. However, after Rome abandoned its republican traditions, its emperors also began to limit the color to a special few, and the freedom of wearing the purple was lost.

As the eastern part of the Roman Empire evolved into the Byzantine Empire, the conception of the emperor was transformed from being the first citizen to being the dynastic heir to an imperial throne. Although Constantine was the first Roman emperor to realize that monotheistic Christianity could help unify the empire, it was not until Justinian's reign (527–565) that the religion became the symbolic umbrella of the empire, and its rulers and subjects began to identify the empire with Christianity. Justinian used the military to regain central control over a large part of what had once been Roman territory in the west, mostly against Germanic conquerors who had overrun the southern parts of Western Europe and northwest Africa, and he also established Christianity as the official state religion. To consolidate this renewed empire, Justinian oversaw the compilation of a law code that would have a significant impact not only in Byzantium, but throughout Europe in the centuries to come. It legislated a hierarchical imperial structure in which the purple-dyed silks were used to differentiate the status of imperial persons. Only the emperor and empress could wear completely purple silk regalia. Those below them in the royal hierarchy could wear varying amounts, depending on their rank.

The Cathedral of San Vitale in Ravenna, Italy, contains a well-known portrait of the Byzantine royal family and their retinue, rendered in two famous mosaics that can still be seen today. It clearly displays the purple color scheme of the imperial hierarchy. The center of one of them is Emperor Justinian who holds the bread for communion, and the center of the other is Empress Theodora who holds the container of wine. Both wear long robes that are entirely purple. Images of the three magi who brought gold, frankincense, and myrrh to the newborn Jesus appear on the lower hem of the empress's robe, a reminder that the emperor and empress were great patrons of the religion. All members of their entourage have some purple on their clothing, but the amount gradually becomes less as one's eyes move from the center of either mosaic to its sides.

To mark Christianity's status as the only officially recognized religion in the empire, Justinian not only built the great cathedral Hagia Sophia in Constantinople, but also garbed the religious hierarchy in purple robes. As in the imperial hierarchy, only the highest-ranking clergy wore fully purple robes. Thus, purple became the color of power, both imperial and divine. Byzantine emperors often were described by the phrase, "born in purple and die in purple," meaning that not only did they wear purple regalia during their lives on this earth, they also were born in a room lined with porphyry, a purple stone, and buried in a sarcophagus made of the same stone. Within their territory, the Byzantine emperors were willing to share the prestige of entirely purple garments with their own royal families and with the church hierarchy, but with no one else.

To ensure that the purple silks were used exclusively by royalty and the church hierarchy, the Byzantine emperors created state monopolies to control the silk and purple dye industries. Byzantine authorities kept the purple dye industry completely under government control, and they never divulged the secret of its production. Indeed, for some 900 years they kept the secret so well that after 1453 and the fall of Constantinople to the Ottoman Turks, the production of this purple dye ceased altogether. Thereafter, the Roman Catholic Church, which had always relied on Byzantium to supply the purple silk used to make the cardinal's robes, had no choice but to change the color of the robes from purple to a red color made from cochineal worms. In contrast, monopolizing other types of silk production and trade was a much more complicated matter than monopolizing the purple dye. The weavers of Byzantium were borrowers of sericulture, not its inventors. They were never Eurasia's only source, and their ability to control the distribution of silks was limited in space and time.

In order to ensure that the finest silk textiles were manufactured exclusively for the benefit of the most powerful in the imperial and ecclesiastical hierarchies, Justinian oversaw the creation of a state-run silk industry that monopolized the supply of silk threads and yarns throughout the empire. According to Procopius, a historian and a contemporary of Justinian, the emperor employed a price scheme in order to drive the private silk industry out of business. He set an artificially low ceiling on the price that private-sector workshops could pay for silk yarns and other silk raw materials, a ceiling price that was so low that yarn dealers could not make any money selling their products to them. Since it would have been illegal, weavers from the private workshops did not dare pay the dealers what these materials were worth, and thus the dealers would not sell to them. The government, however, was exempted from this artificially low price, and government officials in charge of the silk industry were thus able to pay what the materials were worth and thereby purchase all the available materials at a higher, more appropriate price. Without raw materials, the private workshops could not function and went out of business, and the weavers who had worked in them either had to seek employment in the government shops or move to Iran.

The state-run silk workshops that wove textiles for the palace and the empire's churches also wove gifts for churches outside the empire as well as for diplomatic gifts to foreign powers. During the reigns of Justinian and his immediate successors, the supply of silk yarns was still inadequate, even when the only purchasers were state-owned workshops. Imperial officials known as commercial agents were put in charge of buying all the silk yarns available from foreign traders. However, because there were occasional problems on either the overland routes or the sea routes, or both, they often could not find enough silk materials in the markets. The commercial agents could then go to Sasanid Iran, which was closer to Chinese sources, to purchase silk materials, but Iran had its own silk-weaving industry and its products were in competition with those of Byzantium. If Persian traders possessed a surplus of yarn or plain silks, they might be willing to sell some of the merchandise to Byzantine buyers, but they charged them unusually high prices since they were not enthusiastic about supplying an industry in competition with their own.

The silk yarns and materials that came by the maritime routes first went overland from China to ports on India's west coast, and then reached the Mediterranean via the Arabian Sea and the Red Sea. During Justinian's reign the Jewish Himyarite kingdom controlled present day Yemen, and from there they could control access to the Red Sea. As a result this kingdom was in a position to monopolize the silk yarn coming from Indian ports. Justinian, following a policy of his predecessors, established an alliance with Ethiopia in order to get control of the southern end of the Red Sea and thus the silk supply coming from Indian ports. Even so, there were still many problems in securing supplies from foreign countries, so it is not surprising that the Byzantine emperors sought to establish a domestic source of materials for the state industry.

Apparently the Emperor Justinian decided to solve this problem by establishing sericulture in Byzantium. According to the historian Procopius, Justinian asked some Nestorian monks to smuggle silkworm eggs out of China, which they did, and thereby sericulture, the actual production of silk threads from the larvae's cocoons, was established in the Byzantine Empire. Historians today doubt the accuracy of Procopius's account of the arrival of sericulture in Byzantine territories, since the mere possession of silk worms is no guarantee that silk can actually be produced. As discussed previously in the Introduction, the feeding and care of the larvae, the supervision of cocoon spinning, and the retrieval of the threads from the cocoons are all complicated processes, requiring much knowledge and skill.

Yet another complication is that one has to have well-established mulberry trees before one can even contemplate raising silkworms. The eggs can only survive one winter, and without an abundant supply of freshly opened mulberry leaves to feed them in the early spring, they would quickly starve to death. Furthermore, it seems unlikely that Nestorian monks would have been willing to smuggle silkworms for Justinian since the Byzantine church had already declared the Nestorian church to be heretical. Nor does it seem likely that Justinian, an emperor whose imperial strategy included the promotion of a strict orthodoxy throughout the Christian world, would seek help from a sect that had been labeled as heretics.

Looking at the issue from the Chinese perspective, there does not appear to be any reason why someone would have had to smuggle silkworms out of China. First of all, the Chinese did not realize that they had a monopoly on sericulture, so it seems most unlikely that they would be trying to protect a monopoly that they did not know existed. They had known for centuries that weavers within the Roman Empire wove beautiful silk textiles, and in the sixth century they still assumed, as they always had, that these weavers knew sericulture and produced their own silk thread. It still had not occurred to them that all the weavers of silk textiles west of them were using silk threads and yarns from China. Furthermore, during the reign of Justinian, China was going through a period of political instability that would last until the Sui dynasty reunified the empire in 581, sixteen years after Justinian's reign came to an end. Given that there was no single political and military authority capable of ruling all of China at this time, much less able to secure its monopoly of a production process that was ubiquitous within its borders, it seems that smuggling the insect larvae out of China would have been unnecessary.

It is, however, quite likely that Justinian was the emperor who began the effort to bring silkworms and sericulture to Byzantium. By the seventh century sericulture was firmly established in the Byzantine Empire, and the supply of silk threads and yarns in the eastern Mediterranean became abundant. Nevertheless, the advantages that Byzantium gained by establishing sericulture were relatively short-lived, since it was also in the seventh century that Islam emerged in Arabia and that Muslim cavalries subsequently conquered lands that stretched all the way from North Africa to Central Asia. Included in these conquests were all the Byzantine lands south of Anatolia (more or less south of present-day Turkey's southern border), as well as Egypt. Byzantium thus lost most of its famous weaving centers to the Arabs, and thereafter it was mostly Arab traders who were delivering silk yarns and textiles to Constantinople. The Byzantine government even maintained a mosque there to accommodate them. Furthermore, by the end of the seventh century sericulture could be found all the way from China to the Byzantine Empire and thereafter neither Byzantium nor China had a monopoly on sericulture.

By the ninth century the Byzantine emperors no longer made any attempt to monopolize the supply of yarn and other raw materials within their shrinking empire. However, they never gave up their monopoly on the exquisite silk textiles that were made with the rare purple dye. Also, within their own empire, they never gave up the government's monopoly (within the bounds of their own empire) on the patterned silks woven with golden threads, a technique that probably came from Iran. According to the *Book of the Eparch*, a set of regulations issued by the mayor of Constantinople during the reign of Leo VI (886–912 CE), traders who tried to export these closely regulated silks and artisans who leaked the technology involved in making them still faced severe punishment. The only foreign visitors who could carry them through customs to their own homes were those who had received them as gifts from the emperor. Otherwise, people leaving Byzantium, even if they were Christian priests or diplomats who had somehow obtained these silk textiles unofficially, were subject to arrest and the confiscation of these goods at the border.

Thus, the emperors reserved unique and regulated silks for strategic and diplomatic purposes. Purple silks and silks decorated with such things as eagles, *simurghs*, and equestrian riders were given out sparingly to foreign rulers and Christian churches outside Byzantium, especially to high-ranking and highly valued foreign allies. Such gift giving did serve to distribute these silks outside the borders of Byzantium. Indeed, most of the Byzantine silks that we know today were preserved in the churches of Western Europe, where they were used to adorn the bodies of the medieval kings who were buried or interred in churches.

The demand for fine silks in Western Europe far exceeded the Byzantine supply. Most of Western Europe was still poor at this time, and most of the market for such luxuries was concentrated in the churches. The bishops sought to purchase fine silk textiles in an effort to make their churches as beautiful as paradise. Since Byzantium could not completely supply this demand, these churches found additional sources. Thus, silk textiles made in Persia, Central Asia, and even China found their way to church treasuries in Western Europe. For example, the *Zandani* silk textiles made in Sogdiana, which were much sought after in China, also made their way to Western Europe.

Also, plain silk textiles, which were much cheaper, could be traded all the way to the western edges of Eurasia. Since the Western Europeans did not have the Byzantine knowledge of how to weave complicated patterns into a silk textile, they began to embroider elaborate patterns with silk thread on plain silk. The papacy in Rome set up a factory for embroidering the portraits of saints on plain silks, and thus they were able to award certain churches a silk portrait of their particular saint. Soon many of those Western European women who could afford silk yarn were also busy embroidering plain silks for their churches. With the increasing supply and spread of embroidered silk, the Byzantine monopoly on the regulated fine silks became increasingly irrelevant.

THE TANG EMPIRE AND GOVERNMENT RESTRICTIONS ON SOME VARIETIES OF SILK

Not long after the Byzantine government had monopolized the weaving of silks within its bounds, established a color-coded hierarchy, and restricted the availability of the finest silk products, a somewhat similar development took place in Tang dynasty China (618–906 CE), at the opposite end of Eurasia. In China, there was no attempt by the government to monopolize all silk materials, nor was there any scarcity of silk materials there. China was the homeland of silk, and silk textiles were commonplace. Nevertheless, the imperial government did seek to restrict the use of certain colors and types of silk.

Actually, there were historical precedents in China for some of these restrictions. As early as the Han dynasty (206 BCE–221 CE) specific types of weaving and specific patterns had been reserved for the ruling elite. After the Sui dynasty (581–618) reunited China bringing an end to several centuries of division and war, its rulers set about restoring a Han dynasty tradition in which the central government controlled the appointment of both central and provincial officials and selected them on the basis of the quality of their education, rather than the social significance of their lineage. However, during the time of imperial disintegration when the north had been ruled by nomads, Confucianism, including the value it put upon an education in the Chinese classics, had been relegated to the sidelines. In order to remedy this problem, the Sui dynasty set about establishing schools all over the country and recruited officials by written examinations based on the classics. Previously, during the Han dynasty, the recruitment of scholars had generally been done through oral examinations or interviews, and this Sui practice of written examinations was entirely new.

As in the Han dynasty, the hiring of officials on the basis of their performance on examinations was one important way that the central government could cope with the arrogance of local aristocracies and their resistance to central government policies. The officials thus recruited were assigned to positions in the bureaucratic hierarchy according to their achievements, and their rank in the system was indicated by the colors and patterns of their silk garments. Curiously, even in China, purple happened to be the color worn by the highest rank. There is no evidence that the Chinese ever used Tyrian purple dye, or any dye resembling it. Instead they almost always used a purple dye made from a grass called *zicao*, which literally means purple grass.

The Sui dynasty did not last long, but the Tang dynasty that followed it continued these policies. To weaken the local aristocracies, the Tang rulers made new lists of noble persons, including only those who had passed the imperial examinations and risen to a high rank. They also enacted and continuously revised a clothing code for each rank of officialdom. Lavish ceremonies at the court displayed this new color-coded hierarchy, and sought to impress upon the consciousness of society the importance of those in high positions. Both a color and a set of motifs were assigned to each rank. Yellow was the color reserved for the ceremonial robe of the emperor, as it always had been. However, the emperor's everyday garments were purple, the same color as the official robes of the highest court officials. Crimson was assigned to the next rank down, followed by green and black. During the first few decades of the Tang dynasty the meaning of the colors was adjusted several times, but even so, purple was always at the top.

This ranking of the colors is curious, since in Chinese antiquity purple and crimson had been colors of low status. Confucius had even condemned the color purple, saying that it was impure, just a tainted version of pure red, since it was a mixture of red and blue. It would seem that Confucius preferred to honor the primary colors, especially red and yellow. In this context crimson (a somewhat darker red), as opposed to a pure red, was also considered to be a mixed color since it had traces of other colors mixed into it. Although no one seems to know why purple had gained such prestige in China by Sui and Tang times, one can speculate. An obvious possibility is that its rulers during the centuries between the fall of the Han and the reunification of China were influenced by the imperial customs of Iran and Byzantium and that their tastes persisted into the Sui and Tang dynasties, which otherwise tended to promote many of the classical Confucian values.

During the Tang not everyone was at ease about purple. The Buddhist monk Yijing, for example, was concerned about the propriety of purple. He had made a pilgrimage to India, and thus knew that people in the homeland of Buddhism rarely used this color for any purpose. This surprised Yijing, who then assumed that there must have been some rule about it, but even though he searched industriously for some Indian or Buddhist prohibition, he could not find one. In any event, the color purple retained its high status in China until modern times.

In the capital of Chang'an, in addition to many private silk establishments, there were twenty-five state-run textile workshops that were under the supervision of a special government department in charge of making textiles for all the official garments. To ensure that certain colors and motifs were worn exclusively by the imperial family and the bureaucratic hierarchy, the government promulgated sumptuary laws forbidding ordinary people from wearing silk robes intended for officials, especially the purple ones. Those who wore or hoarded clothing of the forbidden colors and patterns faced dire consequences, including death, if they were discovered.

However, the more the government tried to prevent commoners from wearing these government-made silks, the more appealing they became. "Wearing purple" became the greatest desire of students, especially those who had failed the examinations required for high office, and of merchants, who had the means to buy them, but were not entitled to wear them. Some people were so intent on trying these forbidden fruits that they wore tight jackets made of purple, crimson, green, or black under their dull-colored robes. Even this practice did not escape the watchful eyes of the Tang government. In 681, Emperor Gaozong issued an edict to chastise those who committed this particular transgression and ordered officials in charge of the matter to enforce the regulations strictly.

The clothing code was in effect until the end of the Tang dynasty, but long before its demise these sumptuary laws were either gradually losing their power, or had never been successfully enforced. The Tang Empire was even less successful than Byzantium with regard to controlling its imperial silk textiles. Many factors impeded successful enforcement of the sumptuary laws. Except for the restriction on official garments, the Tang Empire was a remarkably open society. Many foreigners came to the empire to preach, to trade, or to immigrate. If they mastered the Chinese language and the literary canon and passed the examinations, they could even serve in the imperial bureaucracy. Foreigners brought in splendid silk textiles, glassware, silver objects and many other luxuries that were quite distinct from Chinese products. The Tang rulers appreciated these exotic items, but due to their foreign source and the quantities available, they could never have monopolized them, even if they had wanted to. Thus, the official silks lost some of their appeal since the market offered so many beautiful, and legal, alternatives. Silk textiles from Persia, Byzantium, India, and Central Asia were all available in Tang markets. Most of the colors and motifs on the foreign silks were not on the list of forbidden official insignia, and many of them were copied by Chinese weavers, thus entering the repertoire of artistic designs on Tang textiles. If both the court and the affluent sectors of urban society appreciated these foreign styles, Chinese weavers were willing to learn new techniques in order to produce them. Silk yarns were plentiful and Tang weavers had fully mastered the eastern Mediterranean weaving techniques developed on foreign looms that were originally for woolen textiles.

Sogdian traders and immigrants played a significant role in the introduction of foreign textiles and the methods used to make them. He Chou, for example, a second generation Sogdian-Chinese, served the Sui government as the head of a department in charge of producing fine artifacts for the court. (His father, who had immigrated to China, was a famous jade carver, and his uncle had made a great fortune in China by selling Iranian-made silk brocades that had golden threads woven into the cloth.) The Sui emperor especially liked the gold-threaded brocades of Iran, and he ordered He Chou to produce similar ones. He not only succeeded in reproducing the Iranian-style silk textiles in China, but also oversaw the production of lapis lazuli glassware in the imperial shop. His efforts were so successful that he earned a well-deserved promotion. In Tang times, the presence of the Sogdian community was even more obvious than it had been in earlier centuries, as were the numerous establishments where foreign-style silks were made. With such an abundance of beautiful artifacts and exotic textiles in China's markets, wealthy buyers without official rank became less interested in wearing the forbidden official textiles, and apparently officialdom no longer scrutinized people so closely looking for this particular transgression.

These sumptuary laws were also undermined by the fact that people who were not entitled to wear the restricted types of clothing were allowed to purchase these items in the markets in order to donate them to religious institutions. Although the Tang emperors never declared Buddhism to be the state religion, Buddhism by this time had grown deep roots in China. This was especially true regarding the Buddhist concepts of rebirth and retribution, and it was generally believed that making donations to Buddhist establishments was the best way to accumulate merit for a better rebirth after death. Both the rulers and the ruled tried to gain merit and please the Buddhas and bodhisattvas through their generous donations to monasteries and their sponsorship of pilgrimages to India. The rulers, especially, donated many official silk robes and other precious items to Buddhist monasteries and other religious establishments. Large quantities of silk items such as cloth, robes, and religious banners flowed out of state treasuries and into nongovernmental storage facilities in the monasteries. And since monasteries were allowed to sell these textiles in order to obtain funds for various projects, they then flowed from the monasteries into the domestic and foreign markets.

In 630, when the newly established Tang dynasty was at war with Turkic peoples along its western frontier, the famous Chinese Buddhist pilgrim and scholar Xuanzang set out for India. In fact, Xuanzang did not have permission to make the trip and sneaked out of China, eluding government authorities. He was thus without gifts for his Indian hosts. This serious problem was solved, however, by the king of Gaochang, an oasis state at Turfan (in the eastern part of China's Xinjiang Uighur Autonomous Region, near the Jade Gate). Thirty horses were loaded down with gold, silver, plain silk, silk clothes, and 500 bolts of damask silk, plus many additional gifts for other rulers along the way to India. Twenty-five laborers helped Xuanzang manage the horses that he would use during his journey on the steppe.

He and many other Chinese pilgrims who went to India in Tang times transported many goods, especially Chinese silk textiles, which were very welcome commodities there. Thus, the pilgrimage procession was, in essence, a caravan. Like Xuanzang, some of the pilgrims went out and came back by land routes, but others used sea routes that went from China to India by way of Southeast Asia. All of them went loaded down with silk textiles to pay their traveling expenses along the way and to make donations to the Indian monasteries whose stupas housed relics of the Buddha.

In 640, about ten years after Xuanzang's departure from Gaochang, the Tang dynasty took over the kingdom whose ruler had so generously hosted the monk. Tang officials then chose Jiaohe, a small town in Gaochang, to be the site of a new headquarters for the Western Frontier Office, which managed both trade and military campaigns. They carried out an extensive building program, and the town grew into a city. Given the dynasty's close relationship with Buddhism, it is not surprising that a Buddhist temple, overlooking a large square, marked the center of this garrison city.

Though Xuanzang left China illegally, fourteen years later when he returned to China he received a warm welcome since he returned with many Buddhist texts and numerous relics of the Buddha in his baggage. He had

**ILLUSTRATION 4-5   THE BUDDHIST CONCEPT OF REBIRTH: SILK BANNER FROM
DUNHUANG, TENTH CENTURY.**

The main figure is the Bodhisattva attended by two clerks who oversee the possible
afterlives to which an individual might be reborn. Those who had the most merit are
located in the two top sectors above the head of the Bodhisattva, a heavenly inhabitant (on
the left) and earthbound humans (on the right). In the next segment down, are those with
less merit, who are reborn as animals (on the left) or as spirit creatures *(asuras)*, on the right.
In the third section down those with the least merit become ghosts in one of the two hells,
one on the left, the other on the right. In the large fourth segment down are portraits of the
donors who paid for the wall-hanging. This Buddhist vision of the afterlife had become
deeply rooted in China by the time of the Tang dynasty. This banner is now in the collection
of the Museum Guimet in Paris. *(Source: Buddhist banner depicting Dizang and the Six Roads to
Rebirth, from Dunhuang (painting on silk), Chinese School (tenth century)/Musee Guimet, Paris,
France, Lauros/Giraudon/Bridgeman Art Library.)*

ILLUSTRATION 4-6   THE RUINS OF JIAOHE, FL. SEVENTH TO THIRTEENTH CENTURIES.

After its 640 conquest of the oasis kingdom of Gaochang, the Tang dynasty built a new garrison city at Jiaohe, which was then only a small town. It became the headquarters of the Western Frontier Office, which managed both trade and military campaigns. A Buddhist temple was built at the center of the new city. In the now-empty shrine facing the viewer, a large statue of the Buddha kept watch over the many activities that took place in the square in front of the temple. *(Photograph courtesy of Xinru Liu.)*

also gained a deeper knowledge of Buddhism, the Sanskrit language, and the countries of Central and South Asia. After his return he became a consultant and priest for the Tang royal family and served the court under two emperors. Although he received numerous prestigious silk robes and piles of exquisite textiles, it seems that he did not wear them. He was very particular about his clothing, and he would wear only Gandharan-style robes made of cotton. He gave many of the royal silk textiles away to his Indian guests or entrusted them to traders to take to his friends in India, and his friends there sent back cotton robes to keep him well supplied.

Late in his career, Xuanzang wanted to have a stupa built in the Indian style to preserve the precious texts that he had brought back to China. When he asked the court for funding, he received many silk items that had been in the wardrobes of women in the royal harem who were deceased by that time. Although these clothes were not brand new, they were beautiful and highly valued royal textiles. One may assume that monks in Xuan-zang's monastery did not wear them but sold them in the market in order to finance the building of the stupa. This is just one example of how royal silk textiles flowed into the markets through religious institutions.

The Tang Empire, most of the time, was open to all religions. In addi-tion to Daoism, an indigenous Chinese philosophy and religion, and Bud-dhism, which by this time was treated as if it were indigenous, royal largess was also extended to Zoroastrianism, Manichaeanism, Nestorian Christianity, and Islam. Royal patronage often took the form of granting purple robes to honored priests, regardless of which religion they prac-ticed. Religions clearly benefited from such recognition. One example of the significance of this imperial patronage is a tablet that records the his-tory of Nestorian Christianity in Tang China, wherein it is clear that a "purple-robed priest" was a source of great pride within this Christian community.

Nevertheless, there came a time in the mid-ninth century when there was a great persecution of religions. The Tang dynasty was experiencing serious economic and political problems at the time, and the Tang court blamed many of these problems on the extravagance of various religions' establishments. Buddhist monasteries, in particular, controlled a consider-able amount of land, and, in addition, people pretending to be monks and nuns in order to avoid taxation were an even more serious problem. Be-cause of these persecutions, all the foreign religions but Buddhism were ei-ther wiped out entirely or pushed into remote areas. Buddhism, too, was attacked, and the large land holdings of many monasteries were confis-cated. However, the emperor, even in his great rage against religions, dared not close the major monasteries that performed rituals for the heav-enly well-being of deceased ancestors of the ruling family. Only a few months after most Buddhist monasteries were closed and monks and nuns had been sent back to their family homes, court officials reported to the emperor that there was much suffering in the land. The monasteries had provided charity such as shelter to the homeless and medicine for the poor, and once they were closed people could no longer find such services. The emperor relented and Buddhism soon recovered from its losses and grew with even greater vigor.

Clearly the participation of religious institutions, especially Buddhist temples and monasteries, in the commercial markets of China was a major factor in the failure of the Tang dynasty's attempt to monopolize high-quality, royal silk textiles. The court itself was implicated in these activities since it donated such textiles to the monasteries for the explicit purpose of financing various projects. By the end of the dynasty in 906 CE, the monasteries' sales of such restricted products in the markets, in combination with the large quantity of highly valued foreign goods available there, created a situation in which neither the imperial court nor the wealthy purchasers of such luxuries paid much attention to the sumptuary laws.

One reason that foreign luxuries became so plentiful in China during the Tang dynasty was the rise and rapid spread of Islam in the seventh century. It was during the early part of the Tang dynasty that this new religion was founded and its followers conquered much of Eurasia between the Mediterranean and the frontiers of China in the seventh and eighth centuries. These new Muslim powers had emerged within the context of already-established Eurasian trade networks, and Muslim caliphs and sultans responded positively to this environment, promoting the production and trade of silk and many other commodities. Thereafter, the abundance of goods available in international markets generally made sumptuary laws and restrictions on luxury goods obsolete. After the end of the Tang dynasty, no government in China ever again tried to enforce sumptuary laws. The next chapter examines the impact that Muslim rule over this large expanse of territory had on the silk trade as well as the cultural changes that the silk roads facilitated during the time of the caliphates.

For Further Reading

Liu, Xinru. *Silk and Religion: An Exploration of Material Life and the Thought of People, AD 600–1200.* Oxford: Oxford University Press, 1996.

Foltz, Richard. *Religions of the Silk Road, Overland Trade and Cultural Exchanges from Antiquity to the Fifteenth Century.* New York: St. Martin's Press, 1999.

TIMELINE

Trade and Communication under the Islamic System

Early Seventh Century	Islam emerges in two cities in the Arabian Desert, Mecca, and Medina.
629–645 CE	Xuanzang's pilgrimage to India.
634–644 CE	The reign of Caliph Umar. He initiated the *jizya* in newly conquered areas. In order to distinguish Arabs from the local population, he established an extra tax on non-Muslims. Otherwise local populations were free to practice their own religions. They were allowed to convert to Islam, and many did. Converts did not have to pay the *jizya* tax.
656 CE	The *Koran* became a written scripture.
661–750 CE	The Umayyad caliphate forms, with its capital at Damascus.
671–695 CE	Yijing's pilgrimage to India.
685–705 CE	The reign of Caliph Abdal Malik. He and the Byzantine emperor Justinian II (r. 685–695 CE) engaged in a dispute about inscriptions on textiles and other goods made in Egypt. This dispute led to the development of an Islamic coinage, and then to war. The *tiraz* system in Egypt also resulted from this dispute. The system involved embroidering inscriptions (which came to function as trademarks) on textiles. After 750, other caliphs established the system throughout the Muslim world.
726–843 CE	Byzantium's iconoclast period. During this period Rome was unable to acquire Byzantine silks with images of the saints. The Roman popes set up workshops where plain silks were embroidered with images of the saints. Most likely the plain silks came from China via Muslim merchants.

Mid-eighth Century	The pilgrimage of Hui Chao, a Korean Buddhist. He describes numerous Buddhist monasteries still flourishing in Tukharistan (in present-day Afghanistan) after the Arab conquest, but before the Battle of Talas (751). Buddhist monasteries typically were centers of paper-making and printing. Thus, Central Asian Buddhists may have been a link in the chain of transmission of Chinese paper-making to the Muslim world.
750–1258	The Abbasid caliphate.
751	The Battle of Talas. Battle on the Talas River (in present-day Kyrgyzstan) in which the armies of the Abbasid Caliphate defeated those of Tang dynasty China, taking many thousands of prisoners. Chinese paper-making then spread throughout the Islamic world. Until recently, scholars attributed this development solely to Chinese artisans captured during the battle and put to work in the caliphate.
754–803	Several members of the Barmakid family became close advisors to the early Abbasid caliphs and some served as wazirs in Baghdad. They were from Afghanistan and were among the earliest converts to Islam in this region. One of their ancestors had been the chief priest of a large Buddhist temple. Since the Buddhist monasteries frequently used paper and printing techniques to publish Buddhist scriptures, scholars now believe that the Barmakids were instrumental in the promotion of paper-making throughout the caliphate.
762	The second Abbasid caliph moved the capital from Damascus to Baghdad. After this move, the government established its own *tiraz* factories to produce textiles for the caliphs and their palaces and for gifts to honored persons. *Tiraz* inscriptions became required for both silk and cotton textiles. Concern about the religious implications of wearing too much silk waned, and caliphs began wearing silk robes as well as silk hems.

813–833 CE	Reign of Caliph al-Mamun. He founded and endowed the House of Wisdom in Baghdad, which served as a library, an observatory, and a scientific academy. It lasted until the Mongols sacked the city in 1258.
d. 835 CE	Muhammad Musa al-Khwarizmi, of Central Asian background, joined the House of Wisdom in the early ninth century. He translated a Sanskrit manual on mathematics into Arabic, introducing the Indian decimal system and its zero to the Muslim world, whence it eventually spread to the rest of the globe.
820–912 CE	Ibn Khordadhbeh, an Iranian Muslim scholar who wrote a geographical study of the known world. His work served as a government training manual for officials of the empire, as an important source for travelers, and as a reference for scholars.

TRADE AND COMMUNICATION UNDER THE MUSLIM SYSTEM

> **GETTING STARTED ON CHAPTER FIVE:** Why did long-distance trade increase after the Muslim conquests? What issues fueled disputes and hostilities between the Umayyad Caliphate and Byzantium? What sorts of political, social, and religious concerns did the wearing of silk raise? How did paper-making spread from China to the Muslim world? What impact did paper have on cross-cultural exchanges after it spread to the Muslim world?

CHAPTER OUTLINE

The Islamic Attitude Toward Trade

Islamic Currency and the *Tiraz* System

The Significance of Textiles

Sericulture and Trade in the Islamic Domain

The Spread of Paper-Making and Books

Scholarly Pursuits

In the early part of the seventh century the wealthy and powerful were prospering in the Byzantine Empire, Sasanid Iran, and Tang China, from one end of the Eurasian landmass to the other. Their elites enjoyed sophisticated material cultures, wore elaborately woven silk textiles, and lived in homes where the walls were hung with silk draperies. Little did they know that their world was about to change dramatically. From a most unexpected corner, a new force, inspired by a new religion, was about to descend upon them. It was at this time that Islam emerged in Mecca and Medina, two cities in the Arabian Desert. The cavalries that its leaders assembled would soon transform political boundaries, as well as trade and communications, all across Eurasia. Byzantium would lose much of its empire, including most of its territory on the eastern and southern shores of the Mediterranean. The empire of the Sasanids would be completely overrun; and Tang China's presence in Central Asia would be noticeably curtailed. Nevertheless, in spite of these hostilities, these cavalries did not destroy the commercial links that stretched across Eurasia. Quite the contrary, long-distance commercial activity actually increased soon after the Muslim conquests.

The Muslims, the followers of this new religion, had few qualms about the pursuit of commercial profits. Islamic traditions differed from those of Christianity and Buddhism in that they explicitly endorsed the pursuit of commercial profits as a totally acceptable and, indeed, virtuous way to make a living. This attitude may have been related to the relatively weak agricultural base on the Arabian Peninsula. Nomads, in particular, tend to value merchants and demean farming. The founder and prophet of Islam, Muhammad, was himself a merchant and Islam's earliest foundations were in the cities of Mecca and Medina, both of which had long been important destinations on the caravan routes across the Arabian Peninsula. Ever since ancient times there had been many experienced and talented Arab traders, and thus it is not surprising that the religion that emerged on this peninsula would explicitly endorse commerce. Nor should it be surprising that soon after the Muslim conquests the scope of Arab trade would expand to an extent even Muhammad could not have dreamed of. In addition, it should be noted that it was not just the conquest of territory that brought about this expansion of Muslim commerce. In the process of conquering and consolidating their imperial position, the various Muslim powers created new commercial facilities and promoted various developments in communications that would both play a major role in the expansion of Eurasian commerce.

Islam served to unify the various tribes of the Peninsula, among whom there had been a long history of rivalry and hostilities. To understand the

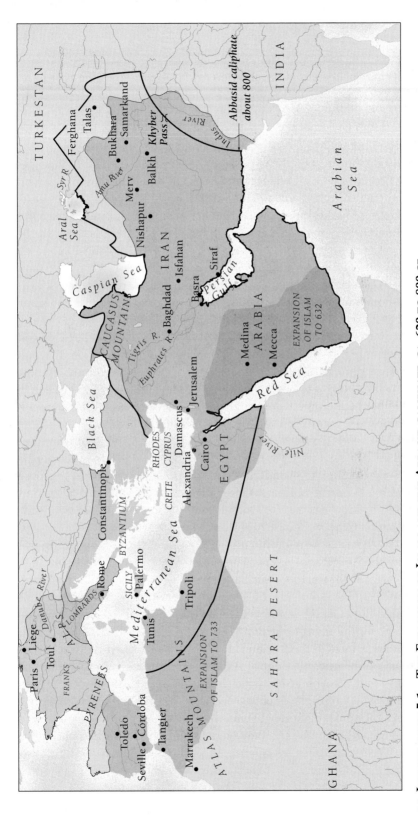

ILLUSTRATION 5-1 **THE EXPANSION OF ISLAM AND THE ABBASID CALIPHATE, CA. 620 TO 800 CE.**
(Source: Used with permission from Traditions and Encounters (2nd ed.), by Jerry H. Bentley and Herbert F. Ziegler. Copyright 2003 by McGraw-Hill.)

complexities of the situation, it is important to note that the word *Arab* refers to an ethno-linguistic group, essentially those people who are native speakers of Arabic and various closely related languages, all of which are Semitic languages that originated on or near the Arabian Peninsula. The word *Arab* does not indicate anything about what religion a person is or what occupation a person has. The Arab tribes were essentially lineages, that is, descent groups. Each of these tribes might include among its members merchants in the caravan cities and the cities that border the nearby shores of the Mediterranean Sea, farmers near the coasts and in the oases, and camel herders in the desert. Prior to the emergence of Islam at the beginning of the seventh century, some Arabs, especially those along the eastern and southeastern shores of the Mediterranean, were Christians, but most, especially those living on the peninsula, were polytheists.

Although most Arabs did convert to Islam, some did not, and there are still, to this day, many Arab Christians living along the shores of the eastern Mediterranean. To those who were polytheists Islam offered its converts not only a new, but an indigenous monotheistic religion. It would also offer a standard language, the language of the *Koran*, the holy book that Muslims believe to be a collection of the revelations of God (Allah) to his prophet Muhammad. Although for many decades its message was maintained as a memorized oral tradition, by 656 it had become a written scripture. Thereafter, both the dialect in which the messages were transcribed and the script used to produce this written version would soon become the sacred literary standard for all Muslims. Thus, for those believers who were already Arabic-speaking, it meant the creation of a standard written language and script. Once Islam spread outside the peninsula, many people who were not Arabs and did not speak Arabic joined the faith. For them, conversion often meant, at least for religious purposes, learning the Arabic spoken language as well as the standard script.

By 656, the first Islamic state had already pushed its boundaries far beyond the Arabian Peninsula, overrunning Byzantine-controlled Palestine, Syria, and Egypt, and Sasanid-controlled Mesopotamia (present-day Iraq) and Iran. By the eighth century Muslim cavalries had conquered all of North Africa, most of the Iberian Peninsula (that is, present-day Spain and Portugal), and much of Central Asia. Not only those who had become Muslims, but also non-Muslim residents living within territories controlled by Muslim rulers, often learned to speak and read Arabic. Many of these Arabic-speaking non-Muslims were Jewish. They spoke another Semitic language, Hebrew, and they were frequently the trading partners of Arabs. They sometimes even wrote in Arabic, but when they did, they wrote it with a Hebrew script, not the standard Arabic one. On the other hand, in Iran, where the overwhelming majority of the population converted to Islam, most continued to speak Persian, which is not a Semitic, but an Indo-European language.

After the Muslim conquests, the elites in Iran, especially the scholars, did read and write in Arabic. Also, since most Iranian Muslims studied the Koran, they did learn some Arabic for religious purposes, and they did begin to write the Persian language in a new way, using the Arabic script of the Koran instead of an older Aramaic writing system. The Iranians also incorporated a great many Arabic words into the Persian language. Thus, rather suddenly the Arabic language emerged as a lingua franca throughout much of the eastern part of Eurasia. For the first time in history, the Arabic language and an Arabic script served a large communications network that stretched from the Mediterranean basin to Central Asia. Thereafter, the long distance that separated the Mediterranean shores from the frontiers of eastern Asia suddenly seemed much shorter.

Muslim trading networks linked all of Eurasia for about six centuries, from the seventh until the thirteenth century, when the Mongolian conquests destroyed much of their traditional commercial infrastructure. During these centuries the international community of Islam would eventually include a wide variety of nationalities and ethnic groups. This was true not only in the places that the Muslim cavalries had conquered, but also in places where there were Arabic-speaking traders, but no Arab conquests, such as West Africa, East Africa, and parts of Southeast Asia.

The spread of Islam across such distances created a highly diverse community of believers that together created what became known as Islamic civilization. Indeed, in the Arabic literature of that time writers often described this expanse of territory as "from Ghana to Fergana," in other words, from the Atlantic shores of West Africa to the frontiers of China. The scholarly community within Islam, which superceded national and ethnic boundaries, was as diverse as the community of believers, and they all brought their learning and cultural traditions into the process that created a new Muslim civilization.

Some of the Muslim scholars, due to their pre-Muslim heritage, were already familiar with one or more of the highly influential classical traditions of the Greeks, the Iranians, and the Indians, and within this newly created diverse community, individuals not only studied their own earlier traditions but also those of others. They steeped themselves in the learned traditions of many countries and cultures, some of which had previously been limited to one culture or region, and transmitted this amalgamated scientific and cultural knowledge along with new technologies, especially paper-making, from one end of Eurasia to another. Because they were all now part of the same community of scholars, discussions among them that involved material from the various traditions that they brought with them were profound. The end result of this sort of cross-cultural communication across traditional intellectual boundaries was exceptional creativity, and their achievements in art, literature, and science were extraordinary and paved the way for the dawn of the modern world.

Although during these six centuries there were many political distur-bances and regime changes in the Islamic world, the trading networks en-dured and survived them, and, to a limited extent, a few even survived the Mongolian conquests of the thirteenth century. Many factors contributed to the strength and tenacity of the networks, but the following four were among the most important. The doctrine and the religious practice of Islam encour-aged trade and communication. The solidity and stability of the coinage, that is, the currency, facilitated transactions over a large geographical area. The Is-lamic invention of a trademark system, known as the *tiraz*, created a market for particular styles and thus stimulated the production and distribution of expensive, finely woven textiles. And the spread of Chinese paper-making technology and book binding throughout the Islamic lands and to Europe not only added another important commodity to international trade but also provided a new means for communication. These were the most significant factors underlying the network's vitality and longevity.

THE ISLAMIC ATTITUDE TOWARD TRADE

Except for its prohibition on usury, which was defined as charging inter-est on any loan of money, the *Koran* encouraged both trade and commer-cial profits. The taboo on charging interest did cause problems for Muslim traders, especially when their trading networks were expanding. They of-ten needed to borrow money at the beginning of a project in order to buy the trade goods and cover the transportation costs of delivering them to a far-off market, where they hoped to reap a large profit. The problem was that if lenders could not charge the borrower interest, there was little if any incentive for them to loan anyone money. There was, however, a solution. The merchants used a special type of partnership that solved the credit problems posed by this prohibition on usury.

From the very beginning of Islam, there were many questions raised within the Muslim community about issues related to trade and commerce. Even during Muhammad's lifetime it became apparent that the *Koran* did not provide detailed guidance on many questions relating to trade, nor about a variety of other issues that arose when the political boundaries of Muslim empires were expanding. While he was alive, Muhammad, personally, was called upon to explain what was meant by the many messages from Allah in the *Koran*. His followers collected his answers in the *Hadith*, a compilation of his remarks and comments, and from the *Hadith* it is clear that Muhammad had many complimentary things to say about merchants, including the following:

> The honest, truthful Muslim merchant will stand with the martyrs on the Day of Judgment.
> I commend the merchants to you, for they are the couriers of the horizons and God's trusted servants on earth.
> The cowardly merchant is deprived; the brave merchant is rewarded.
> Nine-tenths of livelihood is trade; the tenth is livestock. (Al-Muttaqi, Kanz al-'Ummal, ii pp. 193–203, 212–213, Bernard Lewis, ed. transl. *Islam*, 126–127)

And the last quotation reflects Muhammad's own interest in the trade in textiles and perfumes, the ancient trading goods of the Arabs:

> If God permitted the inhabitants of paradise to trade, they would deal in cloth and perfume [meaning such things as frankincense and myrhh].
> (idem)

These sayings ascribed to Muhammad certainly were consistent with the pre-Islamic trading patterns of the Arabs, as well as the trading patterns of many of the converts from other nearby cultures, such as the Iranians and Egyptians.

Mecca, the city where Muhammad first preached, became the spiritual as well as the commercial center of Islam. To achieve unity among a widespread and diverse community of believers, the religion requires that at precisely the same time, five times a day, all its followers physically turn toward Mecca and pray. It also requires that all Muslims (or at least all those who are capable of long-distance travel) should make a pilgrimage to Mecca at least once in their lives. Mecca thus became the center of Islam even though the city's polytheistic leaders had once forced Muhammad out of town when he first began preaching there.

Well before the emergence of Islam, Mecca had been both the meeting place and the most important sacred site of traders on the Arabian Peninsula. Long before the time of Muhammad, the black meteor stone in the Islamic Kaaba, the square structure that enshrines the stone, had been a revered object in the folk religions of Arabia. Islam incorporated this reverence for the stone into its own monotheistic belief, maintaining that there was only one spirit, Allah, within this traditional sacred object. Thereafter, all Muslims, whether or not they were Arabs, made the pilgrimage to Mecca in order to worship at this site.

The requirement of Muslims to turn toward Mecca whenever they prayed, regardless of where they were on the globe, created a need for knowing precisely where they were located in terms of this caravan city. In addition, the requirement that Muslims travel to Mecca also necessitated and brought about an increased awareness of how one could get from any given location in the Eastern Hemisphere to Mecca. Thus, it is not surprising that Muslims learned and developed the scholarly fields of astronomy (used among other things for navigation across deserts and seas), mathematics (which was required for astronomy), and cartography, the science and technique of map drawing. This knowledge not only helped pilgrims, but also helped traders. In any case, in medieval Eurasia commerce and pilgrimage were so closely linked that it is often difficult to disentangle them. Thus, it is not surprising that Mecca became not only the center of the Islamic religious world, but also a major center within the Islamic trading networks.

Although Islamic doctrine and religious practices did not initially stir up any difficulties within the trading networks located east of Arabia, Islamic monotheism had a head-on collision with the Christian rulers of the Byzantine Empire. During the seventh and early eighth centuries when early Muslim empires were encroaching upon Byzantine territory, the Byzantine Empire was still a model of material culture for all of Christendom. In addition it was a major empire with an unusually strong central government that was closely tied to the Christian hierarchy of the eastern Mediterranean region. Both its political and religious structures were hierarchical. One may recall from the previous chapter that the status of the political and religious elites was marked by their regalia, and that they were the only people allowed to wear the expensive silk textiles that were colored with the rare purple dye. Although the Byzantine church at Constantinople was not as involved with the saints' bone relics as were Rome and the rest of Western Europe, its members were proud of the true cross of Jesus' crucifixion and had made Mary the patron saint of the city. Despite the many theological debates among the Christians, most of them accepted the Holy Trinity of "Father, Son, and the Holy Spirit in one God" as the orthodox theology.

It was Constantinople's introduction of this Christian belief in the Holy Trinity into an international commercial situation that caused the initial troubles on the eastern Mediterranean trade routes. The Muslims saw the Christian division of the divinity into three parts as unacceptable from a monotheistic point of view, and they saw the worship of saints as a kind of idolatry. Also because Islam recognized only Allah's authority, its followers believed that there should not be any ecclesiastical hierarchy among the faithful, at least in theory, and, in general, in practice. Within the community of believers, the faithful should only submit to Allah and not to any religious hierarchy. Muslims also were puzzled by Byzantine efforts to limit the wearing of finely woven purple silks to a very small political and religious elite. Although there were Islamic restrictions on how much silk a person could wear, these restrictions applied to all Muslims, without exception. A policy that allowed some people but not others to wear these silks did not make sense to them, especially within a religious context.

Initially, trade between the new Islamic state and Byzantium had been unaffected by these religious differences. After the Muslim conquest of Egypt, which had previously been a part of the Byzantine Empire and thus a bulwark of Christianity, Constantinople was in an awkward position. It was dependent upon Egypt for its supplies of certain basics such as grain, for which they had other possible sources, and linen textiles and papyri, for which they had no other sources. Egypt's new Muslim rulers were quite willing to continue exporting these products to Byzantium. The confrontation between them developed only after the Arabs discovered the meaning of Greek-language inscriptions put on these products by their Egyptian manufacturers. When the Muslim caliph in Damascus learned that these inscriptions were a confession of faith in the Christian Holy Trinity, he objected to their use in Egypt. Ironically, the controversy that ensued led to the creation of an Islamic currency.

ISLAMIC CURRENCY AND THE *TIRAZ* SYSTEM

The first Islamic empire, known as the Umayyad caliphate, had its capital in Damascus. Its ruler at this time was Caliph Abdal Malik (685–705 CE) who is famous for creating several important institutions, including a system of Muslim currency and the *tiraz*, a system of embroidering inscriptions onto the fabric of textiles. Under Byzantine rule, some Egyptian products, such as textiles, papyri, and pottery, had carried Greek-language inscriptions giving the name of the reigning Byzantine emperor. After the Muslim conquest this was obviously unacceptable to the Muslim governor of Egypt, since such inscriptions would have implied that Byzantium still ruled Egypt. There was thus a compromise. There could still be Greek-language inscriptions on Egyptian products, but their content would not be political in nature. In fact, it was even agreed by both the Byzantine officials and the Muslim officials in Egypt that the inscriptions could be a reference to Christianity's Holy Trinity. Thereafter, the Byzantines continued to receive their supply of papyri with the new Greek inscriptions, and the new Muslim regime in Egypt accumulated great profits by exporting it. However, Caliph Malik, in Damascus, was not a part of this agreement. When he discovered the meaning of the Greek inscriptions on the Egyptian goods, he ordered the governor of Egypt to ban the Greek inscriptions and mark all the papyri and textiles with an Islamic inscription, written in Arabic, proclaiming its strictly monotheistic belief, "there is no other god but God."

Byzantium, the most literate part of the Christian world at that time, and thus the major importer of Egyptian papyri, found Caliph Malik's order to use the Arabic-language inscription, "there is no other god but God," to be unacceptable. Because the emperor of Byzantium, Justinian II (685–695), did not want to break the treaty with the caliphate, he sent generous gifts to the caliph in order to initiate negotiations with him. Caliph Malik, however, was determined to carry out the new policy and refused to negotiate. An outraged Justinian II then threatened the caliph, saying that he would put profane inscriptions against the Prophet Muhammad on all Byzantine coins. Since Byzantium's gold coins were the standard currency of the time and were widely used by many nationalities on many of the Eurasian trade routes, Justinian II was assuming that the Muslims would have no choice but to use the coins with the inflammatory inscriptions, and that Caliph Malik would thus back down.

That, however, was not what happened. The caliph retaliated by stopping all exports of papyri to Byzantium, and set out to cast his own gold and silver coins. Furthermore, he put his own image, holding a sword, on the face side of these coins. Then he sent the first specimen to the Byzantine emperor with a message informing Justinian II that he would be making his own currency. He also indicated that he also would continue to accept Byzantine currency, presumably including the coins with the objectionable inscriptions. Justinian II then declared war on the caliphate.

Caliph Malik won the war against the Byzantines, both on the battlefield and on the coins. However, Islamic scholars soon pointed out to him that under Islamic law he could not use his own image on the coins. In many contexts, Islam forbids the use of any human figure as a religious symbol. The caliph was considered to be a successor to the Prophet Muhammad, although without Muhammad's powers of prophecy, but it was nevertheless deemed inappropriate to use the caliph's figure, or any human figure, as a symbol of the religious community or the empire that it ruled. Caliph Malik thus had to remove his sword-waving image from the coins, and he replaced it with just his name, the year of his reign, and a pious inscription.

The central government of the caliphate guaranteed the quality of the coins, and with this new design, they enjoyed a wide circulation both inside and outside the empire. In terms of their denomination, the coins were very much in the tradition of the Greek, Roman, and Byzantine currencies, which is to say that the actual value of the metal used to make them was the same as that used in the older Mediterranean coins. While the Arab *dinar* corresponded to the Roman denarius, the Arab *dirham* was the equivalent of the Byzantine *drachma*. As a result, traders, whether or not they were Muslims, could recognize and appreciate a coin's value, even if they could not read the Arabic legend. What was different was that the legends on the coins (the name and reign date of the caliph and the religious inscription) established an effective way for the Commander of the Faithful, one of the caliph's titles, to communicate with his Islamic subjects. Muslim traders and consumers thereby knew who was issuing the coins and who was in charge of imperial finances.

Caliph Malik initiated another important institution, the system known as the *tiraz*. The word *tiraz* comes from the Persian language, in which it simply means embroidery. However, in Arabic, during the Umayyad caliphate, the word came to mean the inscriptions that were embroidered on the hems of textiles. This Arabic association of embroidery with hems probably came about because of an old Iranian custom of sewing patterned or embroidered hems on expensive garments. The hems were highly decorative, and were made either by weaving various patterns into silk brocades or tapestries, or by embroidering the patterns onto the hem with silk thread. In Iran this fashion can be dated back to the very beginning of the first millennium CE, since many of the statues that date from Parthian (ca. 239 BCE–224 CE) and Sasanid (ca. 224–640 CE) times portray people wearing robes with patterned hems.

THE SIGNIFICANCE OF TEXTILES

The Islamic domain ruled by Caliph Malik stretched from Iran to Egypt, and thus his empire had inherited a wide variety of textile industries. Sasanid Iran and the cities along the eastern coast of the Mediterranean had been famous for silk weaving for several centuries before the Muslim conquest, and Egyptian linen had been a popular product in both the Greek- and the Arabic-speaking lands. The Arabs themselves were from a tent culture that had a great appreciation for textiles. People who live in tents do so because they need to move their homes on a regular basis, and thus their belongings need to be easily portable, which textiles are. Both the camel herders and caravan traders spent much of their time in tents, which were made of a heavy woolen felt. People, who spent a lot of time in their tents, often sought to decorate the floor and walls with more luxurious textiles, thus creating a steady demand for these items. Even when they moved into ordinary houses, they carried their upholstery decorating traditions with them into their sedentary residences. Also at that time textiles were the major form of wealth in the tent culture, as well as in the sedentary societies that the Muslim cavalries had conquered. After Caliph Malik went to war with Justinian II over the issue of an Arabic inscription on Egyptian-made papyri, he also had *tiraz* borders with an Islamic message put on all the linen made in Egypt. The inscription could either be woven into the silk tapestry on the border, or it could be embroidered on a border with silk threads. Thus, these consumer goods carried a political as well as a religious message.

Unlike the production of coins, which the Islamic rulers borrowed from the Byzantines, the *tiraz* system was an innovation sponsored by the new Islamic empire. The older inscriptions put on commercial products in Byzantium and Iran had been utilitarian, conveying information about the place and time of manufacture in an ordinary script. The *tiraz* inscriptions were different. With the coming of Islam, calligraphers turned the Arabic script into an extraordinary art form. Although these inscriptions also conveyed information, they were written in a calligraphic style that added significantly to the aesthetic value of the textile. Also, because they were an aesthetic addition, they were not limited to borders and hems. Some *tiraz* inscriptions were embroidered on strips of cloth that were sewn across the main body of the material.

The system arose at a time when the caliphs were seeking to maintain Arab identity and power while ruling over an empire that contained extraordinarily diverse peoples and traditions, and who in most places outside the Arabian Peninsula greatly outnumbered their conquerors. Although the Arab caravan traders who had founded Islam were familiar with the wealth and luxurious life of the elites in the lands they had just conquered, that was not the case for many of the troops that made up the Muslim cavalries. For the most part, their ranks were made up of Bedouin herdsmen, who had lived a relatively spartan life in the deserts, and the caliph worried that they would be easily overwhelmed by what they saw in areas once ruled by Iran and Byzantium. The first few caliphs were thus equally concerned with exploiting the conquered lands on the one hand, and on the other hand keeping the Arab military elites from becoming assimilated into the cultures of the conquered peoples.

To get the funds necessary to support themselves and their government in style from the newly conquered lands, caliphs had to employ members of the local elite, Persian- and Greek-speaking literati, to run the administration and collect the taxes. Caliph Umar (634–644), for example, had implemented a poll tax called the *jizya*, which was intended to distinguish the non-Muslim local population from the Muslim Arab rulers. Christians and the followers of other religions could continue to practice their religion without interference from the Muslim government, but they did not enjoy the same status as the Muslims. In particular, they had to pay an extra tax. However, if members of the conquered nationality wanted to, they could convert to Islam, and if they did, they no longer had to pay the *jizya*.

In these conquered lands many members of the former elites were eager to take government jobs working for the Arab conquerors, and thus share the privileges of their Arab rulers. These non-Arab clients of the Islamic regime were called *mawalis*, and they were the ones who actually ran the state machinery, since the rulers of the caliphate maintained only small staffs and kept most of their Arab soldiers in separate garrison cities such as Basra on the Persian Gulf, Kufa on the Euphrates, and Fustat on the Nile. The *mawalis* generally converted to Islam and learned Arabic. By the time of Caliph Malik, that is, by the end of the seventh century, a whole new generation of *mawalis* was in charge of the business of governing the caliphate.

The economy of the conquered lands recovered quickly from the shock of the conquest, and, in addition, the garrison cities in the empire also developed into flourishing commercial centers. The *mawalis* who served the new rulers drew their Arab masters into the luxurious lifestyle of the ruling elite of those ancient cultures. However, the practice of Islam required a disciplined life. All the conquests had been carried out in the name of God, and even the Commander of the Faithful, the caliph, was supposed to follow all of the religious protocols. The *ulama*, religious scholars who had a strong moral authority within Muslim communities, studied the *Koran* and compiled the *Hadith*, and they always expected both the rulers and Muslims in general to strictly follow the requirements of the religion. They did not like to see the Commander of the Faithful acquiring what they believed to be the bad habits of the conquered, who were in their minds, the products of old, corrupt, and idolatrous cultures. Even so, they could not prevent the caliphs from rewarding their brave soldiers and themselves with the booty collected from the conquered peoples.

One of the major religious controversies had to do with silk. In a world where textiles represented wealth, silk had long been the most prestigious and precious fabric both for clothing and household decoration. Those believers who could afford to buy silk saw no reason that Muslims, rulers or commoners, could not enjoy silk attire, especially when former Iranian rulers and contemporary Byzantine rulers could wear silk robes. To resolve this controversy, the religious scholars searched the *Koran* and the sayings of the Prophet looking for guidance.

In fact, the *Koran* does not say whether or not a Muslim can wear silk garments. The only places where silk is mentioned in the *Koran* is in descriptions of the wondrous paradise that awaited devout Muslims when they died. For example:

> Verily, God will make those who believe and do right enter into gardens, beneath which rivers flow. They shall be bedecked therein with bracelets of gold and with pearls, and their garments therein shall be of silk, and they shall be guided to the goodly speech, and they shall be guided to the laudable way. (XXII 22-4)

It is interesting to note that this Islamic vision of paradise very much reflects the most desirable things in the world of the Arab caravan traders who stayed in oases in the midst of the desert. Oases can only develop where there is water, and oasis gardens must be irrigated. There are no rivers on the peninsula, except for those that dry up during much of the year. Water in the desert generally comes from underground sources. In addition, the gold, pearls, and silk, so abundant in paradise, were also some of the most valuable commodities in the caravan trade.

Although the *Koran* says nothing about whether or not those faithful who are still alive on earth should or should not wear silk garments, the *Hadith* do address this issue. In passing, the Prophet during his lifetime made a number of negative comments, some harsh and some mild, about Muslims wearing silk. For instance:

> Yahya related to me ... that Abdullah saw a silk robe for sale near the door of the mosque. He said, "Messenger of Allah (the Prophet Muhammad), would you buy this robe and wear it on Jumu's and when envoys come to you?" The Messenger of Allah, may Allah bless him and grant him peace, said, "No-one wears this but a person who has no portion in the Next World." The Messenger of Allah, may Allah bless him and grant him peace, was brought some robes of the same material and gave one of them to Umar ibn al-Khattab. Umar said, "Messenger of Allah, do you clothe me in it when you said what you said about the robe of Utarid?" The Messenger of Allah, may Allah bless him and grant him peace, said, "I did not give it to you to wear." Umar gave it to a brother of his in Makka who was still an Idolater. (Malik ibn Anas, *Al Muwatta*, 48.8, 18)

The meaning here is clear. Those who enjoy silk garments in this world will not be going to paradise, hence the wearing of silk robes was a reward reserved only for those who had died and gone to heaven after living a good and faithful life on earth.

Nevertheless, peoples' desire to wear silk was apparently irrepressible, which is not surprising given that the caliphate was ruling over peoples who considered fine silk textiles to be status symbols and highly desirable luxuries. People then asked another question, if wearing a purely silk garment is too extravagant, what about a garment that only has some silk decorations on it. After much deliberation and debate among the learned *ulama*, a general agreement emerged. Good Muslims could still go to paradise if they wore a robe decorated with a silk strip that was less than two or three fingers in width, or if they wore a robe made from a textile that was woven with a silk warp, as long as the weft was of some other kind of yarn. The use of silk threads to inscribe borders on textiles such as those used for *tiraz* fit neatly within this standard of silk strips, and at the same time it spread the Islamic religious message and communicated to consumers the name of the caliph and the year of his reign. In time, Islamic weavers invented a kind of half silk called *mulham*, which had a silk warp forming the shiny surface and used linen or some other fabric for the weft, to support the textile's structure from underneath. Thus, for several centuries the making of *tiraz* and *mulham* became the most common uses of silk in the textile workshops within the Islamic domain.

After Caliph Malik had established the *tiraz* system within Egypt, the caliphs who followed him extended it to the entire Islamic empire. As a result, all textiles were supposed to have silk borders inscribed with the name of the ruling caliph, the date (given as the year of the caliph's reign), and a phrase praising Allah. Nevertheless, unlike the rulers of Byzantium, the caliphs never attempted any sort of government monopoly on the textile industry, nor did they ever create sumptuary laws specifying who could wear what. Although there were state-run *tiraz* workshops, most workshops were privately owned. The system thus was no more than a government regulation requiring manufacturers to recognize the authority of the government and the religion that provided its legitimacy. In addition, the system ensured that products carried what was essentially a trademark by which their quality and reputation could be judged.

It was only after the Abbasid caliphate (754–1258) moved the capital from Damascus to Baghdad in 762 that the government set up its own *tiraz* factories, which manufactured textiles for the caliphs' palaces and for distribution by the caliph to honored persons. In these government-controlled factories a typical *tiraz* inscription began with the phrase, "In the name of God the Compassionate, the Merciful," the same phrase that appears at the beginning of most chapters of the *Koran*. It was followed by the name and the title of the ruling caliph, and a blessing, such as "may God prosper him," or "may God strengthen him." In addition, there was also supposed to be the name of the *wazir*, the minister in charge of the caliph's *tiraz* industry. Because the government's *tiraz* enterprise was large and became an essential part of the state machinery, the *tiraz* minister became someone of high status. In the new capital of Baghdad, there was a "house of silk," a "house of cotton," and a *tiraz* street. By this time, both silk and cotton fabrics, if they were produced under government auspices, were supposed to be marked with a *tiraz* inscription. The caliphate also had *tiraz* factories in provincial textile cities. By the time the Abbasid caliphate had established its power over most of the Muslim world, the caliphs no longer confined themselves to linen robes with silk *tiraz* but also wore silk robes with a silk *tiraz* often with an inscription that was embroidered with threads of gold.

The caliph in Baghdad maintained a large *tiraz* enterprise because he, himself, had a large wardrobe and because he needed robes to give away, that is, to bestow as robes of honor upon his especially meritorious subjects. The reader may recall that the contemporary Byzantine and Tang emperors granted robes of honor to high ministers and priests. Both the Byzantines and the Chinese considered purple robes to be the highest honor, but the leaders in the Muslim world did not care for the color purple. The Umayyad caliphate was known for its white robes, and the Abbasids were known for their black robes.

After about 800 CE, the Abbasids began to have political problems in the empire and power tended to migrate to various local rulers. In this situation these robes took on new meaning. When an Abbasid caliph appointed a sultan for a territory, he granted him a whole set of regalia starting with a robe of black silk satin with a golden *tiraz* border, followed by a gold necklace, a pair of gold bracelets, a sword with a gold-covered scabbard, a horse with a gold saddle, and a black standard, bearing the name of the caliph in white. This seven-piece grant was the symbol of the caliph's recognition of the sultan as the ruler of a given territory, as well as the sultan's recognition of the caliph as overlord. Many of the sultans were largely autonomous, and some of them had not been granted their territory by the caliph, but had conquered it with their own armies. Nevertheless, receiving the black robes from Baghdad was a great honor and bestowed legitimacy upon their rise to power.

Caliphs granted many robes of honor with *tiraz* to scholars, brave generals and soldiers, artists, poets, and other high achievers in their empires. The most spectacular *tiraz*, however, were the ones made for the Kaaba that enshrined the black stone in Mecca. Not only had the Kaaba been an object of worship for Arabs long before the coming of Islam, the custom of covering the square structure with precious textiles also dates to the pre-Islamic period. Prior to the emergence of Islam, it had been the king of Yemen who had supplied a famous striped cloth for covering the structure.

During Muhammad's lifetime, the textile covers came from many lands. In addition to the striped cloth from Yemen, there were also carpets and silks. When the Islamic empire expanded after Muhammad's death, the caliphate took over the responsibility of covering the Kaaba. The caliph ordered precious textiles from all the Muslim domains and had the names of the caliph and the *wazir*, if they came from a government workshop, inscribed on them. Since the Kaaba was the central focus of the pilgrimage for all Muslims, precisely whose names were inscribed on the cover's *tiraz*, visible to all, was of the utmost significance. All pilgrims noted the inscriptions, and scholars studied the variations in the listed names, looking for changes in the balance of power in the caliphate.

Since these precious textiles were draped over the outside of the square structure, they deteriorated rapidly, making it necessary to order a new cover every year. The quantity of material necessary to cover the entire structure, though not enormous, was considerable and inevitably expensive. Nevertheless, all the sultans who controlled textile resources and had *tiraz* workshops under their control seemed to be eager to contribute one of their textiles for the cover and considered it a great privilege to do so. Thus, the caliph always had many choices when he selected the materials, and these choices also presented an opportunity for him to manipulate the power structure. For instance, in the year 892 CE, Egypt was supposed to be the supplier of the cover for the Kaaba. However, the governor of Egypt had deleted the name of the caliph's brother, the man actually in charge in Baghdad, from locally made coins, prayers, and *tiraz* textiles. This act was obviously a challenge to the authority of Baghdad. The caliph, fearing that the governor would do the same thing on the Kaaba cover's *tiraz*, decided to cancel the order from Egypt and transferred it to Tustar in Khuzistan (in present-day Iran).

Even after the central power of the caliphate declined, rulers throughout the Muslim areas all still vied with one another for the honor of contributing the material for the Kaaba cover. They probably were even more keen on contributing the material than they had been before because their own names could be inscribed on the cover and thereby displayed to the entire Islamic world. Even after the caliphate was gone and the empire was replaced by local powers, the *tiraz* system survived.

After the power of the center weakened, local sultans took over the *tiraz* system as well as currency production, and had their own names inscribed on the borders of textiles manufactured in their jurisdictions. There were, in addition, some places where the inscriptions on textiles were abbreviated, using only short religious phrases, such as "victory from God," or "the kingdom of God," leaving out the name of the ruler and the year of his reign. Nevertheless, in one form or another, *tiraz* inscriptions continued to function as trademarks on textiles in these regions even into modern times.

Between the seventh century when Caliph Malik implemented the *tiraz* system and the mid-thirteenth century when the Mongolian conquests broke up the system, an international textile market formed within the Islamic world. The markets of Baghdad, especially, and other cities as well across the entire region sold a great variety of textiles. Although there were many regime changes, a number of the local styles from southern Spain, Egypt, Mesopotamia, Iran, India, and Central Asia persisted, and were still recognizable in any given market by the silk inscriptions on the borders of the fabrics. The very best pieces, with large inscriptions, would be sent to Mecca and displayed on the Kaaba. Some of these textiles would even find their way to the Byzantine markets and the church treasuries of Western Europe.

While the *tiraz* system promoted the production and trade of many different kinds of textiles, it had the greatest impact on the production of silk. Because the caliphs required that the borders and inscriptions on all textiles be made of silk, which had been relatively scarce outside China, its production increased and spread throughout the Islamic domains. Ultimately this growth included not only the long-standing weaving of silk using imported threads, but also sericulture (the raising of silk worms to harvest the cocoons), and filature (the separation and reeling of the cocoon fibers to make thread). Thus, the system led to an overall growth in the supply of textiles, in general, and silk, in particular, and thus made a significant contribution to the breakdown of the Byzantine silk monopoly in the western part of Eurasia.

SERICULTURE AND TRADE IN THE ISLAMIC DOMAIN

Although sericulture had spread from China to some of the more eastern parts of Central Asia soon after the silk roads became established during the Han dynasty, any silk industry west of the eastern parts of central Asia was confined to the weaving of silk with imported threads at least until the sixth century. It was only then that the Byzantine Empire started to build its own sericulture industry so that it could supply its own silk yarn for its many looms. However, as late as the seventh century, when the Arabs took over the eastern territories of Byzantium that lay south of Anatolia (more or less south of present-day Turkey), sericulture still was not a well-established industry in the eastern Mediterranean area. It was only after the Muslim armies took over the Central Asian oasis states in the eighth century, that they inherited a well-established sericulture industry, which had long been supplying the numerous royal silk-weaving workshops of Sasanid Iran. In the following centuries, mulberry trees (a good marker for sericulture since they supply the food for the silk worms) appeared in several new places, including the western parts of Central Asia such as Khwarizm in Uzbekistan, the Armenian region near the Caspian Sea, Mesopotamia, Tripoli in North Africa, and Granada in Spain. (There may have been other places, but they do not appear in the extant sources.)

Tending mulberry trees and raising silk worms requires much specialized knowledge regarding the technical details, as discussed in the Introduction. The most complicated part of the process is the unraveling and reeling of the filature which has to be done without doing any damage to the integrity of the fiber. As a result, even after the spread of mulberry trees and silk worms, silk producers in areas that were new to sericulture remained less competitive, and the Chinese and some Central Asians still continued to produce the best silk and still supplied the bulk of Eurasian production. In order to make the best silk fabric one has to have the longest and strongest filaments, and this means maintaining the integrity of the single filament that makes up the cocoon and unraveling it without damaging the fiber. One of the requirements in this process is to kill the larvae inside the cocoons before they become moths, since the moth will damage the fiber while gnawing its way out of the cocoon. This is now done either by boiling or baking the cocoons. The special techniques required in these processes and taboos against killing any creature, even a worm, as among Buddhists outside China, limited the mastery of these filature techniques to the Chinese and some Central Asians for a few centuries longer than the spread of the more basic techniques in sericulture.

Although many Chinese had become Buddhists by 500 CE, very few of them ever felt compelled to stop making silk in the traditional way. China was the home of silk, and Chinese had been making silk and killing larvae for many millennia before the arrival of Buddhism. No silk-maker in China, Buddhist or not, was going to stop making the best-quality silk yarns for fear of killing the larvae and thereby damaging his (or more accurately her) position in the next life. However, in China there were devout Buddhist monks who wrestled with this religious problem. Even though some went on pilgrimages to the Buddhist homeland in India, carrying large quantities of Chinese silk with them to help finance their trips and to use as gifts upon arrival, a few of them clearly were worried about the religious consequences of killing silk worms.

In the early seventh century, for example, when the Buddhist monk Xuanzang was on his way from India back to China, he stayed for a while in the oasis of Khotan in the Takla Makan Desert. This was long before there had been any Islamic influence in this region, and the people there were devout Buddhists. He noted that the local silk-makers did not kill the silk larvae. Instead they allowed the moths to gnaw their way out of the cocoons, and collected and used the broken cocoons to make silk yarn. Although Xuanzang never openly addressed the issue of killing silk larvae, it appears that he, personally, was concerned about the issue, and that this was the unstated reason that he refused to wear silk robes. He insisted on wearing cotton clothing, most of which was sent to him from India, even though a significant part of his own wealth was held in the form of silk textiles.

In 671, another Chinese pilgrim, Yijing, went to India to study Buddhist texts and monastic laws. He, too, was concerned about whether or not a devout Buddhist should wear silk. While in India he realized that Indian monks did wear a variety of silk called *kaushya*, which was made from the cocoons of wild species of silk worms. He thus reported to his colleagues at home that monks in China need not worry about wearing the silk robes that were given to them by donors. What Yijing did not realize was that the *kaushya* silk worn by monks in India was different from Chinese silk. Not only was the species of the worm different, but they were not fed mulberry leaves. They fed themselves off of local trees, since different species of silk worms eat leaves from different trees. What would have been most relevant to Yijing, had he known it, was that the Indians did not boil the cocoons in order to preserve their integrity, and thus did not kill the larvae. They, like the people in Khotan, made their silk from broken cocoons, left over after the moth had emerged. Broken cocoons do produce good silk floss and some yarns, but because the single filament of each cocoon is broken up into pieces, the silk made in this way is not suitable for weaving fine textiles, making tapestries, or embroidering.

In the Islamic domains there was a variety of silk that was called *khazz*, a word that was most likely a derivative of the Indian word *kaushya*. *Khazz* was a course silk, made from silk floss and broken cocoons, and it was acceptable material for making ordinary textiles. However, it could not be used to make the finely patterned silk tapestries and embroideries, including the *tiraz* inscriptions, which required silk yarn of a much higher quality. There was another word, *ibrism*, in the Islamic domains that meant long-fibered silk. The word *ibrism* was of Persian origin, and in books on silk production written in Arabic, the directions say that cocoons should be sun-dried before being unraveled. Baking the cocoons out in the hot sun would kill the larvae, just as boiling does, and it was thus a fitting modification of the Chinese method, especially since in many parts of the Islamic domain sunny and hot days were plentiful and water for boiling was scarce. This technique, which spread from Iran throughout the Islamic world, may well have been from a Persian-speaking area, either in Iran or adjacent parts of Central Asia, and in the latter case might even date back to the days of the Sasanid Empire.

After mastering the technique of making long filaments, silk workers in Muslim areas produced a greater quantity and a finer quality of silk textiles. In addition to textile types that already existed in the Eurasian market, such as brocade, tapestry, and embroidery, Muslim weavers invented new products. For example, the artistic quality of the silk *tiraz* borders on Egyptian linens was so high that a product called *qabati* became famous throughout the Muslim world. *Qabati* was made in the Coptic areas of Egypt and the workers were usually Coptic Christians. In addition, silk velvets and other textiles made with piles were probably an invention of the Muslim weavers. (A pile is a smooth, raised surface produced by an extra set of filling yarns that are added to the fabric in the form of raised loops, which are then cut and sheared.) Driving the filling yarns into base fabrics was an old technique used to make woolen carpets, and Arabs, Iranians, and Central Asians had a long history of making such carpets. In addition there were the half-silk textiles, with their silk warp shining on the surface (concealing the weft), which were aimed at a market of consumers who were either concerned about how much silk they wore for religious reasons or had less means.

The markets in Islamic countries also sold silk textiles imported from the Byzantine Empire and China. Byzantine brocade was well known, and it did not matter to Muslim consumers that Byzantium's purple silks were not available, since they did not care for the color purple. Chinese silks, which often had many patterns and figures, were popular, and so was the good-quality silk yarn that came from China. The overall increase in the supply of silk materials and textiles in the markets must have brought down the prices, and in addition, the availability of a variety of grades, qualities, and features helped to make silk textiles a common commodity in the Muslim lands. Although the caliphs and sultans never made any effort to limit certain kinds of textiles to political or religious elites within their domains, it was, nevertheless, true that they and their wives often did set fashion trends and thus have an impact on market trends. For instance, when Caliph Mutawakkil (847–861) came out in public wearing a robe made from the half silk *mulham*, people in the caliphate quickly followed his lead.

Silk textiles made in Islamic lands also made their way to both Byzantium and the Christianized parts of Western Europe. One may remember from the previous chapter that the Byzantine government guarded its regional silk monopoly with vigilance, and banned the commercial export of its finest silks. As a result, there was an unfilled demand for silk textiles in the Christianized areas of Western Europe, where they used silk textiles to venerate the relics of saints and to decorate their churches.

In the Byzantine capital of Constantinople, there was a group of Muslim traders known as Saracens, who settled there on a long-term basis in order to sell silks to Christian customers. There was also a caravanserai in the city that accommodated the Muslim traders who traveled back and forth, bringing silks and other goods from the eastern Mediterranean and Baghdad. The *Book of the Eparch*, a late ninth-century market code issued by Emperor Leo VI to the eparch (the mayor) of Constantinople, contains a whole chapter of detailed regulations pertaining to traders from the Muslim regions. In Byzantium, Muslim merchants could only sell silk and other textiles that they had brought in from eastern Mediterranean cities and Baghdad, which is to say that their inventory could not include local silks sold by Byzantine silk merchants and dyers.

When the merchants arrived in Constantinople, they were supposed to declare all the goods that had been entrusted to them for sale and to deposit all the goods that they had brought with them in a particular warehouse. They were to allow access to these goods by other caravanserai merchants and the Muslim merchants who had taken up long-term residence in the city. The latter were organized as a guild that specialized in importing manufactured goods from the eastern Mediterranean and Baghdad, and the mayor of Constantinople appointed a special official to supervise them. In addition, the travelers were supposed to stay in the caravanserais, and they were not supposed to remain in Byzantium for more than three months at a time. Those who violated these regulations faced stiff penalties. According to the *Book of the Eparch*, "All persons who do not conform to these rules shall be flogged, shaved, and have their property confiscated" (Chapter V, Variorum Reprint, 1970, p. 240).

In spite of these harsh rules, Muslim traders persisted in coming to Constantinople to sell their silks, which suggests that there was a good market for the silk textiles and yarns from the Muslim domains. Although the royal factories of Byzantium might well have been producing the most beautiful silk textiles, they were available only to the highest echelons of the empire's secular and religious elites. People of lower status, such as eunuchs in the court, were thus happy to purchase the half-silk *mulham* textiles imported by the Muslims. Although the silk textiles from Muslim regions might be less prestigious in Constantinople, they found a large number of consumers there, in the very heart of one of the world's most renowned centers of silk culture.

Many pieces of silk textiles made within the Islamic domains ended up in the churches of Western Europe, where they have been found and identified by modern historians. One example is a famous *Zandani* silk, a patterned silk textile woven between the seventh and at least the tenth century in Zandan, a Central Asian town near Bukhara, as discussed in the previous chapter. Although the *Zandani* silks appear to have been made from Chinese yarns and dyes, and definitely have a Chinese color scheme, the designs and the weaving technique are those of Sasanid Iran. Although many of the surviving samples were produced after Muslim rule was established in the area around Bukhara, the silks still managed to make their way to various Christian shrines in Western Europe, including the Cathedral of Toul in France, the shrine of St. Lambert at Liege in Belgium, and the tomb of St. Landrade at Bilsen in Austria.

At this point in time the Christians who lived in the more western parts of Europe were not particular about the origin of any silk textile that they might buy. In part, this was because there was no local silk industry in their region, and thus all silks that could be found there were imported. They even imported many silk textiles with *tiraz* borders that had been decorated with Islamic religious messages and used them to make the shrouds of Christian saints and the covers of Christian altars. Most likely their use of these silks was due to the increasing amount and variety of silk textiles available in Muslim regions, and thus the increasing use of *tiraz* borders. In any case, it does not seem to have mattered, since the inscriptions were indecipherable to anyone who could not read Arabic, and the caligraphy on the borders was very decorative, and may well have been mistaken for some sort of abstract design.

The increasing supplies of silk products arriving in the western part of Europe from the Muslim regions helped the Christians in Western Europe to cope with the Byzantine silk monopoly. They could purchase ready-made patterned silk textiles from the Islamic areas, or they could purchase plain silk textiles and embroider their own patterns on the material. In the markets there were many plain materials, some of them coming from as far away as China, via the Muslim merchants. Among the numerous ready-made patterned silks found in the Western European churches, there are very few, if any, that are typically Chinese, but it is quite likely that the bulk of the supply of plain silks and yarns did come from China. During the Tang dynasty (618–906 CE) Chinese farmers still paid their taxes in rolls of plain silk, woven in their own households, and the Tang government continued to use many thousands of these rolls to supply the nomads to their north and west and traders coming from all directions.

Although the Western Europeans did not have the sort of silk looms that Byzantium had that could do the compound weaving necessary for making complicated patterns, they did have needles and imported silk thread with which they could embroider designs on the plain silk. Even the popes in Rome adopted the strategy of embroidering plain silk in order to counter Byzantine silk policies of monopoly and manipulation. During Byzantium's iconoclast period (726–843), the availability of plain silk and silk yarn and thread was especially useful in the western part of Europe. During these years Christian authorities in the eastern Mediterranean prohibited both the worship of saints and the making of any sort of image of Jesus or the saints, believing that it was a form of idolatry. In the west the Roman papacy disagreed and ignored this policy, and continued its patronage of western churches by giving images as gifts.

In particular, the popes set up workshops in Rome where images of the saints were embroidered on plain silks using golden threads. Giving embroidered silks with images of their patron saints to churches endeared the papacy to these Christians even more than giving them patterned Byzantine silk textiles would have. Embroidery subsequently became a popular pastime of European women with means, many of whom expressed their religious devotion by embroidering silks for the church. The irony of the situation is obvious. Very few people in Western Europe were aware of the source of the silk products that made their churches look heavenly and their clergy majestic. Little did they know that during these centuries before the crusades, the prestige of the papacy and the splendor of the churches west of Byzantium depended at least in part upon Muslim trading networks and Muslim and Chinese made silks.

THE SPREAD OF PAPER-MAKING AND BOOKS

In the seventh-century dispute over inscriptions between Caliph Malik and Emperor Justinian II, the Byzantine Empire was the loser. Not only did the Muslim caliphate begin to mint its own coins and create the *tiraz* system, it also shipped very little Egyptian papyri to the Byzantines. The peoples in the Muslim domains had learned how to make paper, and thus the Egyptians were no longer interested in producing papyri. At the time the Byzantines were unfamiliar with paper, and even if they had been willing to use it as a substitute, they would have had difficulty buying it from Egypt given the various disputes between the two powers. As a result palace and church libraries in Byzantium began to shrink.

Paper, which was invented in China around the first century CE, first appeared in the Muslim lands around the mid-eighth century, after the Abbasid dynasty replaced the Umayyads, and moved the capital from Damascus to Baghdad, which was closer to the center of the newly expanded empire. Within just a few decades paper spread throughout the Muslim areas, providing the best medium for developing literature, art, science, technology, and last, but certainly not least, bureaucracy. Previously most writing in this part of Eurasia was done on parchment. Although today some superior types of paper are referred to as parchment, during these centuries the word referred only to writing surfaces that were made from the skins of sheep and goats. Compared to other writing materials such as papyri and parchment, paper was cheap, and thus its introduction enabled many more people in Muslim areas to write and copy books. Within a short time, the Muslim world could boast of many institutes of learned scholars and large libraries. In short, due to paper, the Muslims became much more effective merchants and communicators.

Apparently, the transition in the Abbasid lands from parchment to paper was not an altogether smooth one. Still in the ninth century writers were arguing about whether parchment or paper was the better choice. Among those engaged in the controversy was Amr ibn Bahr al-Jahiz (d. 868), one of the most significant and admired authors of the century. The descendant of East African slaves, he had an unusual perspective on Abbasid society, and his writings are often both critical and satirical. His attack on parchment apparently was provoked by a suggestion from a colleague that he should not use paper when writing his books. He was told that he should use parchment because then it would be easier to scratch out mistakes and make corrections, and the books would stand up better to wear and tear. Furthermore, said his colleague, books written on parchment were more revered and perceived to be more serious, and thus they had a better market value than anything, no matter how significant, that was written on paper. The reply of al-Jahiz leaves no doubt about his own preferences.

> Explain why you have pressed on me the advantages of using parchment and urged me to write on hide, when you know very well that parchment

is heavy and cumbersome, is useless if it gets damp, and swells in wet weather—so much so that were its sole disadvantage to make its users hate rainy days, and its owners regard a shower as a nightmare, this alone would be reason enough for giving up the stuff. You know well that on rainy days copyists do not write a single line or cut a single skin. Parchment has only to get moist, let alone left out in the rain or dipped in water, for it to bulge and stretch; and then it does not return to its original state, but dries noticeably shrunk and badly wrinkled. What is more, it smells worse, is more expensive, and lends itself more readily to fraud.... You are obliged to leave it to age in order to get rid of the smell and for the hair to fall out; it is fuller of lumps and flaws, more is wasted in scraps and clippings, it turns yellow sooner, and the writing very quickly disappears altogether. If a scholar wished to take with him enough parchment for his journey, a camel-load would not suffice, whereas the equivalent in [a variety of paper] could be carried with his provisions.

You did me a grave disservice when you made me take to using parchment instead of paper, and were the cause of my misfortune when you made me exchange light writing books for volumes too heavy to hold, that crush people's chests, bow their backs and make them blind. (Charles Pellat, ed. and trans. from the French, *Al-Jahiz, 'Amr ibn Bahr. The Life and Works of Al-Jahiz*. University of California Press, 1969, pp. 211–212)

It has long been accepted by scholars that Chinese prisoners, taken by the Abbasids at the battle of Talas in 751, were responsible for the spread of paper-making technology throughout the Islamic world. Talas, a city located on the Talas River just after it crosses the border between present-day Kyrgyzstan and Kazakhstan, was the site of this famous and momentous military confrontation between the Arab Abbasid caliphate and Tang dynasty China. On the banks of the river, the Arabs defeated the Chinese army and took twenty-thousand Chinese prisoners, including paper-making artisans. For many decades people have believed that these Chinese prisoners were the individuals responsible for the spread of paper production from China to the Muslim domains. However, in a new study published in 2001, Jonathan Bloom, a historian of technology in the Muslim world, has suggested that this is an oversimplification of what actually happened. He agrees that there must be some merit in this traditional view, since it was around the year 751, when the Abbasids took power and Baghdad was about to become one of greatest cities in Eurasia, that paper and paper-making first appear within the Muslim empire.

His problem with the old view, however, has to do with the quality of the sources upon which it is based. Indeed, the main source for the traditional version comes from an Arabic book that was written some three centuries after the battle was fought. Bloom, however, has found an earlier

Chinese source that suggests that the Arab estimates of the number of prisoners taken at Talas were exaggerated. Also, he points out that paper-making technology, like sericulture, had already spread from China to Central Asia long before 751, and was already well established there prior to the famous battle between the Abbasids and Tang China. Since by the time of that battle the Arab conquerors already had power over many Central Asian peoples, Bloom suggests that the Arabs would have had no need to resort to the use of Chinese prisoners of war in order to disseminate the techniques of paper-making throughout the Muslim domains.

Bloom may well be right that the technology transfer was not just the result of a single military victory. It is quite likely that the spread of paper-making throughout the Muslim areas was related both to the Muslim conquest of parts of Central Asia and to the strong economic demand for the product, which fueled many ongoing efforts to produce it. In a way, the spread of paper-making was quite similar to the spread of sericulture, in that one cannot give sole credit for the transfer of a whole set of techniques to the Nestorian monks, who supposedly stole some silk worm eggs and smuggled them from China all the way to Byzantium. There were, nevertheless, a large number of Chinese prisoners taken at Talas, and some of them did migrate to various parts of the caliphate, and some may well have helped promote paper-making.

Du Huan, for example, was one of the prisoners taken at Talas. He belonged to a renowned Tang literati family, and after spending at least twelve years in several different Muslim lands, he returned to Tang China and wrote about his experiences in these foreign lands. Unfortunately, his book, *Jingxing Ji*, has been lost. Only a small fraction of it remains, as quotations in an important historical study written by his uncle Du You. These fragments reveal that Du Huan personally knew Chinese artisans working in the Abbasid Empire. Although these artisans were weavers, painters, and gold and silver smiths, there may have been paper-makers as well, either unknown to Du Huan or described in the parts of his book that his uncle did not quote.

It seems that many different people helped spread paper-making technology throughout the caliphate. Buddhist establishments in China, for example, had long been making paper and printing on paper. Printing was actually invented in the early seventh century in a Chinese monastery. Given the level of interaction among members of various Buddhist establishments, it is quite likely that paper-making and printing were well known in the many Central Asian monasteries. It is also known that these monasteries continued to flourish for quite a long time after the Muslim armies occupied parts of Central Asia. Before the battle of Talas, in the first half of the eighth century, for example, the Korean pilgrim Hui Chao passed through Tukharistan (in present-day Afghanistan) on his way to India. He noticed that even though the Arabs had controlled this region for some time, people there were still devout Buddhists, and its many monasteries were still filled with monks. Thus, it is quite possible that the Buddhist monasteries in Central Asia contributed to the spread of paper-making in the Muslim world.

Bloom also found relevant material in the world historical studies of the renowned fourteenth-century North African scholar Ibn Khaldun that suggests a strong connection between Buddhist establishments in Afghanistan and the spread of paper-making in the Abbasid Empire. According to Ibn Khaldun, in the latter half of the eighth century, several members of the Barmakid family served in the important position of wazir in Baghdad. They were the descendants of an influential family based in Balkh, the medieval and modern name for the ancient city of Bactra in Afghanistan. One of their ancestors had been the chief priest of a large Buddhist temple in that vicinity.

This Buddhist family appears to have been among the earliest Central Asian converts to Islam, and it soon gained influence in Baghdad due to its experience in administration. Bloom suggests that during their fifty years of service (752–803) the Afghani Barmakids promoted paper-making throughout the caliphate, and had all documents and diplomas written on paper instead of either papyri or parchment. Thus, his account suggests that the transfer of paper-making technology may very well have been a part of the much larger story of the absorption of Central Asian material culture by the Abbasid caliphate.

The transfer of paper-making technology was also propelled by the demand for the product and thus the desire to learn the technology. The Muslim world in the eighth century was a vigorously growing society and one eager to absorb new knowledge from other cultures. Furthermore, the expanding bureaucracy in Baghdad desperately needed better writing material for its documents. Not only was paper cheaper, it also had other advantages. An important one was that paper absorbs ink more readily than parchment or papyri, making it more difficult for someone to subsequently alter the text for dubious purposes. Thus, there were many opportunities for talented and skilled converts to Islam among the conquered peoples, and they made substantial contributions in many different fields. In contrast, the Byzantine Empire, with its sophisticated silk-weaving technology and its artistry, apparently was not interested in the new paper-making technology, and in time, it would be Italy, in the fourteenth century, that became the first European locale known for its manufacture of paper.

SCHOLARLY PURSUITS

Paper-making happens to be a technology that not only produces a useful product in great demand, it also provides a commodity that facilitates the production of other products, both material and cultural. It happened to be the best means of recording knowledge and communicating information at that time. And because people were writing more, paper also indirectly aided thinking and promoted discussion, especially within the scholarly world. Without it, many of the remarkable achievements in science, technology, art, and literature in the Muslim world during the time of the Abbasid caliphate would have been unimaginable.

Caliph al-Mamun (813–833) established in Baghdad a scholarly institute called the House of Wisdom. Many scholars from all parts of the empire came there to study and translate into Arabic scientific works written in Greek, Sanskrit, and Persian. Given that the translations were written on paper, one can say that the availability of paper was an important factor in this effort. A community of scholars studying such diverse traditions led to the creation of numerous new questions, and the work they did on these problems led to advances in many fields. Thus, the ninth century saw a peak in scientific scholarship within the Muslim lands.

They were particularly strong in mathematics, astronomy, and geography, and it was in the ninth century that the Arabs began to use the Indian numerals, the numerals that in the West are called Arabic. The Islamic practices of always praying facing the direction of Mecca and making pilgrimages to Mecca created interest in geographical research on how best to determine the cardinal points of the compass and how to improve navigation across the seas. Observing the stars and calculating the angles and distances between the stars and the horizon were essential to navigating across the seas that were otherwise without landmarks.

One of the most famous among those who studied mathematics, geography, and astronomy was Muhammad ibn Musa al-Khwarizmi (fl. ca. 825). He joined the caliph's House of Wisdom in Baghdad in the early ninth century, and his translation of a Sanskrit manual on mathematics introduced the Indian decimal system to the Muslim world. Because this system was the first to have a functional zero, it was by far the most useful for making complicated calculations. Thus, this translation of the Indian manual, along with his own works, spread throughout the Muslim scholarly community. His importance with regard to the development of modern mathematics is indicated by the fact that the word *algorithm* is derived from his name. The name also reminds us of the many learned men of Central Asia who played a part in this new scholarly world. The name al-Khwarizmi indicates that his home was in Khwarizm in present-day Uzbekistan. These numerals spread throughout the Muslim world along with paper, and this combination not only facilitated scholarship, it also helped traders by making accounting and bookkeeping much more efficient.

Arabs had been experienced travelers and sailors even before the advent of Islam, but by this period they could chart their routes and record their observations on paper. Map drawing became much easier, and so was traveling. Many Muslim travelers were scholars who recorded their experiences and observations on paper and compiled them into books, which in turn increased geographical knowledge within the Muslim world. They often traveled throughout the Muslim domains, visiting places both within and without the jurisdiction of the Abbasid caliphate. Islamic religious establishments such as mosques and saint's tombs provided hostels for them, regardless of the local ruler's relationship to Baghdad. Nor did it matter to which variety of Islam the traveler belonged. All sojourners were welcome. Meanwhile, a group of outstanding geographers tried to describe the entire known world using a variety of classical sources and information from contemporary travelers. Among their sources were the works of the Greek scholar Ptolemy and various Arabic traditions, such as those of the Nabataeans who were based in the northern part of the Arabian Peninsula. Long before the advent of Islam, they had traveled and traded over long distances.

The Iranian scholar Ibn Khordadhbeh (ca. 820–912) is a good example. His geography book, *Kitab Al-Masalik Wa'l-Mamalik*, was about roads and peoples. It starts with a general description of the known world, and how Muslims in various parts of this world could find the right direction to Mecca. The narrative follows the road system of the Abbasid caliphate, and the trade routes, overland and overseas, which extended outside the Islamic domain. He described the mountains, rivers, and local landmarks that one could see along the way, as well as the special products, social customs, and religious practices of the peoples who lived along these roads. Other topics include the Arab ships that sailed to India and China and the goods that could be purchased in Chinese ports, such as silk, swords, saddles, sable furs, and porcelain. Also available in these ports were aromatic materials from the north such as musk, as well as Southeast Asian aromatics, such as camphor and various other resins. The list of goods in the Indian ports included many kinds of tropical spices and fragrances, plus jute, cotton, pearls, diamonds, and many other precious stones. In addition to traditional commodities traded on the Indian Ocean, Muslim traders also had direct links to the far north, the source of sable and musk, and to the tropical regions that lay south of them. The inventory of Arab traders during the Abassid caliphate was obviously much richer and much more extensive than that of the first-century CE Roman Empire traders described in the *Periplus Maris Erythae*.

Muslim routes were also linked to the trade routes of peoples of other faiths. Slavic traders from Rus (in the vicinity of Moscow) carried northern products such as black fox furs and weapons to the Black Sea and the Caspian Sea, whence camel caravans carried the goods to Baghdad. Slavic slaves, previously captured by the Muslim armies, interpreted for the Rus traders once they were within the caliphate. The most renowned traders in this type of trade were the Radhaniyyah, or Ladino-Jewish traders, who were superb linguists. They spoke Arabic, Persian, Andalusian, and Frankish languages, among others, and could be found on virtually all the trade routes of Eurasia.

Ibn Khordadhbeh created the model that later geography books would follow within the Muslim world. No doubt, many times over, his words were copied on paper by hand and bound into books. His study of geography served as a government training manual for officials of the empire, as an important source for travelers, and a reference for scholars as well. By this time, the Muslim world was indeed a society of books. It has been estimated that approximately 600,000 of these hand-written books still survive, but that is only a fraction of the number that then circulated (Bloom, 93). Scholars had many books to study, and traders had numerous reference books. Caliphs and sultans, proud sponsors of learning, established research institutes and built libraries. With the emergence of the profession of calligrapher and book-copier, calligraphy reached an unrivaled level of excellence in both Arabic and Persian, the two official languages of the Muslim domain from Abbasid times.

Calligraphers made their name by copying the *Koran*, and rulers competed with each other to sponsor such projects. The technology of paper-making had been improved such that the paper was smoother and the size of the pages was larger. Although some preferred paper from China, the paper from the Baghdad factory was also of especially good quality. Under the lavish patronage of rulers, calligraphers copied the words of the *Koran* on large pages, illuminated with gold speckles and borders. Though other sorts of books were not so lavish, the improvement in paper-making, bookbinding, and calligraphy in general helped to produce more and more books. Many books were written on a wide variety of a secular topics, including science and technology as well as art and literature, and there were those written simply for entertainment. The vast travels of Muslim traders and pilgrims provided the material for many anecdotes, the sources for wonderful stories, from near and far.

The *Arabian Nights*, also known as the *One Thousand and One Nights*, was a collection of such stories popular among Muslim readers. It was copied many times and circulated for many years. The descriptions of Baghdad in these stories make it clear that in the eighth and ninth centuries the city was a world trading center parallel in importance to the Tang dynasty capital of Chang'an.

There were two significant differences in the books made in the Muslim world and those made in China. Beginning in the eighth century Chinese books were printed using carved wooden blocks. Although it took longer to carve the characters onto a wooden block than to write them on paper, printers could use each block to make a large number of copies, so it was a much more efficient way to make large quantities of the same book. Had this technology made its way to the Muslim realm, there would have been even more books there, but for reasons that are unclear, it did not.

The second difference was in the materials used to make paper pulp. In the Muslim world, the most common material in paper pulp was rags from clothing, that is, recycled plant fibers, since most clothing there was made from plant materials such as cotton or flax (in the case of linen). In China, from the beginning of paper-making around the first century CE, people used many different kinds of plant material to make pulp. Some of the more common items were tree bark, bamboo, fibers from ramie, and sometimes recycled fibers from ramie nets and rags were mixed in.

Although silk, an animal product, was the most common textile in China, its rags were rarely used in paper-making, and then only in small quantities, since they did not make good pulp. Chinese did write directly on pieces of plain silk, as well as on thin slips of wood or bamboo, but they rarely used recycled cloth, or rags in paper pulp. The best as well as the most popular paper was made using the bark of the paper mulberry tree and some other varieties of mulberry. However, when paper-making spread to Central Asia, and thereafter to the Abbasid Empire, many of the sources of paper pulp used by the Chinese were not available.

Thus, throughout the history of paper-making in the Muslim world, rags that came from clothing made of plant fibers and sometimes the raw plant fibers, themselves, were the main source of paper pulp. Although rags were cheap, the supply was limited, and thus even though paper was cheaper than parchment, it was still expensive. In those lands where wool was the main fabric used to make clothing and sheep raising was the main economic pursuit, such as in Sicily, the Maghrib (the western part of North Africa), and some parts of Spain, paper was less competitive than parchment. In these areas plant-fiber rags and plant fibers generally were scarce. Sheep skins were relatively plentiful and local workers were adept at producing parchment. Thus, paper-making was not established in the Maghrib until the eleventh century, and even then parchment remained the most common writing material for several more centuries. The technology of making rag paper eventually spread to Italy, and by the fourteenth century quality paper was being produced there. Thereafter, paper-making in the Muslim world declined, apparently due to the higher cost and the relatively limited availability of linen rags.

One should point out, however, that even in the midst of this impressive development of paper-making all across Eurasia, China remained the world's largest paper-maker and book-printer for a few more centuries, at least until the eighteenth century, when Western Europe moved into the lead. Despite the impressive development of silk and paper-making in the Muslim areas, China remained the single largest producer of both silk and paper until modern times. Muslim traders thus continued to enthusiastically include China in their commercial networks. Regardless of the costs and the dangers, they continued to go to China seeking silk and paper, and they continued to carry these goods not only to their own homelands, but even to the western end of the Eurasian landmass. Yet there was even more to come from China. Soon Chinese teas and porcelain would start to make their way along the Eurasian trade routes. And the Chinese would introduce the compass to the maritime routes between China and India. In the next chapter, these maritime routes will take center stage in this story of commerce, communication, and cultural change.

FOR FURTHER READING

Islamic regulations on trade and silk textiles can be found in Bernard Lewis, *Islam, from the Prophet Muhammad to the Capture of Constantinople*, Volume II, Religion and Society. Oxford: Oxford University Press, 1987.

There are several catalogues of *tiraz* textiles preserved in various museums worldwide. *Islamic Textiles* by Robert Bertram Serjeant, Beirut: Librairie du Liban, 1972 is the most comprehensive collection of literary sources on textile production and trade in the Muslim world.

Bloom, Jonathan M. *Paper before Print, the History and Impact of Paper in the Islamic World.* New Haven and London: Yale University Press, 2001.

TIMELINE

Origins of Sri Lanka—Southeast Asia-China Maritime Route

Fourth Century	After nomads invade northern China, 60 to 70 percent of northern elites flee south of the Yangzi River, creating a market for "Persian" goods in the south. (Not all "Persian" goods were from Iran.)
	Southeast Asian sailors begin to supply "Persian" goods to southern China by sea.
By Early Fifth Century	Hostilities occur along the overland silk roads coming into China. "Persian" goods become scarce.
	Persian Gulf traders establish themselves in Sri Lanka, where Southeast Asian sailors can purchase "Persian" goods to supply the market in southern China.
	Southeast Asians introduce their own Southeast Asian goods to the southern Chinese market. Many of the earliest ones can be construed as substitutes for "Persian" goods such as Arabian frankincense and myrrh.
	Buddhism spreads from India to some parts of Southeast Asia via this maritime route.
ca. 411 CE	Buddhist monk Faxian goes home to China by a maritime route. He boards a ship in Sri Lanka that takes him to Southeast Asia. There he boards a ship destined for China. He writes an account of his pilgrimage, including this voyage home.

Maritime Trade During the Umayyad and Abbasid Caliphates

Seventh to Ninth Centuries	Arabs still sailed to ports in northeastern India, such as those in the Konkan area and in Gujarat. (During the Kushan Empire these had been silk ports that provided luxury goods such as spices and gems.) In the seventh century they mainly export Indian products such as large quantities of indigo and cotton textiles.
	Silk remained the most important export from China. Muslim Arabs and Iranians sailed to China to purchase it.
	In the *Arabian Nights*, the hero Sindbad the Sailor sails to China and back, as did many real-life sailors, departing from the Persian Gulf and the Red Sea.
	Sulayman's *Records of China and India* describes the maritime trade between the Muslim heartland and China.
	China-bound ships depart from Persian Gulf port Siraf and stop at Quilon (on India's southwestern coast) on their way.
	Archaeological finds at Siraf have revealed thousands of pieces of Chinese porcelain, and early Islamic coins from Muslim Spain, Russia, and Syria.
671–695	During Yijing's pilgrimage he takes an Iranian ship from China to Srivijaya (on Sumatra), which has already become a center of Buddhist studies. He studies Sanskrit there for six months before going on to India. On his way home he also stays in Srivijaya in order to transcribe Buddhist texts.

Muslim Maritime Trade During the Fatimid
Caliphate and the Ayyubid Dynasty

Tenth Century	Population and economic growth shift from the Persian Gulf area to Egypt.
	Chinese ships begin sailing to India.
967–1171	The Fatimid caliphate. The Fatimids, Shiites from the Maghrib, establish the Fatimid caliphate in defiance of Baghdad and establish Cairo as their capital.
	Thereafter, the Fatimids establish the Karim system of convoyed merchant ships to facilitate their maritime trade with Indian ports.
	Traders use commenda-style partnerships to acquire investment funds. Jewish traders work closely with these Muslim organizations.
Eleventh Century	Arab ships rarely go to China. Chinese ships deliver Chinese goods to Quilon, on India's southwestern coast, and Arab ships based in Red Sea ports acquire them at Quilon.
Twelfth Century	Saladin (a Kurdish general from Iran) prevents the Western European Christian crusaders from gaining access to the Red Sea and takes over the Fatimid dynasty.
1169–1250	Saladin (d. 1193) establishes the Ayyubid dynasty in 1160. It lasts until 1250.
1182	Saladin's deputy oversees the construction of the *Funduk al-Karim* in Cairo. It continues to flourish under the Mamluks who ruled until 1517.

Mediterranean Trade, Tenth to Thirteenth Centuries

Tenth to Late Eleventh Century	Partnerships between Muslim and Jewish merchants in the Mediterranean are quite similar to those in the Arabian Sea, and extend all the way to Muslim Spain.
	Trading networks of Christians on the Mediterranean's northern shore, especially those of Byzantium, Italy, and the Franks, are linked to Muslim-Jewish networks on the southern shore.
	Silk yarns and textiles are by far the largest part of this trade in terms of the percentage of value of the cargo. Silks include Zaytuni silk from China, but most of the silk traded in the Mediterranean comes from Muslim Spain. Also some parts of the Maghrib produce silk.
	Venice emerges as the preeminent port on the Mediteranean's northern shore.
Late Eleventh to Thirteenth Century	Western Christian crusades against Byzantium and the eastern shores of the Mediterranean controlled by Muslim Turks.
Late Thirteenth Century	Ships sailing on the Mediterranean use compasses.
	Close cooperation between Muslim and Jewish traders comes to an end. Jewish traders migrate to Europe.

The Indian Subcontinent as the Center of Southern Ocean Trade and the Rise of the Colas

First to Third Centuries	Yuezhi-Kushan and Roman Empire trade routes meet in ports on India's northwestern coast.
Fourth to Sixth Centuries	Iranians establish a trading station in Sri Lanka that provides "Persian" goods to Southeast Asian sailors. Southeast Asian sailors deliver these goods to southern China. Indian traders (mostly Hindus) use this route to purchase silks in China.

Seventh to Eighth Centuries	Iranian and Arab ships use the Indian port of Quilon (on the southwest coast) and join routes that stop in Southeast Asia before going to China, mainly to the port at Canton.
844–1279	The Hindu Cola Kingdom is established, on India's (southeastern) Coromandel coast and becomes a maritime power. Cola Hindus have a well-established presence in Quanzhou, China, where they build Hindu temples. At home they hosted both Hindu and Buddhist traders and built a Buddhist monastery to accommodate the latter.
Tenth Century	Chinese ships begin sailing the routes between China and India.
Eleventh to Thirteenth Centuries	Once Chinese ships become the most numerous on the routes between China and India, Iranian and Arab ships rarely go to China. They meet Chinese ships at Quilon, in India, in order to acquire Chinese goods.

Chinese Seafaring from the Tenth to Thirteenth Centuries

Tenth Century	Chinese ships begin sailing to Southeast Asia and India after the fall of the Tang dynasty in 906. The most important Chinese port is Quanzhou in present-day Fujian Province.
	China's imports enjoy a large market, and many are no longer luxuries destined for a small market.
	Tea and porcelain join silk as important Chinese exports.
	The overland routes out of China become inadequate, considering the volume of international trade and also because of new products that are too bulky or too heavy for long-distance trips by camel or horse.

Eleventh Century	According to the earliest written source, the compass is used on Chinese ships, but only during bad weather.
	Chinese ships outnumber all others on the route between India and China. They use the port of Quilon in India. Arab and Iranian ships rarely go to China, and buy Chinese goods at Quilon.
Thirteenth Century	According to the earliest written source, the compass has become the principal means of navigation on Chinese ships. Also by the thirteenth century the compass had spread from China to the Mediterranean.

 CHAPTER SIX

OCEANS AND SEAS, 900–1300

GETTING STARTED ON CHAPTER SIX: What were the advantages and disadvantages of transporting silk products and other goods by ship rather than by overland routes? In what ways was shipping related to the quantity and type of goods being traded? What were the circumstances surrounding various changes in the routes taken and the ports used? What geographic region was always involved in the maritime routes over which silk was transported? How did governments facilitate overseas trade and make their ports more attractive? What skills and technologies contributed to the success of long-distance sailors?

CHAPTER OUTLINE

The Chinese referred to all the seas and oceans south of China by a single term, the Southern Ocean. By this they meant all the waters from the northern end of the Red Sea to the easternmost islands of present-day Indonesia, a distance along the equator of roughly 3,500 miles. One part of this ocean, the sea routes between Egypt and India had been an important part of the silk roads as early as the first century CE, during the time of the Roman and Kushan empires. However, after the emergence and expansion of the Iran's Sassanid Empire in the third century, the Kushan Empire had fallen and Roman Empire sailors had disappeared from the sea routes between Egypt and India.

By the fifth century yet another maritime trade route had emerged on the Southern Ocean, a route used not only by international traders but also by Chinese Buddhist pilgrims going to and from India. This was an all-sea route that linked the ports of southeastern China and Sri Lanka, an island country less than fifty miles off the southeastern coast of India. It differed from the sea route that had flourished during the time of the Roman and Kushan empires in at least two ways. One difference was the route's location east of the Indian subcontinent rather than west of it. A second was that when the Kushans had controlled the silk roads out of China the silk left northern China by overland routes and only took to the sea once it had arrived in ports on India's northeastern coast. However, this fifth-century route was an all-sea route, and silk and other Chinese products were leaving China by sea from its southeastern coast.

The Southeast Asian sailors who developed this route were intrepid monsoon sailors who had long been familiar with China's southern ports and had already explored much of the Indian Ocean as well. There was, however, one disadvantage on this route. Because they used winds blowing off the continent to leave either Sri Lanka or China and sail to a port in Southeast Asia, and used winds blowing toward the continent to go from Southeast Asia to either Sri Lanka or China, it required a layover in Southeast Asia no matter which way one was sailing.

By the seventh century Iranian and Arabian ships would also be using this route to go to and from China. And by the tenth century, Chinese ships began using it to sail west to ports on India's southwest coast, where Muslim ships from the Fatimid caliphate in Egypt could also be found. Thus, by the latter part of the tenth century the entire Southern Ocean was covered by interlocking maritime trading networks. Furthermore, since in Egypt there was also a short overland portage from the Red Sea to the Nile River, these Southern Ocean routes were also closely linked to the maritime routes of the Mediterranean Sea.

From the fifth century on, the amount of shipping on these Southern Ocean routes was steadily increasing. By the twelfth century the amount of silk and other Chinese exports leaving southeastern China by ship had increased to the point that the original overland silk routes out of northern China had lost much of their significance. By far, the majority of China's exports were leaving China by ship from ports on its southeastern coast. The increase in shipping led to another development of great import. The types of goods moving on these maritime routes were becoming more diverse, and by the twelfth century, one could no longer refer to this commerce as simply a luxury trade. Although the ships on the Southern Ocean still carried the rare and expensive goods purchased only by those with extraordinary means, much of their cargo space was taken up by large quantities of less-expensive goods that ultimately were meant for a much wider audience.

THE ORIGINS OF THE ROUTE BETWEEN CHINA AND SRI LANKA

In 1967 O. W. Wolters, a specialist on the early history of Southeast Asia, published a book entitled *Early Indonesian Commerce: The Origins of Srivijaya*. This study illuminates the role played by Southeast Asia sailors in the development of the maritime route that carried international traders and pilgrims between China and Sri Lanka, at least by the early fifth century. One of the reasons that his study is so interesting is that it attributes the development of this route more to a Chinese demand for foreign products than to the rest of Eurasia's desire for Chinese silks.

Wolters points out that during the centuries of turmoil that afflicted China after the fall of the Han dynasty, it was in the fourth century, after northern China had been overrun by invaders, that approximately 60 to 70 percent of its elite families fled south of the Yangzi River. This refugee population had long been accustomed to purchasing what they called "Persian" goods, by which they meant all those goods that Iranian or Sogdian merchants carried to China by way of the overland routes, regardless of where the goods had actually been produced. Although these foreign goods were still able to make their way to northern China via overland routes during the fourth century, and thus could be carried south to this displaced Chinese market, the Southeast Asian sailors nevertheless saw an opportunity. They could purchase many of these goods in the ports of India and Sri Lanka and supply this southern Chinese market by sea. By the fifth century, hostilities along the overland silk roads that came into northern

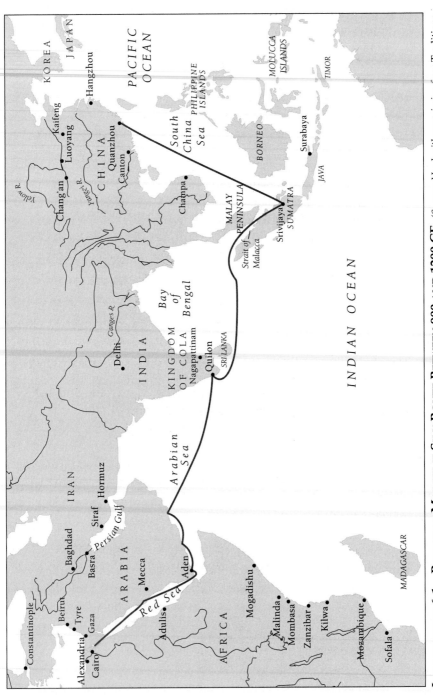

ILLUSTRATION 6-1 PRINCIPAL MARITIME SILK ROUTE BETWEEN 900 AND 1200 CE (*Source: Used with permission from Traditions and Encounters (2nd ed.), by Jerry H. Bentley and Herbert F. Ziegler. Copyright 2003 by McGraw-Hill.*)

China had made these "Persian goods" scarce throughout China, and Persian Gulf traders had established themselves in Sri Lanka, which made these trade goods even easier to acquire. Thus, the Southeast Asians could sell even more of these "Persian goods" in the ports on China's southeastern coast.

They also took advantage of the opportunity to introduce a number of their own products to the international market, almost all of which came from islands that are now part of Indonesia. Many of the earliest Southeast Asian specialties sold to this refugee market could be construed as substitutes for some of the "Persian goods." In particular, they were able to substitute Sumatran pine resins for frankincense and benzoin for myrrh. They also introduced a number of other products, including gharuwood, sandalwood (a specialty of Timor), and Sumatran camphor.

Fortunately for historians, one of the early passengers on this route, the Chinese monk Faxian, wrote an account of his pilgrimage to India, including his travels by sea. Leaving China, he made the outward leg of his pilgrimage to India (399–414) via the land route that crossed the suspended rope bridge, but he returned home to China by sea. After a long stay in the Buddhist homeland along the Ganges River in northeastern India, he started making his way back to China by going south to the island country of Sri Lanka. By this time Sri Lanka had become an important pilgrimage site due to its possession of a most sacred relic, the tooth of the Buddha. It was also in Sri Lanka that Faxian would be able to find a ship that would carry him from there to a port city in Southeast Asia, the first leg of his journey home by sea. Thus, he boarded a large ship carrying 200 passengers, almost all traders who were going east to China. Most of these traders were Hindus, but there were also some Buddhists among them.

At this point in time no one was sailing the seas with a compass and in only two places, on the Arabian Sea and in Southeast Asian waters, were there monsoon sailors. These were the only sailors who ventured far from shore, navigating by the stars, the winds, and the waves by night, and by day the cloud formations, the swell and wave patterns and the color of the water, and bird and fish behavior. Because monsoon sailors did not cling to the coasts but rode the winds across the open seas, traveling on their ships considerably reduced the usual sailing times between ports. Violent storms, however, could blow these ships far off course.

It took ninety days for Faxian's ship to reach Yepoti, in what is today Indonesia. Historians are not sure exactly where this port was, but some have suggested that, most likely, it was on the western coast of the island of Borneo. Ninety days was not the ordinary sailing time. Faxian's ship had encountered a terrible storm that inflicted much damage to the vessel and blew it off course. It was only because the crew happened to encounter a single small, uninhabited island that the ship's crew and its passengers did not perish. The sailors were able to beach the ship on the island, make the necessary repairs, and finally proceed to their destination.

The passengers stayed at Yepoti for five long months, waiting for the seasonal winds to shift back toward the mainland. Finally Faxian and the other passengers boarded another large ship that was destined for China, but this leg of the trip turned out to be even more harrowing than the first. On the South China Sea the ship encountered a dangerous storm that blew it off course. After the storm had passed, Hindu traders on board the ship accused the Buddhist monk Faxian of jinxing the journey, and they had every intention of putting him off the ship on an isolated and uninhabited island. However, his Buddhist patron managed to persuade them not to do this, arguing that such an act would anger the many Buddhist rulers in China where all the traders hoped to do business. Due to the storm, the ship was totally lost on the high seas and missed its destination of Canton (in present-day Guangdong Province). When the sailors realized that they were lost on the Pacific Ocean, they just turned the ship westward toward the Asian continent, and after 82 days at sea they beached it on a shore that turned out to be in China's Shandong Province, more than 1,000 miles north of their intended destination. Despite the dangers on this monsoon route, it persisted and by the late seventh century the Southeast Asians would be sharing this route with Arab and Iranian sailors making their way to China from the Red Sea, the southern shores of Arabia, and the Persian Gulf.

THE MARITIME TRADE OF THE UMAYYAD AND ABBASID CALIPHATES

Prior to the late ninth century the Muslim caliphates had extended their trade networks throughout much of Eurasia primarily by means of land routes. Outside of Eurasia, they had also conquered the Mediterranean coast of Africa and much of Spain and extended their trade routes across the Sahara to West Africa. Meanwhile, the military force that had begun as desert cavalries was cautiously approaching the seas and acquiring a navy. The early founders of the Muslim Empire, whose roots were in the overland caravan trade on the Arabian Peninsula, didn't show much interest in the sea. They were from inland cities, and were more familiar with camels and horses than with ships. Though their cavalries occupied a significant part of the eastern and southern coasts of the Mediterranean, the cities in this area that were most important to them, such as Damascus and Fustat-Cairo, were located somewhat inland from the port cities.

Nevertheless, some caravan leaders did have contacts with the Arab traders of aromatic resins, woods, and spices who were based on the peninsula's southern coast, and these coastal people had been active on various maritime trade networks from ancient times. Thus, after southern coastal Arabs and Egyptian-Greeks began to convert to Islam, or just agree to participate in Muslim networks, their seafaring skills helped to promote Muslim trade on the sea routes.

The people who lived on the shores of southern Arabia had never really abandoned sailing even during the downtimes of the seafaring trade. When there wasn't much traffic from overseas traders, they resorted to fishing to make a living. Nevertheless, when the traffic increased, they could bring in much larger profits by offering transportation to traveling merchants. Even in the years when the overseas trade fell off, the coastal people had to maintain some of their long-distance maritime activities. The southern shores of Arabia had very little wood for ship construction, and teak lumber and coconut fiber for making seaworthy ships had to be acquired in the ports of India and various islands in the Indian Ocean. On Egypt's northern, Mediterranean coast, the situation was similar. Even though the political and economic importance of the Muslim city of Fustat-Cairo had diminished much of Alexandria's prestige and prosperity, the latter continued to export Egyptian flax, linen, and wheat, and to import timber for boat construction from the Palestinian coast and even from Western European ports.

In Iran as well, the Arab conquests had brought long-established maritime traders into the realm of the Muslim caliphate. Persian Gulf sailors had a long history of foreign trade, especially with India, that dated back to ancient times. Archaeological excavations at the Persian Gulf port of Siraf have revealed that it was still an important international port in the early Islamic period. Among other things, the archaeologists found thousands of pieces of Chinese porcelain, lapis lazuli from Afghanistan, glassware from Egypt, and some very early Islamic coins, as well as coins from Muslim Spain, Russia, and Syria. There is also an abundance of evidence from China that both Arab and Iranian ships were coming into the ports of southeastern China during the seventh and eighth centuries.

By the late seventh century, many Chinese pilgrims were going to and from India by sea. One of them was the Buddhist monk Yijing (635–713), who left China on an Iranian-owned ship in 671. In his baggage was a large quantity of silk, which he had brought along for donations to Buddhist establishments that he would encounter on his journey through Southeast Asia as well as in India. Yijing sailed from Canton, which until the ninth century would be the most important port on China's southeastern coast. It only took him twenty days to reach Srivijaya on the southeastern coast of Sumatra. (One might compare this to Faxian's 82-day trip from Yepoti to Canton, during which his ship was blown out onto the Pacific Ocean, and never found the port of Canton.)

By this time the maritime routes between India and Sri Lanka and various ports in Southeast Asia had already facilitated the spread of Buddhism to parts of Southeast Asia. When Yijing first stopped there in 671, Srivijiaya was already an important center of Buddhist studies, and its king was also a generous supporter of pilgrims. Yijing's layover in this port city lasted for six months, but unlike Faxian, he found the layover useful since he could study Sanskrit in preparation for his journey to the Buddhist homeland in northeastern India. When it was time for Yijing to depart for India, the king even provided passage for him on a royal ship, which stopped at a place called Jietu on the Malay Peninsula for two months, before proceeding to the Indian port of Tamralipti, on the Ganges River delta.

By the early eighth century, when Yijing returned to China, it seems that navigation on the two-part sea route between China and India was routine. He did not record what sort of ship he took on his way back to Srivijaya, but once there, he had no difficulty finding a ship back to China. The traffic between Srivijaya and Canton seems to have been quite heavy, and there were also many ships from India and the Abbasid caliphate that frequented this Sumatran port. Knowing that he would have no trouble getting back to Srivijaya, Yijing even made a quick round trip from there to Canton just to get paper and assistants for copying Buddhist texts in Srivijaya. Thereafter, he finally ended his pilgrimage and returned home to Tang dynasty China in 713.

During the latter half of the eighth and the ninth centuries, when Baghdad was the economic center of the Muslim heartlands, Sindbad the sailor, the hero in the *Arabian Nights*, assumed the risks of sailing all the way to China, as did other real-life Muslim maritime traders who generally departed from the Persian Gulf or the Red Sea. According to a book compiled in the late ninth or the early tenth century, *the Akhbar al-Sin Wa'l-Hind* (*Accounts of China and India*), which is attributed to a merchant named Sulayman, most ships destined for China sailed from the Iranian port of Siraf, on the Persian Gulf. The traders usually stopped at Quilon, on India's southwestern coast, where they had to pay a port tax, and then proceeded on to Canton. In Canton the Tang government appointed a Muslim to settle disputes within the Muslim trading community and lead prayers at Islamic festivals, and Iraqi merchants all followed his leadership.

Sulayman was a keen observer of the commodities imported to and exported from China. Silk was still China's most important export. He noticed that all Chinese wore silk textiles, and that during the wintertime some wore many layers of silk. He greatly admired the delicate pale green celadon porcelain ware, but thought it strange that Chinese drank a beverage made by sprinkling some kind of leaves in hot water. Apparently neither celadon nor tea had yet become a significant part of the Southern Ocean trade. Large quantities of porcelain did not leave China until the early tenth century, and tea, likewise, was almost unknown outside of China and the Buddhist communities of East Asia until the tenth century.

Apparently, the ocean traffic between the Persian Gulf and China had been increasing well before Sulayman wrote his *Accounts of China and India*. By that time shepherds from inland areas had already left their homes, and found work on ships sailing the Southern Ocean. Sulayman recounts the story of one of them, Captain Abharah, who had long since become a famous captain on this route due both to his valor and his skills.

> Among the yarns of seamen and shipmasters is that which is told about Captain Abharah. He was originally from Kirman [Kerman, in central Iran], a shepherd in one of its districts, then he became [a]fisherman, then one of the sailors on a ship trading with India. He then changed to a China ship, of which he afterwards became captain. He was well versed in the ways of the sea and made the voyage to China seven times. No one had crossed to China before him except [without] a perilous adventure. No one had ever . . . heard of [anyone] who had made the voyage without accident and returned, if anyone made the outward voyage safely, that was a wonder, and safe return was rare; and I have never heard of any but him who made both the outward and the return voyage wholly without mishap. (George Hourani, *Arab Seafaring*, 114)

By this time Arab and Iranian sailors were not only going much further east than they had in Roman times, Arabs who sailed the Mediterranean were also going much further west, all the way to Muslim Spain. The traders' inventories reveal that they still carried many of the traditional goods bought and sold in Roman times, such as olive oil from the Mediterranean, frankincense and myrrh from Arabia, and silk from China, but there were also many new, more bulky goods.

Agricultural development in Western Europe had transformed the region into a profitable hinterland for Italian traders. Members of the political and religious hierarchies in this region also bought silks from Byzantium and various parts of Asia, while other purchasers began to demonstrate a demand for large quantities of somewhat less-expensive textiles such as Egyptian linens and Indian cottons. Muslim traders, who were already delivering paper, books, and *tiraz* textiles, also introduced many new agricultural products to these markets. China continued to supply silk textiles and yarns, but by this time there were more patterns and styles, as well as new products such as porcelain and tea. The sea routes were critical to the growth of this trade since the overland caravan routes did not have the capacity to carry the increased quantity of goods that were being traded. Nor did horses or camels have the capability of carrying some of the larger and heavier cargoes that were being carried by ships.

THE FATIMID CALIPHATE AND THE AYYUBID DYNASTY IN EGYPT

By the tenth century, just as commercial activities on the Southern Ocean were gaining greater significance, the centers of population and economic growth within the Muslim heartlands began shifting in a southwesterly direction, from Mesopotamia to Egypt. This transition was in large part due to political instability and hostilities in Mesopotamia and surrounding areas. It was already underway when in 969 the Fatimids annexed Egypt, took over the old capital Fustat, and built their new capital of Cairo right next to it. The Fatimids were Shiite Muslims who were originally based in what is now Tunisia. They had rebelled against the local authorities in the Maghrib in 909, and took Egypt only after establishing their control, directly or indirectly, over the western part of North Africa. Once in Egypt, their leader declared himself caliph, in opposition to Baghdad. The Fatimids also extended their rule onto the Eurasian landmass, taking control of the Mediterranean's eastern coast and eastern Arabia, including the holy cities of Mecca and Medina.

Cairo quickly became a busy inland port, shipping trade goods up the Nile to the Mediterranean port of Alexandria. Many of the trade goods that passed through Cairo had originated in China, Southeast Asia, or India. Once they were unloaded on the shores of the Red Sea, they were portaged to the Nile River. Thus, Cairo had become a major transshipment point between the Southern Ocean and the Mediterranean Sea. At the same time the significance of the river and land route from the Persian Gulf to the Mediterranean had declined. The Fatimids also succeeded in turning Cairo into a prestigious cultural center, famous for its scholars and its architecture.

By the eleventh century there was yet another transition. The maritime trade of the Muslims became primarily a trade with India. Rarely did their ships go past India to Southeast Asia and China. Muslim maritime traders still sought goods coming from China and Southeast Asia, but they purchased these items on India's southwestern coast. By this time Chinese shipping was predominant on the routes from China to India, and Chinese ships (some of them owned by Arab and Iranian traders based in China) unloaded their cargoes on this same coast.

The founding of the Fatimid caliphate in Egypt had occurred almost simultaneously with the establishment of the Song dynasty in 960. Given the strength of the Song economy in general and the dynasty's focus on the development of its maritime capabilities, one can only imagine just how much of the India trade was actually fueled by products arriving from China, and how much of the India trade of the Cairo-based Islamic and Jewish traders was actually an indirect trade with China. Beginning in the tenth century, after Chinese ships started going to India, the volume and variety of commodities in Indian ports increased rapidly.

Sea voyages between Egypt and India were still dangerous and still involved long voyages, as well as long stays in harbors where they waited, sometimes for several months, for the winds to shift directions. As in ancient times, piracy also caused substantial losses on the Red Sea and the Indian Ocean. To protect themselves, Muslim merchants organized *Karim*, convoyed merchant fleets, in order to safely sail the Arabian and Red Seas. The Fatimid caliphate provided an armed escort, first sending five ships, and later three, to escort the fleets. Even though the *Karim* convoys could not totally guarantee the safety of the seafaring trade, they nevertheless succeeded in making the trade between the Red Sea and India a government-protected, regularly accomplished endeavor.

The merchants who joined the *Karim* were called *Karimis*. They were large family firms with substantial assets, business experience, and clients in markets all over the trading networks. Young members of the family were often sent to faraway markets to learn the business. The family enterprises also used slaves as their representatives in some places. Slaves in Islamic society were often upwardly mobile and thus loyal to their masters, and often were emancipated in return for their good services. When a trader had young sons, he might well send slaves to manage the overseas branches of the family firm. Once the boys had grown up and could be trained, the slaves might be freed to pursue their own lives.

The *Karimi* trade in Indian ports flourished and the convoy system soon spread into the Mediterranean, west from Egypt to the Maghrib and Muslim Spain. However, these convoys, unlike the ones on the Arabian Sea, did not enjoy the benefit of armed escorts. On the Mediterranean the most serious threats to *Karimi* business, or the seafaring business of the Islamic world in general, came from the Western European crusaders. In the twelfth century, the Franks attempted, by military means, to get access to the Red Sea, but did not succeed.

In the end, it was Turkish commanders, not Arabs who defended the Muslim position in the eastern Mediterranean from the Christian crusaders. After the Abbasids conquered Iran, various Turkic peoples on the steppe, especially those who lived relatively close to Iran, began to convert to Islam and establish nomadic states on the steppe. Eventually some of them began to venture into agricultural areas. Mahmud of Ghazni, for example, established an emirate, a tribal confederacy, in Afghanistan in 999. By the end of the eleventh century, the Seljuk Turks had conquered Iran and captured Baghdad. For purposes of legitimacy, they chose to maintain the already enfeebled line of the Arab Abbasid caliphs, but the lands of the caliphate were now ruled by a people from the Eurasian steppe.

Saladin (ca. 1137–1193), a Muslim hero, was the commander who had prevented the crusaders from getting access to the Red Sea. Although he was not a Turk, but a Kurd from the Iranian highlands, his father had risen to a high command under the Seljuk Turkish Zangi Emirate, and Saladin followed in his footsteps. After defeating the Franks, Saladin went on to conquer Egypt for the Zangi Emirate in the years from 1169 to 1171, thus bringing an end to the Fatimid caliphate. Once he had gained control of this strategic area, he established the Ayyubid dynasty, which lasted until 1250.

Although Saladin was an enthusiastic supporter of the *Karim* system, he also taxed the *Karimi* merchants heavily in order to support his military campaigns against the crusaders. Nevertheless, these were probably the golden years of the *Karimi* merchants. It was one of Saladin's deputies who in 1182 oversaw the construction of the famous *funduk al-Karim*, the *Karimi* market in Cairo. Even after the Ayyubid dynasty fell, the *Karim* system continued, protecting the Indian Ocean trade until well after the founding of Egypt's Mamluk dynasty in 1250.

During the time that the numerous *Karimi* family firms operated in the Indian Ocean and on the Mediterranean, a complicated system of finance and partnership developed to help traders acquire investment funds and collect debts. The Islamic law code also became more and more comprehensive on these matters. The problem confronting the traders and the investors was the Koranic prohibition on usury, which was defined as any loan that had to be paid back with interest. The Koran, however, did not forbid partnerships, so the person with capital to invest and the actual trader, who needed money to invest in goods, could form a partnership rather than have the former make an interest-bearing loan to the latter. Islamic law did allow various forms of partnerships, which had been derived from Arabic customary law. The most common one was a *commenda*-type partnership. During the medieval period in European history a *commenda* was a partnership in which the owner of capital or merchandise entrusted one or the other to an agent, expecting him to sell the trade goods or invest the money in trade goods and then sell them at a profit.

The owner and the agent agreed that after the trade was done, the agent would return to the owner the original capital that he had been given or the value of the goods that he had been given, plus a share of the profit that the agent had made. The agent could keep the remainder of the profit as payment for his labor. In the event that the capital or goods were lost, and the loss was not due to the negligence of the agent, but happened for uncontrollable and unforeseeable reasons, the agent was not liable for the loss, which is to say he did not owe his partner the amount of the initial investment. His loss was limited to the time and labor that he had contributed to the partnership.

During this era of the Indian Ocean trade, the *commenda*-type partnership flourished. In Arabia it was actually a very long-standing variety of partnership that predated the rise of Islam, and there were several words for it in Arabic. In the seventh century, the Prophet Muhammad himself had acted as an agent in a *commenda*-type partnership with Khadija before their marriage. Khadija was a widow with capital, but she could not run the caravans herself. Thus, she formed a partnership with Muhammad, entrusting her capital to him. Once the Islamic leaders were in power, they used this type of partnership for yet another purpose. The first few caliphs all entrusted the money of orphans under their care to traders who established such a partnership with the caliphs.

In the Indian Ocean trade, as well as the trade on the Mediterranean, Muslim traders not only dealt with other Muslims, but also Hindus, Parsis, Christians, and frequently with Jewish traders. Although the followers of the three monotheistic religions took off different days of the week for their Sabbath—Muslims on Fridays, Jews on Saturdays, and Christians on Sundays—traders of various religious backgrounds boarded the same ships or stayed in the same caravanserai. In Cairo, many Jewish traders actually operated their businesses within the framework of Islamic networks, most likely because it was advantageous to the growth of their businesses.

Numerous letters written by Jewish traders who resided in Cairo reveal frequent economic collaboration and close interfaith partnerships between Jews and Muslims. The collections of those letters are called the *Geniza*. Jewish people did not like to casually discard paper if it had any writing on it, for fear that it might contain sacred words invoking the name of Jehovah. They therefore deposited old correspondence and accounting books in a storage facility called the *Geniza*. The Cairo *Geniza* happened to survive into modern times, providing a wealth of material for scholarly study. The letters were written in the Arabic language, using the Hebrew script. A study of those letters has revealed that in the time of the *Karim* trade, even independent Jewish traders often transported their cargoes on ships that had Muslim captains.

According to S. D. Goitein, a leading authority on the *Geniza* collection, *Karim* was a household word in twelfth-century Cairo. Any woman in Cairo whose husband's business was linked to someplace on the Indian Ocean could expect to receive goods that he sent to her through the good offices of the *Karim*. The *Karim* convoys had a reputation of carrying high-quality goods from India, both from its eastern and western coasts. The fleets sometimes sailed back and forth between the Red Sea and India, without making any stops, and sometimes they stopped at Aden, on the southern coast of the Arabian Peninsula. Since the seafaring ventures were strictly seasonal, due to the biannual shift in the winds, there were schedules that kept all the traders informed about departures and arrivals. The schedules were based on the calendar of Egyptian Christians known as Coptic Christians. Jewish traders had large consignments on these *Karim* ships and were thus familiar with the shipping processes, the schedule, and the calendar.

Jewish traders formed *commenda*-type partnerships among themselves or joined Muslim *commendas*. In Jewish court, this type of partnership was referred to as a "mutual loan according to Muslim law," to distinguish it from the Jewish partnership. This shows again that the Jewish community in Cairo, operating within Islamic trading frameworks, was willing to adapt to local customs. Since Muslim powers had spread so far afield, this was the case in most regions surrounding the Indian Ocean, and in addition, even in those places not ruled by Muslims, there were Muslim diaspora communities that possessed extraterritorial powers within their own enclaves. Also, Jewish traders who had business in remote ports often hired legal representatives, and these people were often Muslims. In fact, usually they were Islamic *qadis* or judges.

Since Cairo, or Egypt in general, had become the principal transit station between the Indian Ocean and the Mediterranean, the close partnership between the Jewish and Muslim communities in the Indian Ocean trade also extended into the Mediterranean trade. Most of the goods obtained in India—the silks, cottons, spices, aromatic woods and resins, and so forth—whether they were from India or from further east, were sold in the market at Cairo, but that was not necessarily their final destination. From there some were transported to Alexandria, where they were loaded on larger ships and hence made their way to ports on the Mediterranean's northern and southern shores.

THE MEDITERRANEAN TRADE

From the tenth to the early twelfth century, the partnerships between Jewish and Muslim traders in the Mediterranean networks were quite similar to those that characterized the Indian Ocean trade. In the Mediterranean Jewish traders used the same Islamic institutions and experts, such as the *commenda*-type partnership and Muslim legal advisors, to carry out their business. Even without military escorts the *Karimi* merchants did extend their business westward to the Maghrib. The Fatimid government taxed the traders, including those who were Jewish, and the traders inevitably tried to evade some of the taxes. Meanwhile, since Jewish traders often made trips to Tunisia and Spain to purchase olive oil directly from the farmers, the Fatimid caliphs entrusted them with the collection of the agrarian tax in Tunisia. In return for this service to the Islamic state, the Cairo caliphs occasionally granted robes of honor to the Jewish traders, following Baghdad's example of bestowing recognition on those who served them well.

The trading networks of the Christian north in many respects depended upon the Muslim-Jewish networks on the southern shore of the Mediterranean. Christian traders from the northern shore, be they Byzantines, Franks, or Italians, participated in the trading networks as buyers of the Asian goods obtained from the Indian Ocean trade. This north-south Mediterranean trade was an important element in the development of the Italian city-states, helped to build a stronger economic foundation generally for Western Europe, and contributed to the end of Roman Christendom's dependence upon Byzantium for its Christian material culture. The many *tiraz* and other Islamic silk textiles found in Western European churches and the plain silks for embroidering images of saints in the workshops of the pope in Rome all came from the Muslim maritime networks.

Muslim traders owned most of the ships plying the Mediterranean, especially on the southern shore and on the coasts of Muslim Spain, just as they owned most of the ships sailing between the Red Sea and India. Goitein collected detailed information about 145 eleventh-century ships and discovered that only a few were jointly owned by Jews and Muslims, and that many among the Muslim elite—sultans, members of the royal families, viziers, military commanders, and judges—owned ships. Thus, it is no wonder that the Fatimid government wanted to protect these ships. Even though the Fatimids in the eleventh century actually controlled little territory outside Egypt, the Muslim and Jewish traders based in Egypt extended their maritime networks to all the Muslim lands of the Mediterranean, including Muslim Spain. The ships in the Mediterranean appear to have been larger than the Arab dhows on the Indian Ocean, similar in size to the middle-sized junks from China. In the *Geniza* letters, there is a reference to a ship going from Palermo, Sicily, to Alexandria with about 400 passengers aboard. Another letter refers to a ship, sailing sometime around 1140, going from Tripoli, Libya, to Seville, Spain, carrying 36 or 37 Jewish passengers and nearly 300 Muslims.

The Mediterranean cargoes were quite valuable. A *Geniza* letter from Alexandria reported a loss of three ships with a cargo valued around 200,000 dinars. The ten Jewish traders on board one of these ships were accompanying a consignment of 7,000 dinars. In general, seafaring on the Mediterranean was less dangerous than on the Indian Ocean, and trips were shorter. The trips from port to port usually lasted for days, not months, and only the voyage between Spain and Egypt could take more than two months.

The commodities traded by the Muslim and Jewish networks on the Mediterranean's southern shore included many items that were traded in Roman times. Silk yarn and textiles were by far the largest items in terms of their percentage of the value of the cargo. However, silks no longer came only from the east via Alexandria. By this time silk was also produced in the western Mediterranean, in Muslim Spain and the Maghrib, as sericulture had developed in most Islamic countries. In fact, silk from Muslim Spain was the most traded commodity in the Mediterranean market. Zaytuni silk from Quanzhou, China, was also available. (Zaytun was the Arabic name for Quanzhou, and in the international market it was also the word for satin, a lustrous, supple, tightly woven silk textile. The English word *satin* is a derivative of Zaytun.) During the Fatimid caliphate silk yarns even served as a kind of cash, or standard of exchange, and not just as a commodity. Olive oil, glassware, flax, corals, and various metals were the traditional goods of the Mediterranean trade, and aromatics, perfumes of plant and animal origins, as well as the many gemstones were mostly imports from the trade in Indian ports.

What was different by this time was that this trade also included many more staple goods such as minerals and chemicals for dying textiles or tanning skins, and raw materials such as lumber and bamboo for carpentry. What was completely different from Roman times was the trade in paper and books made of paper. The scriptures of various religions were traded by the Muslim-Jewish traders, including hand-copied Bibles and Talmuds, as well as legal and otherwise edifying literature, grammars, and Arabic books. Paper, a replacement for papyri, was also one of the exports from Egypt to the north shore of the Mediterranean.

Both Muslims and Jews sought markets for their commodities in the ports on the Christian northern shore. Muslim ships visited a variety of Christian ports, including the Italian cities Salerno, Amalfi, and Genoa, the Frankish port Marseilles, and occasionally Constantinople. The ships from the Italian cities more regularly visited ports in Egypt, Tunisia, Syria, and Sicily. Trading firms based in Cairo sent agents to Alexandria to observe foreign ships coming into that port, including those from Christian Europe. These agents noted the arrival and departure dates of the ships, and kept their Cairo offices well-informed and up-to-date with regard to the nature of the cargoes, prices, shipwrecks, and other losses.

Traders from the northern shore of the Mediterranean were very eager to purchase the useful and attractive goods that the ships from the southern shore had to offer, but they had limited means to pay for them. Agricultural production in Western Europe during the tenth and eleventh centuries was just beginning to increase and had yet to produce enough surpluses to pay for imported luxuries for the church and for prosperous city dwellers. This led to a balance-of-payments problem, causing gold and silver to drain out of the region. Unfortunately for those involved, this lack of balance in the trade was also made up by the sale of slaves, Western Europe's most valuable export. Throughout medieval Eurasia, the slave trade was a pervasive and large-scale business. Warfare from Western Europe to central Asia created many prisoners of war whose captors subsequently sold them as slaves. In the Mediterranean and Indian Ocean trade networks, slaves or bond servants were widely used. However, most of the movement of slaves took place on overland routes, and they were rarely transported by sea.

When Europeans were building their commercial economies, Jewish traders were important contributors. The famous Muslim geographer, Ibn

Khordadhbeh (ca. 820–912), mentioned in the previous chapter, was amazed by the multiple linguistic skills of the Ladino Jews, who traveled to all corners of Eurasia. They went to Slavic countries, Frankish Europe, central and western Asia, and Africa to purchase slaves to supply the markets of Muslim countries. The Ladino traders, however, specialized in trading European slaves. They had Slavic slaves castrated in or near Spain, and then sold the eunuchs to various Islamic countries. Their inventory also included young girls and boys from France and Galicia. If there was any consolation for the slaves, it was that slavery in the Islamic countries allowed for upward mobility and manumission. Masters often released their slaves while they were still young enough to make their own living. Those who were prisoners of war often served in the Muslim armies and could therefore move up in the military and social hierarchy. During the Muslim Turkish conquests slaves, known as *mamluks* (the Arabic word for slave), founded two Mamluk dynasties, one established in northern India soon after 1200, and one established in Egypt in 1250. Whatever the fate of the slaves, their sale brought in essential revenues to those areas that had victorious militaries but could not otherwise pay for all the goods that they imported.

From the end of the eleventh century to the thirteenth century it was the Western European Christian crusades against Byzantium and the Muslim Turks that reversed the commercial balance of power between the southern and northern shores of the Mediterranean. The crusades also brought an end to Muslim commercial collaboration with both Jews and Christians. This change in the balance of power between the shores had actually started as early as the late eleventh century. It was then that Norman knights, whose ancestors were originally from Scandinavia, used their long-established base in northwestern France to take over Sicily from the Muslims. The Normans were as much a threat to Byzantium as they were to the Muslim coasts, not to mention Italy, itself.

By the twelfth century, Western Europe's economic strength was growing as a result of an increase in the production and trade of various goods, including grain, hardware, and textiles. In this transition, the Italian cities were the vanguard. Italians, with their first-hand trading experience with Muslims and Jews from the southern coast of the Mediterranean, began to use notaries and rely on credit transactions, both of which are trading practices that require paper. They became the most sophisticated traders of Europe and also the most eager and knowledgeable crusaders.

Although many Italian cities were involved in commerce, Venice stands out. Its rise as a trading empire best describes the momentous transition in the relative status and power of Western Europe and the Muslim trading world. Venice had once been a Roman province. When the empire began to disintegrate in the west, a northern polytheistic people known as the Lombards attacked the city in 568 CE, and drove its inhabitants off the mainland to the sand banks and islands in the lagoons. There the people of Venice rebuilt the city, with its numerous canals. While most of Italy was occupied by the Lombards, Venice was not. Due to its watery location, the people of Venice were able to keep the Lombards out of their area and to maintain contact with Constantinople by sea. It thus remained under the sovereignty of Byzantium, while most of Italy was controlled by the Lombards. As Byzantine maritime power gradually declined, the Venetians began to build ships and supply transportation to Western Europe and to defend the region from Muslim sea power on the Mediterranean. Meanwhile, the Byzantine emperors granted Venice the privilege of selling silks, garments, and spices to the rest of Western Europe. However, they also threatened to withdraw such privileges from Venice, Amalfi, and other Byzantine enclaves if they tilted too much toward Frankish Europe.

In the ninth century, to enhance their independent status, the Venetians stole the body of St. Mark from its tomb in Alexandria and thereafter made St. Mark the patron saint of the city republic. Once Venice had become wealthy from the trade and had built the strongest naval force of the Mediterranean, the city began to resent its historical subordination to Byzantium. A major act of revenge took place in 1203, during the fourth crusade, when the Doge, or the mayor of Venice, carrying the flag of St. Mark, led an attack on Constantinople and subsequently occupied the city for fifty-seven years.

The crusaders never sank deep roots in Constantinople or the other cities they occupied on the Syrian and Palestinian coasts. They remained a community of male soldiers and did not bring along with them significant numbers of civilians, most especially, women from the European west. Nevertheless, they stayed there long enough to become familiar with the material cultures and the technologies of the areas ruled by Muslims. It was in these eastern Mediterranean cities that the crusaders first developed a taste for granulated sugar (which was originally an Indian product, but by this time its production had spread to various parts of Asia, including the Muslim world). Also, it was in the thirteenth century, during the time of the crusades or soon thereafter, that the compass, long used on Chinese ships, appeared on European ships sailing the Mediterranean.

In the beginning the crusaders expelled and sometimes killed the local populations in these cities. A 1991 French language study by Georges Tate, *L'Orient des Croisades*, includes plates of two miniature paintings from a thirteenth-century manuscript, the *Histoire d'outremer de Guillaume de Tyr*, that graphically depict the slaughters at Nicea and Jerusalem. Eventually, however, many former residents of cities taken by the crusaders were able to move back to their homes, without incident. The crusaders, who were from a variety of different cities and regions in Western Europe, organized their own separate communal centers within the bounds of the old Islamic cities. They transformed mosques into churches or built new churches, and each communal neighborhood had a marketplace, a baking oven, and a public bath.

While in the Muslim areas, the crusaders had much better access to many commodities that they had been purchasing from Muslim and Jewish traders for centuries. In addition, the central marketplace, which had once been regulated by Muslim rulers, was divided up into sections, where each community carried out trade in its own interests. The Venetian community at Tyre, for example, specialized in the trade of medicines since their part of the old market had long been the center of the medicine trade.

The crusaders' days, however, were numbered. Turkish forces in Central Asia had moved into Iran, and from there into the eastern Mediterranean region, and they set themselves the task of throwing the crusaders out of those parts of the region that had been Muslim for something like five centuries. Although the Turkish forces succeeded, the battles between the Western European navies and the Turkish armies of Ayyubid Egypt had destroyed many of the important coastal towns and ports. After the eastern Mediterranean coasts were cleared of crusaders at the end of the thirteenth century, the Muslim traders in Cairo then turned their backs on the Mediterranean. Although some of these traders did attempt to maintain maritime trade along the Maghrib coast, their business there started to dwindle. In addition, Jewish traders in Egypt no longer felt comfortable in a land ruled by Turkish warriors with Central Asian traditions, and they migrated to the north to seek better commercial opportunities in the Christian lands.

THE INDIAN SUBCONTINENT AS THE CENTER OF SOUTHERN OCEAN TRADE AND THE RISE OF COLA

Due to the Indian Peninsula's geographic position at the center of the Indian Ocean, its ports served as the meeting place of sailors coming from both the eastern and western ends of the vast Southern Ocean from the first to the thirteenth centuries. Nevertheless, India's ports were never just a place for foreign traders to meet. Its maritime trading tradition predated the development of the silk roads by more than 2,000 years, dating back to ancient times when sailors went back and forth between the urban civilization of the Indus River Valley (in present-day Pakistan) and Mesopotamia. Even then, India was exporting cotton textiles. Also prior to the development of the silk roads, sailors on India's eastern coast had developed routes to various ports in Southeast Asia. And southern India was already exporting large quantities of pepper to various lands, including the Roman Empire, when the Kushan Empire took over a large part of northeastern India in the first century CE.

As discussed in Chapter Two, since Roman times, the northwest coast, including Konkan and ports on the Gulf of Cambay, had become an essential part of the earliest silk roads, harboring ships that went back and forth to the Persian Gulf or the Red Sea. From the first to the third centuries CE Roman Empire sailors, based on the shores of the Red Sea, had carried Chinese silks from India to Egypt, where they were portaged to the Nile River, and then sailed down the river to Alexandria where they met the Mediterranean Sea. Even after the Roman Empire sailors disappeared from this route, maritime exchanges remained focused on India. With the spread of Buddhism, both the overland and the overseas routes became pilgrimage routes for Chinese Buddhists, and Sri Lanka, home to a most treasured relic, the tooth of the Buddha, became an important stop for pilgrims. By the early fifth century, when Southeast Asian sailors developed the sea route between ports in southeastern China and Sri Lanka, this island nation, less than 50 miles off India's southeastern coast, played a crucial role in the delivery of "Persian goods" to China's southeastern ports and Chinese silks and other products to the Iranian outpost on Sri Lanka.

After the Muslim conquest of Iran, India's northwestern ports were also home to communities of Parsis, the Iranian traders who maintained their Zoroastrian religion, and to Muslim traders, both Arabs and Iranians. Although the trade in luxuries remained important, many more staple goods were now entering the international markets. By the seventh century, India's northeastern ports were much less involved in the trade of foreign goods and mainly exported Indian products such as indigo and cotton textiles. These ports were in the same general vicinity as the ports the Kushans had controlled in the first several centuries CE, when the Central Asian Silk Road had linked up with the Arabian Sea routes of the Roman Empire sailors. Although these commodities might not be as precious as the silks, spices, and gems that were sold there during the Kushan period, the quantity of goods exported was quite large.

Also in the seventh century, first Iranian and then Arab ships joined the Southeast Asian sailors on the eastern part of the Indian Ocean, sailing from Indian ports to Canton on China's southeastern coast. By the latter part of the century, the Sumatran port of Srivijaya had become a center of Buddhist learning. By the late seventh century, the Chinese pilgrim Yijing could find a ship that took him from Srivijaya directly to the mouth of the Ganges, the Indian ports closest to the Buddhist homeland. By the end of the ninth century, there was a steady stream of Chinese Buddhist pilgrims making their way first to Srivijaya and then to northeastern India. And by the tenth century both Muslim and Jewish trading communities in Baghdad were moving their centers southwest to Egypt and managing their trade in Indian ports from this new location. India's Malabar Coast, on the southwestern side of the peninsula where Quilon was located, soon became a transit station on the Indian Ocean routes, and the site of Muslim and Jewish trading diasporas.

By the ninth century the southeastern coast of the Indian Peninsula had acquired two different names. Although Islamic geographers called the peninsula's southeastern shore the Ma'aba coast, the local Tamil name was Cola Mandalam (the realm of the Colas), a term that has survived until today as Coromandel. The rise of two states on this coast, the Pallavas (ca. 550–900) and then the Colas (844–1279), added a new element to the international situation and accompanied the emergence of a new configuration among Indian traders and international routes. In the ninth century Hinduism had consolidated its influence in southern India, and Brahmadeya, or Brahman villages, had become the main agricultural institutions, responsible for bringing more land under cultivation and building and maintaining irrigation systems. The political power of the Hindu Colas was rooted in their control of agriculture, and the Cola kings had enough of an agricultural surplus to support a navy and to export commercial products such as sugar and coconuts. Thus, they revived India's trade with Southeast Asia.

During the reigns of Rajaraja (985–1014) and his son Rajendra (1012–1044), the Colas expanded their territory such that it included all of southern India, and then sent overseas military expeditions against Sri Lanka (1001–1004 and 1014–1017) and Srivijaya (1025). They reached the peak of their power and their seafaring adventures in the late tenth century and early eleventh century. Many of these southern Indian traders moved to Quanzhou, China, and built Hindu temples there. Although the kings of the Colas as well as most of their subjects in southern India were Hindus and worshipped Siva, Buddhism was still the religion of many traders who frequented their ports, especially the foreign traders. Buddhist monasteries continued to host pilgrims and traders in the Cola Kingdom, and the kings made large donations to monasteries. To accommodate this stream of trade, the Cola rulers also patronized Buddhism. In the port of Nagapattinam a large Buddhist monastery was built in the eleventh century, next to a Shiva temple, obviously to accommodate Buddhist traders from Sri Lanka, Southeast Asia, and China.

The hegemony of the Colas in the region began to fade after their early eleventh-century peak, just as Chinese ships became the main carriers between China and India. The transit point between Arab dhows and Chinese junks became Quilon on the southwestern coast of the Indian Peninsula, and thereafter India's southeastern coast lost much of its international significance. Even Chinese traders who wanted to visit the Colas had to go first to Quilon, and then board a smaller ship that would take them back east to the Coromandel Coast.

By the late eleventh century, traders from China and Southeast Asia who wanted to visit the markets of the Persian Gulf, the Arabian Sea, and the Mediterranean had to stop at the southern Indian port of Quilon on their way. Likewise, traders from the Persian Gulf and the Red Sea also sailed eastward to Quilon where they could fill their cargo space before returning home. From these Indian ports they could also venture on to the South China Sea on Chinese junks. Ports on the Indian peninsula provided a convenient stopping place for the traders from both sides, as in ancient times, and the Indian merchants based in these ports also were active participants in this international commerce. Despite all the shifting patterns of the roads that silk traveled, from the first century CE on, India ports always had a crucial role to play on these maritime routes.

An Age of Chinese Seafaring

During the earliest centuries of China's trade with the Western Regions, almost all of the empire's commercial traffic departed from northwestern China and followed the earliest silk roads, the overland routes that headed west, either across the steppe or through the deserts. This was during the time of the Roman Empire, when the maritime trade of the Roman Empire sailors went no further east than the southeastern coast of India. The Greek author of the *Periplus* knew that if ships sailed on further east from India, they could reach China, the land of silk, but during the first to third centuries CE Roman Empire ships did not attempt to follow these routes to China. Also, during the early centuries of the silk roads, Chinese ships did not venture out onto the oceans. This was not so much because Chinese sailors were afraid to leave the coastal waters, but because the lands that the Chinese knew as places of wealth and marvelous things lay to their west, which they reached by overland routes. They knew little about the islands of Japan and Southeast Asia and showed little or no interest in going there.

Significant numbers of Chinese-owned ships started sailing the southern ocean routes only after the fall of the Tang dynasty in 906. At this point in time much of China's foreign trade was turning away from the overland routes of the northwest and toward its southeastern seaports. There were several reasons for this, related both to economic developments in the agricultural sector as well as to political instability in the eastern part of Eurasia. While the power centers of various Turkic peoples had been moving westward on the Eurasian steppe, new confederacies of nomads began threatening the northern border of China in the post-Tang period.

The Qidan (also Kitan or Khitan) Mongols appeared outside the Great Wall soon after the fall of the Tang Empire. After the Song dynasty was established in 960, the Qidan actually conquered and ruled over parts of north China, establishing the Liao dynasty (947–1125) in the northeast, which included seminomadic pastoralists as well as semiagricultural sedentary peoples. This state was then taken over by one of its previously subordinated allies, the Manchu Ruzhen (also Jerchen), who had been threatening the Qidan's northeastern frontier. By 1127 the Ruzhen tribes had conquered the Qidan and taken over their territories. The Ruzhen then pushed the Song court all the way south of the Huai River.

No sooner had these northeastern tribal rulers adapted their administration to a more sedentary Chinese-style administration, than a new Mongolian nomad confederacy began to emerge on the steppe. In the northwest there were similar problems. In the region around the Hexi Corridor, the strip of land between the Qilian Mountains and the Mongolian deserts, a Tangut leader created a new state called Xixia that controlled the gateway to the Western Regions, including the Jade Gate and the silk roads. The Tanguts were a group of nomadic Tibetans who had gained prominence during the chaos of the later Tang and post-Tang periods.

Despite their large size, the Song dynasty's military forces could not cope with these challenges for a variety of reasons, and the rulers of the Song never developed an army that could successfully counter the threats on its northern and western borders. After several military defeats the Song court resorted to sending large quantities of silk and other goods to their northern and western neighbors in order to make treaties with them. Some of the treaties, especially those with the Xixia, made it possible for the Song dynasty to acquire horses, without which they would have had very little military capability in the north. In addition to silks and silver, the Song dynasty found that they could trade tea for horses. Although the Chinese had been tea drinkers since ancient times, this beverage did not become a significant export until the demand for it spread out of China, mostly due to the spread of Buddhist monasteries from China into other parts of eastern Asia. Since tea was a good beverage to accompany a diet of meat, the staple food of the nomads, it quickly became a much desired commodity in these border markets.

Although militarily unsuccessful, the Song dynasty was actually a very wealthy state. Thus, in some circumstances the Chinese government deemed it prudent to give some of its wealth to its stronger neighbors in order to avoid a war with them. The relationship between the Xixia and the Song thus alternated between hostilities on the one hand, and peace treaties and commercial exchanges on the other. For instance, in 1044, after seven years of war, the Xixia and the Song agreed to a treaty that required the Song to give the Xixia 7,000 taels (a tael is roughly 38 grams or 1.35 ounces) of silver, 150,000 bolts of silk, and 3,000 catties or about 1,500 kilograms (about 3,300 pounds) of tea on an annual basis. The pretense was maintained that these goods were not payoffs for peace, but merely gifts or part of some diplomatic exchange. From the Song point of view, the costs were worth the results, since they at least temporarily halted hostilities and kept the border markets open for trade.

Although the Song government managed to keep some border markets functioning—for a price—the carrying capacity of the caravans on the northwestern frontier had become far from adequate to service Chinese markets. The Song economy was indeed very large, probably the largest in the world at that time. It produced large quantities of good-quality iron and steel for tools and weapons, many kinds of textiles, much paper, many books, and many varieties of porcelain, another new Chinese export that was warmly welcomed in international markets.

Much of the prosperity during the Song was due to economic development in the south. Tea will grow well only under certain growing conditions, and the production of tea soon became concentrated in the foggy and hilly regions of the Yangzi River valley. Porcelain, which is much harder and more delicate in appearance than ordinary pottery, must be made from a special clay called Gaoling and must be baked at very high temperatures. Like the main tea-producing areas, most of the sources of Gaoling clay were located in the south.

Even more important, the agricultural surplus at this time came mainly from the south. Rice, the major crop of the marshlands and terraced hills of southern China, always produced higher yields than millet and wheat, the crops grown in the north. Also, during the Song dynasty, a superior variety of early-ripening rice was introduced to China from Champa (a Malayo-Polynesian-speaking kingdom located in an area that is now part of Vietnam's eastern coast). Because of the fast-ripening qualities of this variety of rice, farmers in the south could raise and harvest two crops during a year instead of just one crop. Thus, the south produced a food surplus large enough for many nonfarmers to produce manufactured goods for both domestic use and for export. Consequently, the political situation and the new economic trends drew the attention of both rulers and traders to the ports on China's southeastern coast as outlets for its products and gates for importing foreign goods.

Even if the northwestern overland caravan routes had been accessible and safe, they would have no longer been adequate. From the time of the Song dynasty China's international trade was much more than a trade in luxuries for elite populations. After the Tang dynasty fell, the sumptuary laws that had prevented commoners from purchasing specially controlled items disappeared, and whoever could afford the foreign goods had the right to purchase them. It was also during the Song that the imperial examination system matured and large numbers of people in China became literate. Almost all offices in the national bureaucracy, from local district magistrate to the highest cabinet posts, were filled by men who had successfully passed a series of written examinations based on the Confucian classics. All registered landholders as well as their male relatives were allowed to take these exams. Although only a few could pass at the level that led to government office, all of the candidates, from both small villages and large cities, became highly literate. This exam system created a large demand for printed materials. Thus, book printing became a large industry in the Song. Textbooks, samples of exam essays, and guidance books were intended for students. Encyclopedias and manuals for agriculture, engineering, and pharmacy served the general public, both urban and rural. Publishing houses also printed fictional literature, collections of anecdotal stories about history, and travelers' tales and fantasies about other parts of the world. This large, prosperous, and well-read population was an immense market for foreign goods.

Not only would the overland routes have been unable to cope with the quantity of Chinese exports, they would have been unable to cope with the weight and bulk of some of the newest exports. The production of silk textiles and floss had increased in both quantity and quality, and enjoyed an ever larger market abroad. Also many of the new products exported from the Song were too heavy or bulky to easily transport on the backs of camels and horses. Porcelain vessels and sets of dishes, for example, were not only heavy, but had to be carefully padded and packed in wooden crates to prevent breakage.

Among the many styles of porcelain produced in the Song, those with a celadon glaze were the most popular in foreign markets, namely in India and the lands of the Muslim caliphates. This translucent, pale green, jade-like, glowing celadon ware soon acquired a marvelous reputation in the international market. Some people even thought that it had magical qualities, and believed, for example, that if anyone put poisonous food into a celadon bowl that the bowl would change color. Because sets of porcelain ware were too heavy, bulky, and fragile for transportation over the land routes, it had to go by sea to its many markets. At this time China also exported paper, books, and tea, mostly to Korea and Japan. Although these goods were not as heavy as boxes of porcelain, once packed for shipping they were bulky and heavy, and they too went by sea.

In response to the constant military pressure from the north and the growth of overseas trade in the south, the Song government sponsored the manufacture of a large number of war ships. Since many members of the royal family, which was quite numerous, were engaged in trade, the government also sponsored the manufacture of some cargo ships. It seems unlikely that this large fleet was of any use in the wars on the inland frontiers with the Qidans, Ruzhens, and eventually the Mongols. What they clearly did do was help the emperors and the court flee from danger whenever the enemy was at the gate of the capital cities. This was especially true during the Southern Song (1127–1279) when the capital was at Hangzhou, a port south of the Yangzi River delta.

In any case, the government's program did propel the industry of shipbuilding to a high level, and the ships were purchased not only by the Chinese government and Chinese traders, but also by many traders from Muslim countries. The largest ships, which could be 100 meters in length, were capable of carrying 500 to 600 passengers and had about 600 tons of cargo capacity. The most common seagoing cargo ships were about 30 meters in length, could carry 200 to 300 passengers, and had a capacity of about 200 tons of goods. Ships that carried less than 100 passengers were considered small.

The largest shipbuilding industry was probably the one at Quanzhou, in present-day Fujian Province. It was located in a southern mountainous area that produced lumber from camphor and fir trees, both of which were good for ship construction. Plus, the tung trees of the area produce tung oil, a wood varnish that is popular even today. Shipbuilders mixed tung oil with lime and broken ramie fibers in order to make a glue that was used to seal the seams in the hull. The wooden planks of the hull were first connected by tenons and iron nails, and then sealed with the tung oil glue. The tung oil in the seams made the hulls very watertight.

To make the ships even safer, they often had transverse bulkheads, which is to say that inside the hull there were interior walls that divided up the cargo space into a number of watertight compartments. Thus, even if one of the compartments were to develop a leak and fill up with water, the others would remain dry and keep the ship afloat. (Roughly 1,000 years later, it was the Titanic's transverse bulkheads that made people think that it was "unsinkable." Unfortunately, as the Titanic demonstrated, if several of the watertight compartments are damaged and let in water, the ship will sink. The Chinese, however, never took these ships into waters where there were icebergs. They were designed for the Southern Ocean.)

The large ships, which were known as junks, were both long and wide, and their sails were reinforced with wooden strips called battens. Although the Chinese junk was not as fast and easily maneuvered as the Arab dhow, it provided a smoother ride and was more stable on rough, open seas and oceans. Chinese junks soon became the most numerous ships on both the South China Sea and the Bay of Bengal. These ships also rounded the southern tip of India to reach ports on its southwestern shore, but there, on the Arabian Sea, they were outnumbered by the Arab dhows.

Quanzhou was also the busiest port on the southeastern coast of China. (Since ancient times Canton had been the most important port for Chinese maritime contact with other countries, but local rebellions in the ninth century had devastated the city and diverted much of the commercial traffic to Quanzhou.) In order to collect tariffs from the seafaring trade, the Song government set up a Seafaring Trade Office in major port areas such as Canton and Quanzhou, and in the Yangzi delta ports of Hangzhou and Mingzhou. The responsibilities of this office included maintaining order in the harbor, examining and registering cargoes, registering Chinese sailors and traders, and supplying archers to protect ships coming into and going out of the harbor. Also foreign traders had to be registered and supervised.

China's general policy at that time was one of free trade, although importers did have to pay tariffs. It was also the case that the Seafaring Trade Office had first choice of the goods coming in and could, if it wanted to, purchase an entire cargo on behalf of the government. In addition, it was responsible for holding rituals that they believed would summon the best winds for sailing, at which time they also held banquets where the governor and head officials of the office entertained traders of all origins. And whenever there were shipwrecks, the office was obliged to send out rescue teams.

The officials in charge of the Seafaring Trade Office obviously had enough work to keep them busy, but they also could learn a great deal about other countries through their contacts with the traders and the cargoes passing through the ports. For example, Zhao Rukuo, a very learned scholar-official, was in charge of the office in the Fujian region, which included the harbor at Quanzhou, for four years beginning in 1224. Based on the knowledge that he gleaned while working there he wrote a book called *Zhufanzhi*, or *Records of Foreign Countries*, which includes much interesting information about the seafaring trade of his time. From this book and similar books by his contemporaries, one learns that Chinese junks from Quanzhou generally went first to Srivijaya, on the island of Sumatra, or to ports on Java (also in present-day Indonesia). From there the ships sailed westwards through the Strait of Malacca, still today the world's busiest sea passage. After entering the Indian Ocean, the ships sometimes stopped at ports on the Malay Peninsula or the Andaman Islands. By the eleventh century the final destination was Quilon, a port on India's southwestern coast. At Quilon, traders who were going further west had to unload their cargo and board "small ships," that is, the Arab dhows, since Chinese ships did not go any further west. Similarly, traders from the Muslim countries who arrived at Quilon in dhows, transferred to Chinese junks to go east.

Seafaring during the Song dynasty was still a very dangerous endeavor, even though by this time there were large numbers of sailors who knew how to navigate the routes and were familiar with the facilities at the various ports. They also had a new tool to guide them, the needle compass. The compass was a Chinese invention. As early as the Qin dynasty (221–207 BCE), Chinese had put to use the magnetic qualities of iron and, among other things, were using it to make an early form of compass (which had a rotating ladle rather than a needle). The earliest use of such a compass was probably for jade-hunting expeditions in the deserts of Central Asia. Thereafter, it was mainly used for geomancy (*fengshui*), a large body of lore that determines the most propitious siting of buildings such as houses and palaces, as well as tombs and graves. Among other things, in order to determine the best siting of a structure, a geomancer must rely on a compass to determine the four cardinal directions.

The earliest written record of Chinese sailors using a needle compass for navigation on the seas and oceans comes from the eleventh century. According to Zhu Yu, the son of the military governor of Canton's port, sailors usually navigated by observing the positions of the sun in the day-time and the stars at night, and relied on the compass only in bad weather. When exactly Chinese sailors began to rely on the compass at all times is unclear, but by the time of Zhao Rukuo, in the early thirteenth century, the sailors' use of the compass had changed. Sailors relied on the compass for navigation regardless of the weather, and it was obviously considered a necessary piece of equipment on seafaring ships. Indeed, all the ships on the South China Sea came to rely on the compass in order to find the car-dinal directions. According to Zhao, the sailors watched the compass day and night, "for the smallest negligence could cost them their lives."

During the Southern Song (1127–1279) most of the traffic going from India to China traveled on Chinese-made junks, but not all of the junks were owned by Chinese. Many foreign traders, Arabs, Persians, Jews, Southeast Asians, and Indians came to Quanzhou to trade. Many of them resided in China in order to manage their business there and some of them purchased Chinese-made ships. One Arab merchant family used the Chi-nese surname Pu. They had originally been based in Canton, but had moved from Canton to Quanzhou during the Song. This family owned several hundred Chinese-made ships and was engaged in trade with India and various Muslim countries. Pu family members made generous dona-tions to local public works projects such as building bridges to improve transportation, and some men in this family even gained official positions due to their contributions to these projects.

When the Mongols were in the process of conquering the Southern Song in the late thirteenth century, Pu Shougeng, the manager of the Pu family company at that time, took over the defense of Quanzhou city to protect it from both the remnant forces of the Song dynasty and the Mon-golian armies. He eventually decided to surrender to the Mongol Yuan dy-nasty, handing over all the family's ships and the city of Quanzhou. The new Mongolian emperor Kubilai was pleased with Pu's service to the new dynasty and granted him a position administering the port's overseas trade. The story of the Pu family is just one example of the many foreign traders who made their careers in Quanzhou or other parts of China.

Silk and porcelain were the two leading exports from Quanzhou. Im-ports coming into China at Quanzhou came from the north as well as the south. In Song times it was the major port for Korean goods. Carrying all kinds of silks, porcelain, clothing, turtle shells, tea, wine, medicines, musical instruments, and books to Korea, the ships brought back gold, silver, copper, furs, ginseng, pine nuts, musk, and many other products from the northern forests to Quanzhou. Although traders from Quanzhou rarely visited Japan, Japanese ships carried large quantities of timber to Quanzhou, according to Zhao Rukuo.

Most of the ships arriving at Quanzhou harbor came in from the south, either from Southeast Asia or places west of Southeast Asia. Their cargoes included tons of spices, medicinal herbs and resins, and various materials of both animal and botanical origin that were used to make incense and other fragrant products. The Chinese referred to all of these items, including the spices, as *xiangyao*, literally aromatics and medicines. In 1974, archaeologists found a sunken ship that dated to Song times in an old Quanzhou harbor that is now dry. The ship's cargo hold contained more than 4,700 catties or about 2,300 kilograms (5,060 pounds) of the remains of various spices, herbs, and aromatic woods and resins. Spices such as black pepper, which was originally from southern India, but by this time was also grown on the island of Sumatra, had been incorporated into Chinese cuisine and thus had a large market.

Some of the aromatic wood resins were used for making incense for worshipping Buddhist deities and other local gods, but most of the various products from animals and plants were medicines. Previously, during Tang times, many Muslim Iranians went to China, opened pharmacies, and introduced a combination of Arab, Greek, and Iranian medicine to the Chinese. In the early tenth century, an Iranian scholar with the Chinese name Li Xun compiled a Chinese language manual called *Medicinal Plants from Overseas (Haiyao Bencao)*. Thus, by Song times, many of the prescriptions from Iran, India, and the Hellenistic regions had been incorporated into Chinese pharmaceutical and medical practice, and there was therefore a large market for these goods. The traditional aromatic resins of frankincense and myrrh from Arabia had also become essential components of many important prescriptions, and the same was true of many tropical plants brought in by Muslim traders to Quanzhou. Song China, though shrinking periodically throughout its history, was an affluent society where many people could afford medicine. To feed this large market for medicines, junks carried many tons of herbs and tree resins to Quanzhou. And some of these ships followed the sea routes north to Korea to bring back the forest products of the north, including ginseng, which was yet another medicine.

In the end, the Song dynasty was conquered by yet another steppe invader. In the early part of the thirteenth century a Mongol confederacy led by Genghis Khan (literally Khan Within the Seas) took over northern China (which was then ruled by previous nomadic invaders) and much of Central Asia. In the meantime, other descendants of Genghis Khan were conquering much of Russia, and by 1258 the Mongols had invaded Iran and the last of the Abbasid caliphs had been assassinated. In the second part of the century Kubilai, a grandson of Genghis Khan, was declared Great Khan in 1260 while warring against the Southern Song dynasty. By 1279 he ruled over all of China. These Mongol conquests, which reached all the way from Korea to Eastern Europe, would deal a devastating blow to the overland silk roads. What this meant for the Eurasian silk trade is discussed in Chapter Seven.

FOR FURTHER READING

Constable, Olivia Remie. *Trade and Traders in Muslim Spain: The Commercial Realignment of the Iberian Peninsula, 900–1500*. Cambridge, England: Cambridge University Press, 1994.

Goitein, S. D. *A Mediterranean Society, the Jewish Communities of the Arab World as Portrayed in the Documents of the Cairo Geniza*. Berkeley: University of California Press, 1967.

Hall, Kenneth. *Maritime Trade and State Development in Early Southeast Asia*. Honolulu: University of Hawaii Press, 1985.

Hourani, George Fadlo. *Arab Seafaring in the Indian Ocean in Ancient and Early Medieval Times*, Expanded Edition. Princeton, N.J.: Princeton University Press, 1995.

Miskimin, Harry A., David Herlihy, and A. L. Udovitch, eds. *The Medieval City*. New Haven: Yale University Press, 1977.

Shaffer, Lynda Norene. *Maritime Southeast Asia to 1500*. Armonk, N.Y.: M. E. Sharpe, 1996.

Tate, Georges. *L'Orient des Croisades*. Paris: Gallimard, 1991.

Udovitch, Abraham L. *Partnership and Profit in Medieval Islam*. Princeton, N.J.: Princeton University Press, 1970.

Wink, Andrew. *Al-Hind, the Making of the Indo-Islamic World*. Leiden: E. J. Brill, 1991.

Wolters, O. W. *Early Indonesian Commerce: A Study of the Origins of Srivijaya*. Ithaca, N.Y.: Cornell University Press, 1967.

TIMELINE

The Mongol Conquest of Eurasia and a New Order of Trade

1206	Genghis Khan (b. 1162) is proclaimed ruler of all the Mongols. He established his capitol at Karakorum (in present-day Mongolia).
1218	Yelu Chucai (1190–1244), a scholar in the Chinese tradition, descended from an earlier Qidan royal family, accepted Genghis Khan's offer of a government position. He advised Genghis Khan on policies concerning Chinese agriculture, mining, and industries.
1222–1234	Mongolians take over northern China from previous rulers, including the Jurchen (from the northeast) and the Xi Xia (from Tibet).
1227	Death of Genghis Khan. After his death and further conquests there were four Khanates. Ogodei, based at Karakorum, ruled the eastern steppe and part of China. Chaghadai and his descendents ruled in Central Asia. Descendents of Jochi (known as the Golden Horde) ruled much of Russia, and Hulegu and his descendents ruled present-day Iran and Iraq, known as the Il-Khanate.
1227–1241	Ogodei rules as Great Khan. After being chosen as Great Khan, he moved his capital from Jungaria to Karakorum, his father's capital.
1237	Ogodei (joined by all his brothers) leads the confederacy in the conquest of additional parts of Russia, plus Poland, and Hungary. The campaign ends when Ogodei dies in 1241.
1246–1251	Guyug, a son of Ogodei, rules as Great Khan. His mother, Toregene, served as his regent when he was away campaigning.

1251	Mongke, a grandson of Genghis, becomes Great Khan. The choice of Mongke marks a departure from the line of Ogodei. His parents were Tolui (a son of Genghis) and Sorghaghtani Beki, a woman much admired for her political savvy.
1258	Helugo (a younger brother of Mongke) sacks Baghdad, bringing the final end to the Abbasid Caliphate. Helugo becomes the Il-Khan (the vice-khan) to Great Khan Mongke. Exchanges between the Il-Khanate and China grow rapidly thereafter.
1259	Great Khan Mongke dies.
1260	Kibilai, brother of Mongke, becomes Great Khan. He constructs a new capital at Dadu (in the Beijing area).
1268–1272	The Mongols besiege Xiangfan (in the Wuhan area), a Southern Song stronghold.
1271	Kibilai establishes paper currency in China, which succeeds.
1274	Kibilai's first invasion of Japan fails.
1275–1292	Marco Polo was in China with his father and uncle.
1281	Kibilai's second invasion of Japan fails.
1285	Bolad Aqa is sent to the Il-Khanate by Kibilai. He was a Chinese scholar of Mongolian heritage and a trusted advisor of Kibilai on political and administrative matters. He stayed in the Il-Khanate as an advisor. While there he became a close colleague of the Iranian scholar Rashid al-Din (1258–1318).
1292–1295	Marco Polo and party's sea voyage from China to the Persian Gulf.

1293	Kibilai's invasion of Java fails.
1294	The Il-Khanate establishes paper currency, which fails.
1294	Death of Kibilai Khan.
1333–1345	Ibn Battuta (ca. 1304–1378) was in India, Sri Lanka, and the Maldive Islands during these years. He was a Moroccan who traveled throughout much of the Eastern Hemisphere. His description of his journeys are an important source in this chapter and in world history generally.

Mediterranean Developments

1200s	Italians begin using paper and calculating with Arabic numerals. Growing use of the compass on the Mediterranean.
ca. 1250	A list of the position of ports on the Mediterranean is completed.
ca. 1270	The portolan chart, essentially a map of Mediterranean ports, is completed.
By 1300	The compass, complete with a card showing the degrees, is mounted on the ship in a straight line with the keel, such that the needle indicates the direction the ship is headed.
1300s	Mediterranean ships no longer sit out the winters in ports. Ships begin to make two trips a year instead of one. Double-entry bookkeeping develops in Italy. The compass is used on Western Europe's Atlantic shores.
1420	Prince Henry of Portugal begins to send out ships to map the western coast of Africa.
1487	The Portuguese sailor Bartolomeu Dias sets out on a voyage that ends up rounding the Cape of Good Hope (which he called the Cape of Storms), sailing out onto the waters of the Southern Ocean.

THE MONGOL CONQUESTS AND A NEW ORDER OF TRADE

> **GETTING STARTED ON CHAPTER SEVEN:** How did the Mongol conquests of the thirteenth century change the overland and maritime trade routes? How did the Mongols govern the immense territories that they conquered? What Mongol practices led to numerous cultural exchanges? What was Mongol Tent Culture and how did it spread throughout their empire and even further afield? What was the nature of the relationship between the Mongols and Western European traders and missionaries?

CHAPTER OUTLINE

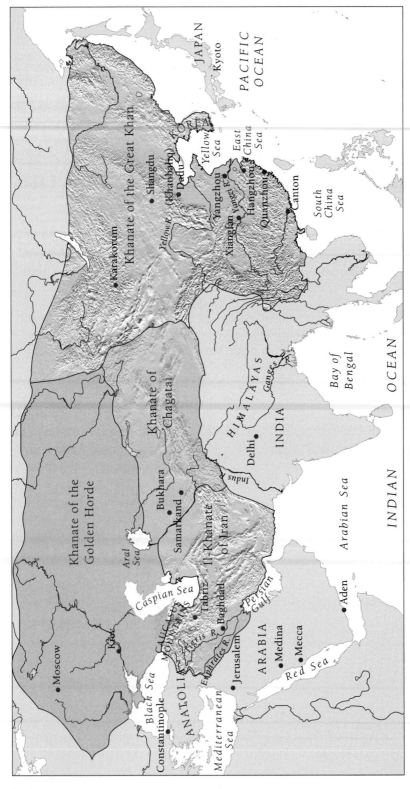

ILLUSTRATION 7-1 **THE MONGOL EMPIRE ABOUT 1300 CE** (*Source: Used with permission from Traditions and Encounters (2nd ed.), by Jerry H. Bentley and Herbert F. Ziegler. Copyright 2003 by McGraw-Hill.*)

In the thirteenth century yet another confederation of steppe warriors emerged on the Eurasian grasslands. Under Genghis Khan and his successors this Mongol confederation would bring about unprecedented devastation to peoples and places all across the Eurasian landmass, from Korea in the east to Eastern Europe in the west. Their conquests destroyed major cities and trading stations all along the overland silk roads. If one were to use the traditional definition of the silk roads, meaning the venerable overland routes along with their infrastructure, one could say that the silk roads were almost completely destroyed by the Mongols. In the aftermath of the Mongol conquests, overland routes shifted to the north onto the steppe. Also, the Mongols were different from earlier steppe conquerors who had formed short-lived imperial confederacies, migrating westwards from the Mongolian steppe or southwards to settle in the agricultural societies. The Mongols, in contrast, intended to build a lasting state structure on the steppe within their own eastern homeland, before setting out to conquer the world.

Even though Genghis Khan, the founder of the confederacy, had been raised on the steppe, he understood what was needed to build a longer-lasting political structure. Although he was illiterate, he enlisted experts to provide the Mongolian language with a written script for the first time. This was done using the Turkic Uighur script. He enacted a code of law and established a standing army. Furthermore, in the process of conquest, he and his successors searched for people with special skills and knowledge, be they merchants, astronomers, weavers, or copper smiths, to serve at the headquarters of Mongol power on the steppe. Even during the most brutal massacres of conquered city residents, the Mongol leaders selected out those with desirable skills, before putting everyone else to the sword. For a century or so, the rulers of the unified Mongol Empire, and then the khanates that succeeded it, distributed these highly skilled and knowledgeable people over a large part of the Eurasian continent, usually in places far distant from their homelands.

Perhaps most remarkable is that these steppe rulers also acquired a formidable navy. Their effort to conquer China, especially the more southern lands still held by the Song in the thirteenth century, spanned nearly half a century. In the process the Mongols learned the value of seafaring after literally chasing the last emperor of the Southern Song to the sea. They commandeered the navies of China and Korea, and launched overseas expeditions against both Japan and Java, neither of which succeeded. By conquering the Southern Song they also had inherited the seafaring networks of the southern oceans. Fortunately they did not attempt to destroy these maritime networks. Instead, they enlarged them, by delivering increased quantities of the northern products of the steppe and the Taiga Forest southward to the sea routes.

Genghis Khan, began a process of fragmentation within the empire when he let his brother and his sons rule over regions of their own. The empire later became four independent khanates, ruled over by four khans, one of whom was designated Great Khan. However, it was not long before they were warring with each other. Furthermore, a grandson of Genghis, the Great Khan Kibilai, near the end of his conquest of southern China de- clared himself the Emperor of China in 1271. No longer following the po- litical customs of the steppe, he set up a Chinese-style dynasty, which he named the Yuan dynasty. Thereafter, the Great Khan Kibilai and his suc- cessors on the Chinese throne maintained a close relationship with only one of the other four khanates, the Il-Khanate that ruled Iran.

THE MONGOLS AND TRADE

In order to conquer the world as he knew it Genghis Khan created some of the tools of empire—an army, a law code, and a writing system. However, some tools of empire were missing from the Mongol state. Under Genghis there were no bureaucratic hierarchies to centrally control and administer the ever-expanding territory. The relationship between the charismatic khan and his followers was still very much in the style of the steppe. The khan distributed booty from the battles—silk, gold, silver, and other sorts of treasure, including prisoner-slaves and territory—to his kinsmen and loyal subordinate chiefs. This political structure did make the Mongol army of Genghis Khan invincible. However, once the chiefs settled in their territories, they adopted local administrative systems, and thereafter cen- tral control further disintegrated.

Furthermore, the military chiefs had pledged allegiance only to the khan personally, not to any confederacy in general, and the Mongol polity never established any strict rules regarding the inheritance of power. In the major agricultural empires, succession usually followed the principle of primogeniture, according to which the first son of the ruler was the heir apparent, the one expected to inherit the throne. In the Mongol polity, however, a new khan was not chosen until after the previous ruler had died. After the death of a Great Khan, the Mongol nobles would gather at a conference called a *quriltai*, where usually one of his male descendants was chosen as successor. Frequently the strong-minded princes who did not agree with the decision of the *quriltai* would wage a civil war against the one who was chosen, or simply desert the confederacy, seeking autonomy in their own territories.

When Genghis Khan died in 1227, the Mongol Empire's conquests were still ongoing. Some fifty years later, once the conquests had ended, his successors divided the empire into four major khanates, which in many ways were four separate and independent states. In the absence of central imperial control, there was never a unified policy among them with regard to trade and communications on the road networks, lodging for travelers, or financial institutions. Even though Mongolian became a written language, it never became an imperial language of the sort that would facilitate communications throughout their immense territories, which is to say that it never became a *lingua Franca*. And even though the Mongols remained true to their own traditional religion, and it remained vital in their own homeland, their beliefs never became the state religion in any of the conquered territories.

Trade, however, did flourish on various parts of the steppe, in large part due to the conquerors' desire to create impressive capitals on the grasslands, a goal that did lead to extraordinary exchanges. Their efforts to create capitals grander and more luxurious than those of the conquered sedentary empires led to the forced migration of a wide variety of skilled artisans and learned scholars from their homelands to various parts of the steppe. Once the four khanates had become settled in their domains, their ritual exchanges and military rivalries stimulated further competition in the display of material grandeur and illustrious courts. Also, the special relationship between the Yuan dynasty of China, where the Great Khan was enthroned, and the Il-Khan in Iran created many exchanges of material items as well as ideas between the two ancient civilizations. It also contributed to the growth and development of the Southern Ocean trade routes. Ironically, even among the horseback-riding Mongols, the sea routes became the preferred means of traveling between the two areas.

While his armies were still in the process of conquering, Genghis Khan assigned the newly acquired lands, called *yurts*, to his brothers and sons. The literal meaning of *yurt* is the felt tent of the Mongols, but the word was also used to refer to the home territory of a chief. During Genghis Khan's lifetime, the two major sedentary areas nearest to the Mongol heartland, China and the combination of what is now Iran and Iraq, had not yet been conquered. The Turkish Seljuk sultanate ruled what was still nominally the Abbasid caliphate, and China was divided between the Jin dynasty in the north and the Southern Song in the south. Genghis gave small territories on China's northern frontier to his brother and several grandsons. His eldest son Jochi received Khwarizm, located south of the Aral Sea in present-day Uzbekistan, along with the Qipchaq Steppe in southern Russia, which was yet to be conquered. Thus, Jochi's descendants later became the khans of the Golden Horde. His second son, Chaghadai, received much of Central Asia, and his successors remained there and enlarged that territory. Genghis Khan's third son, Ogodei, obtained the area of Jungaria in the northern part of present-day China's Xinjiang Uighur Autonomous Region. The youngest son, Tolui, received a piece of territory on the Mongolian steppe.

After the death of Genghis Khan, the *quriltai* met in 1229 and chose Ogodei, his third son, as the next Great Khan. Ogodei then moved his headquarters from Jungaria to Karakorum, his father's capital in present-day Mongolia. The khanates of the Golden Horde and Chaghadai also established their boundaries at this time. Although territorial conquests continued, tensions among the Mongol princes increased. Nevertheless, beginning in 1237, all four lines of Genghis Khan's descendants joined in the expeditions against Russia, Poland, and Hungary. It was only the death of Ogodei in 1241 that saved the rest of Europe from invasion and conquest.

Due to the Great Khan's death, the commanders and other nobles all returned to Mongolia in order to hold the *quriltai* during which they would choose the next Great Khan. In 1246, Guyug, the son of Ogodei, was elected as the Great Khan, but his reign proved to be short. Soon after Guyug assumed the title, civil wars broke out and within six years Guyug was dead. More importantly, the *quriltai* did not choose his son as the successor. Instead the position went to the previously obscure line of Tolui, Genghis Khan's youngest son.

Some of the most important participants in the struggles that determined the succession were not among the warriors, but among the women, especially the mothers of the candidates. One of Ogodei's wives, Toregene, was an ambitious woman accused of manipulating the previous election on behalf of her son Guyug. Ogodei had wanted the succession to go to one of his grandsons (whose grandmother was another one of his wives), but Toregene got her way in that succession dispute. Once Guyug became Great Khan, she acted as his regent whenever he was away on military expeditions. In particular, her tax-collecting methods angered many of the Mongols' subjects in sedentary lands, especially those on China's northern frontier. Evidently, she ran his khanate using foreign Muslim tax collectors, whose methods turned out to be unpopular.

Meanwhile, Sorghaghtani Beki, the Nestorian Christian widow of Genghis's youngest son Tolui, gave all four of her sons a good education and useful training. Furthermore, when administering her sons' territories on China's northern frontier, she collected taxes by more regular means. In large part due to her political vision and savvy, all four of her sons became significant leaders in the Mongol Empire. However, this did not come about without a struggle. Guyug had attempted to annihilate the other lines of descent from Genghis Khan, so Sorghaghtani Beki had allied with Batu, the son of Jochi (the founder of the westernmost khanate later known as the Golden Horde) and they prevailed. After Guyug was killed in a civil war amongst the Mongols in 1251, it was Sorghaghtani Beki's eldest, Mongke, who was chosen as Great Khan.

In 1256, Mongke sent his younger brother, Hulegu, westward to conquer the heartland of the Muslim regions. In 1258 Hulegu sacked Baghdad and brought a final end to the Abbasid caliphate. He established a khanate that ruled over present-day Iran and Iraq, and he himself was known as the Il-Khan, which literally means subordinate khan, or vice-khan. He accepted this title in order to acknowledge his older brother Mongke, the Great Khan, as his superior. Meanwhile, in China Mongke was in the process of conquering the Southern Song dynasty. The Chinese people in this rich land put up a long-lasting resistance to the Mongol conquest, making good use of its numerous deep rivers and marshlands, as well as an effective naval force.

Mongolian cavalries lost much of their fighting capacity in this environment of intricate river systems and rice paddies, since no horse can gallop across an irrigated rice field or easily ford a river. On this front, Kibilai, another brother of Mongke, was the main commander. In 1259, while campaigning in southwestern China, the Great Khan Mongke died, either from cholera or dysentery, or from an arrow wound. Civil wars over the succession broke out again, and in 1260, at a hastily convened *quriltai* Kibilai, yet another son of Tolui and Sorghaghtani Beki, successfully assumed the title of Great Khan. Sorghaghtani Beki lived long enough to see sons Mongke as Great Khan and Hulegu as Il-Khan, but died in 1252, before the rise of Kibilai to the position of Great Khan. Kibilai Khan, after defeating a challenge from his younger brother Ariq Boke, resumed the conquest of the Southern Song. Even before this campaign was successfully finished, in 1267 he began building a new capital, Dadu, where Beijing now stands. Then, in 1271, he declared himself the emperor of a new Chinese-style dynasty, the Yuan.

By the time that the Great Khan of the Mongols transformed himself into the first emperor of the Yuan dynasty, a dynasty that lasted about 90 years, there was no longer a single Mongol Empire stretching from East Asia to Europe. Warfare among the Mongol khanates continued, and it was only the Il-Khanate that maintained a symbolic subordinate status to the Great Khan in China. For many decades the Il-Khanate and the Yuan dynasty maintained friendly relations and engaged in frequent exchanges of personnel and goods. Prior to the Mongols' consolidation of power in these two major sedentary lands, both of which were carried out by sons of Tolui and Sorghaghtani Beki, trade and communications amongst them had been reduced for the most part to the involuntary movement of artisans and scholars and what were essentially private trading partnerships between Mongol nobles and merchants. However, once the line of Tolui had consolidated power in Iran and China, official exchanges between the Yuan dynasty and the Il-Khanate became quite significant.

When Genghis Khan had built his capital at Khara Khorum, a site far out on the Mongolian steppe, its construction had required the engagement of many workers and merchants. The place was distant from sources of construction materials, most sources of food other than animal products, and even from trade routes. Every day 500 cartloads of goods reached the isolated city on the vast steppe, just to supply the luxurious palace life of the Great Khan and his large retinue, plus the army. Thousands of artisans were brought in to work on various projects, including the structures that held up the huge tent palaces. Numerous weavers made textiles for both clothing and tents. And merchants thronged there, where they were paid handsomely in gold and silver for their wares. Under Kibilai Khan, the construction of Dadu, on the site of present-day Beijing, was an even grander project. Most of the artisans and materials were available from nearby locations in northern China, but some of the planners, architects, and engineers came from Muslim countries. Nevertheless, the architecture and the decorations still carried a strong flavor of the steppe's tent culture.

In spite of the civil wars among the princes, Genghis Khan's kinsmen and their followers did spread out to all the various imperial territories, and the inspection of properties and the collection of dues did require various agents from the center to make frequent trips to far-off locations. However, after a short initial period of conquest, even the soldiers on the battlefields were not all Mongols. At the siege of Xiangfan (1268–1272), a Chinese city near present-day Wuhan where the Han River joins the Yangzi, Kibilai Khan mobilized an international army composed of Mongols, Chinese, and Uighur Turks. Jurchen (a people from China's northeast) and Korean artisans helped by building ships for a navy that could cut the Song's riverine supply lines and attack the city from the river. Even so, the Xiangfan garrison did not surrender. Kibilai also asked for help from his nephew, the Il-Khan, requesting Muslim engineers who could build mangonels (weapons that threw missiles) and catapults, which could throw huge rocks or other objects at the city's defenders. It was only after two Muslim military engineers arrived in 1272 and organized this medieval artillery force that this siege of 5 years' duration finally came to an end and the resistance of the Southern Song forces collapsed.

While pursuing the fleeing Southern Song emperor, the Yuan army reached the region of Quanzhou, the famous port city. The head of the Muslim traders in Quanzhou, Pu Shougeng, who was of Arab heritage, decided to throw his lot in with the Yuan dynasty. He killed several thousand members of the Song royal family and surrendered all the Song ships to the Mongols. Thus, overnight the Yuan government became a strong naval power. Kibilai Khan took full advantage of the trading skills and the oversea connections of the Pu family and their associates, sending them as ambassadors to Southeast Asian countries and coastal regions of the Indian Ocean.

Thus, one could say that the Mongol rulers, while pursuing their political, military, and material interests, also inadvertently distributed talents and skills to a vast area of Eurasia. Also, since the early centers of Mongol power and prestige remained on the steppe, land routes across the steppe became major routes of exchange and commerce. The Mongol conquests of the sedentary lands eventually led them to sea routes, and from the late thirteenth century to the end of most Mongol polities in the fourteenth century, the sea routes through the southern oceans became the preferred routes for communications and trade between China's Yuan dynasty and the Il-Khanate. Frequent hostilities among the khans of the Golden Horde in Russia, the Chaghadais in Central Asia and the Il-Khanate made the Central Asian land routes unsafe, even for official travelers with Mongol credentials. Even though Kibilai Khan's new naval force failed in its attempts at overseas conquest, both in Japan and Java, the Yuan dynasty did inherit a strong commercial position on the southern seafaring networks, and these networks remained a major source of wealth for the government and traders.

CROSS-CULTURAL COMMUNICATIONS AND TRADE SPONSORED BY MONGOL RULERS

Trade and communications under the Mongol rulers flourished in many areas, not only because of their control over such a vast amount of territory, but also because of their inclination to disperse people and goods to locations throughout their domains. In his later years Genghis Khan did start a relay postal system, similar to a pony express, to assure rapid delivery of military messages over long distances, and the facilities that it created were heavily used by commercial travelers. However, when the Mongol princes were at war with each other, these facilities became unusable. The Mongols under Kibilai Khan also created a central banking system and a paper currency, backed by silver. The paper currency was first issued in 1271, the same year that Kibilai became emperor of the newly minted Yuan dynasty. This was the first use of paper currency in the world, but it succeeded only in China. When the paper currency was introduced in the Il-Khanate, it proved to be a disaster.

Thus, in the early period, the most significant factors contributing to communications and trade were the employment of foreign nationals and the desire to build the most splendid capitals and headquarters. Genghis Khan and his successors obviously succeeded in finding talented people among those they had conquered and they put them to good use, either in the places they had just conquered or in those they were planning to conquer. They also succeeded in attracting merchants of various origins to deliver the luxuries as well as the necessities to their headquarters and to the newly constructed capitals on the steppe and in the conquered lands.

Because the Mongols hired so many people of different nationalities and religions, some writers have admired them for their religious tolerance. Although they do seem to have been genuinely curious about the various religions that they encountered, it should be pointed out that, for the Mongols, religious tolerance was not a principled goal in and of itself, but the result of purely practical and pragmatic considerations. In short, Genghis Khan had the genius to select and use the expertise of the conquered peoples in order to rule a culturally diverse empire. One of his most important advisors was Yelü Chucai, a man whose ethnicity was Mongolian, even though he was not from the steppe. For about two centuries his ancestors had been residents of the city of Yanjing in the vicinity of present-day Beijing, which prior to the Mongol conquest of the city had been the capital of the Jurchen's Jin dynasty. The reason for the family's residence in Yanjing was that they were descendants of the Qidan royal family, which had ruled the city before the Jin, during the Qidan Liao dynasty. Although the Qidan dynasty was Mongolian in origin, its members had no connections to Genghis Khan or his confederacy. Even more remarkable, Yelü Chucai, a devout Buddhist, was a well-known and highly respected scholar of Chinese language and literature. In 1218, when Genghis Khan was preparing for a campaign to the west, he summoned Yelü Chucai to his camp on the steppe. This erudite man answered the summons, followed Genghis to the west, and became one of his most valued advisors on political and administrative matters.

Before coming back to his Mongol homeland, Genghis Khan in 1223 also summoned to his camp in the west a famous Chinese Daoist teacher Qiu Chuji, who had the religious title of Changchun, meaning "Everlasting Spring." Genghis apparently showed great interest in both religions since Yelü Chucai and Qiu Chuji were both happy with their new patron. Nevertheless, neither one of them succeeded in converting Genghis Khan, and their religious conversations with each other seem to have driven them further apart, not closer together. After following Genghis back to the east, Yelü Chucai returned to the Yanjing area for business in 1227. Answering one of his old friends' inquiries about the Western Regions, from which he had just returned, he wrote a book called *Xiyou Lu* (*A Journey to the Western Regions*). However, the main thrust of this book is not a description of his travels, but an attack on the behavior and the teachings of Qiu Chuji in the camp of the Mongol ruler. The various intellectuals who followed the khans, regardless of their backgrounds, all served Mongol power to the best of their abilities, even though their hometowns such as Yanjing had been sacked and their fellow citizens slaughtered by the Mongol army during the conquests. Thus, due to this policy of religious tolerance, the Mongol khans received the gratitude and devotion of intellectuals from the conquered lands.

Yelü Chucai's most influential and numerous opponents in the Mongol court were the Muslim ministers from Central Asia and Iran. Their loyalty to the Mongol Khan is also surprising when one considers how much damage he had inflicted on their homelands. The Iranian scholar Juvaini who wrote a biography of Genghis Khan in Karakorum around 1252 or 1253, noted that Genghis Khan thought it was sufficient to slaughter and loot in the Central Asian caravan cities of Bukhara and Samarkand only once, but in other areas his armies repeatedly attacked the towns and villages.

> It is otherwise with Khorasan and Iraq, which countries are afflicted with a hectic fever and chronic ague: every town and every village has been several times subjected to pillage and massacre and has suffered this confusion for years. So that even though there be generation and increase until the Resurrection the population will not attain to a tenth part of what it was before. The history thereof may be ascertained from the records of ruins and midden-heaps declaring how Fate has painted her deeds upon palace walls. (Ata-Malik Juvaini, *Genghis Khan, the History of the World Conqueror*, J. A. Boyle trans., Seattle, University of Washington Press, 1997, pp. 96–97)

This is a description of Juvaini's own homeland. Yet the historian calmly ascribed this calamity to Fate, and appears to have served the Mongol regime contentedly.

News of Genghis Khan's interest in other peoples' religions spread even as far as Europe, which was still preoccupied with the crusades. In particular Christian missionaries were attracted by rumors of a legendary sage king, Prester John, who supposedly ruled over a Christian kingdom somewhere in the east. Rumors of his existence had begun circulating in the twelfth century, but as it turned out no one ever found such a person, or if they did, they did not recognize him. The most successful Christians in Asia were the Nestorians, whose church was based in Syria. Much earlier there had been Nestorian communities in central and eastern Asia, but in China they had been closed down in the ninth century by the Tang government.

Under the Mongols, especially among the Mongol nobles, Nestorian Christianity enjoyed a rapid revival, and subsequently its believers prospered yet again in China generally. The papacy and the Frankish kings also sent missionaries to the east. John of Plano Carpini, an emissary from the pope, arrived at Khara Khorum in 1245 or 1246, and was probably present at the ceremony of the accession of Guyug to the position of Great Khan. Another missionary, William of Rubruck, arrived at Khara Khorum about 1254. Although none of the missions from Western Europe was successful in converting the khans to Christianity, the idea of converting Asian peoples continued to motivate Europeans to travel to the Mongol-controlled lands, be they adventurers, clerics, or merchants like the Polos from Venice.

After the dust of conquest settled somewhat, the Great Khan Kibilai and the Il-Khan began exchanging more staff members between them. Bolad Aqa served the Yuan court of Kibilai in several crucial positions. Like Yelü Chucai, he was of Mongolian ethnicity, but not from the steppe. His education and experience in administration had made him familiar with many aspects of sedentary societies. As director of the emperor's household management office, he had close personal contact with the emperor. He also assisted in the establishment of the Office of State Ceremony, which controlled the ruling ideology of China, served in the Censorate, the office that investigated the conduct of governmental officials, and was appointed Director for Agricultural Affairs in 1271, the year Kibilai declared himself emperor of the Yuan dynasty.

Subsequently Kibilai assigned Bolad Aqa another important task. He sent him to the court of the Il-Khan Arghun, accompanied by one of his interpreters, Isa, a native of Syria. The two arrived in Iran in 1285 in order to confer Kibilai's blessing on Arghun's accession to the position of Il-Khan. On their way back to China, they encountered a rebellion and became separated. Isa managed to get back to the Mongol capital Dadu, but Bolad Aqa stayed on in the Il-Khanate, serving as an advisor to the Il-Khan. While serving in the Il-Khan's court Bolad Aqa made significant contributions to the scholarly works of Rashid al-Din (1248–1318), one of the most important and remarkable of the Il-Khanate's *vizirs*, or prime ministers.

Rashid al-Din's father was a Jewish apothecary who specialized in a variety of medicines and herbs. The *son* was a physician who converted to Islam and served in the court of the Il-Khanate during the 1290s. His relationship to the Il-Khan Ghazan (r. 1295–1306) was similar to that of Yelü Chucai's to Genghis Khan in the east. He tried to persuade the Mongol ruler to regularize the tax system and protect farmers from indiscriminate looting. Rashid al-Din also established an academic institute in a suburb of Tabriz, the capital of the Il-Khanate. Among its many parts was a House of Healing, which included both a hospital and a training center for physicians.

Among the many books that he wrote were several on medicine and agriculture that demonstrate a deep knowledge of Chinese studies and practice in these fields. Given that he was a close friend and colleague of Bolad Aqa, the content of these books strongly suggests that the two were intellectual collaborators. Furthermore, given that there is an extant Persian translation of a Chinese medical book with a long introduction by Rashid al-Din, it seems that he also sponsored the translation of Chinese medical books into Persian. In addition *Rashid al-Din* was an important historian, most famous for his *Collection of Histories*. In 1974 Marshall Hodgeson, an American historian whose publications contributed much to current conceptions of world history in the United States, characterized this tome as the first book that has some claim to be called world history. He also commended it for its accuracy and fairness, as well as its coverage, from Western Europe to East Asia.

Mongol rulers in all the khanates thus took advantage of the knowledge and skills of people from the conquered lands. Yet they did not really treat those scholars as their own. Even a renowned scholar like Rashid al-Din was executed, at the age of seventy, because of a false accusation made against him. In addition, his hometown was plundered, and a large portion of his scholarly and literary work was lost to humanity. In the minds of the Mongol rulers, intellectuals from the sedentary societies were too shrewd to be trustworthy.

In China, Kibilai Khan explicitly divided the population into four categories. The supreme status of Mongol, rich or poor, noble or commoner, could not be challenged by anyone, and Mongols were the top-ranking commanders and the directors at all levels of government. Second in the hierarchy were the foreigners, who came from a wide variety of backgrounds. The rulers deliberately imported foreign talent to carry out the ordinary business of government. Muslim tax collectors, for example, were the most hated people in their administration, but from the point of view of the Mongol government, they were among its most useful staff members. One step below the foreigners were the peoples from the north of China, including Chinese, Qidan Mongolians of the Liao Dynasty, and Jurchens of the Jin dynasty. The latter two were peoples who had ruled over parts of northern China before they were conquered by the Mongols. They had been conquered by the Mongols prior to the conquest of southern China, and had then helped the Mongols conquer the Southern Song. The southern Chinese were left with the lowest status within Yuan China.

In the records of the Il-Khanate, there is no such artificial hierarchy. Its absence there may have been due to the extent of depopulation in the lands of the Il-Khanate, where many people were slaughtered and many migrated to other lands such as China. As in China, foreigners in the Il Khanate, including the Chinese who lived there, did have a relatively high status. Chinese physicians, in particular, were much in demand, especially among the Mongol elite.

Migrations of physicians and pharmacists, both in and out of the various khanates, created more demand on the long-distance trade routes for medicinal herbs and minerals. Tea was introduced into the Muslim heartlands as a kind of medicine. Rashid al-Din gives a lengthy description of its medical benefits, and Kibilai Khan began efforts to increase its production in China. This introduction of tea into Iran and Iraq as a rare commodity during the Mongol period eventually led to its becoming a common beverage in Muslim regions at a later time. By this time rice cultivation had also spread to Iran, and in particular Ghazan Khan promoted its cultivation, most likely with the advice of his Mongolian-Chinese ambassador Bolad Aqa. Since the most productive varieties of rice plants require a great deal of water, the plant was not well suited to growing conditions in the Il-Khanate. Nevertheless, it did become a part of the gourmet cuisine of these Muslim lands.

Though the Mongol rulers were always suspicious of the scholars who worked for them, they had no such reservations about merchants, to whom they were generous patrons. From the early days when the Mongol conquerors still lived in camps on the steppe, they depended upon merchants to deliver both luxuries and staples. After they occupied increasing amounts of territory within the sedentary societies, they relied on merchants who had knowledge of the local languages and accounting skills to collect taxes from the conquered peoples. The partnership between Mongol rulers and merchants was an important one from the very beginning of the empire until its demise.

Genghis Khan appreciated the skills and courage of traders who risked their lives for profits, especially the *ortoq* traders. *Ortoq* was the title for those traders who formed a special partnership with the Mongol rulers. It was similar to the *commenda*-style partnerships in the Islamic world. The Mongol nobles, men and women, entrusted the *ortoqs* with gold and silver ingots, gotten as part of their booty, and the *ortoq* traders then used the bullion to purchase and sell other goods. The two parties shared the profits from the trade. If the *ortoqs* lost the principal, due to circumstances beyond their control, they were not required to pay it back, and only lost their time and labor. Genghis Khan understood the risks the traders took and the dangers they faced, especially when transporting goods, and he appreciated how much knowledge was required in their business. According to Rashid al-Din, he once made the following comments on the subject.

> Just as the *ortoqs*, who come with garments of gold brocade expecting to make a profit, become very knowledgeable about these goods and wares, so ought the military commanders train their sons to shoot arrows, ride and wrestle well, and so instill in them these arts of war [so] that they will become as daring and brave as the *ortoqs* are vigorous and knowledgeable [in the pursuit] of their own line of work. (Thomas Allsen, "Mongolian Princes and Their Merchant Partners, 1200–1260," *Asia Major*, 3rd series, vol. II, part 2, p. 125)

That Genghis would use the example of the *ortoqs* to encourage Mongol princes to train their sons in the skills of war indicates the unusual esteem that he held for the merchants and how much confidence he was willing to place in them. The Mongols indeed relied on the merchants for supplying many essential goods and for the profits from their commercial investments, and therefore, after the conquests, he did everything possible to protect the trade routes and facilitate the merchants' travels.

In fact, the very incident that ignited the first westward march of the Mongol army involved caravan traders who had commercial ties with Genghis and his camp. In 1218 the caravan, made up of Muslim traders, was carrying large amounts of gold, silver, silk, precious furs, and elegant wares from China. These items were both booty from the just-finished campaigns in northern China and various indigenous products of northern Asia. The caravan was on its way to trade in Khwarizm, a great trading center then ruled by the Seljuk Turks. It was located south of the Aral Sea, on the lower reaches of the Amu River. The Mongol authorities had previously made a treaty with the shah of Khwarizm, guaranteeing the safety of such caravans. However, the governor of Utrar, a garrison town on Khwarizm's border, decided to treat the merchants as spies and had them killed. Though enraged by this provocation, Genghis was still patient enough in this case to send another envoy to demand punishment of the offending governor in order to settle the case. The shah of Khwarizm rebuked the offer and executed the envoy, thus making war inevitable.

To protect the traders and their goods, the Mongol authorities enacted a law that made the residents of any locale where a robbery occurred, people who were often peasants or herders, responsible for any losses that the merchants suffered. It also required the community to compensate the merchants for their losses. This policy surely burdened ordinary people who were not involved in either trade or robbery. The same Muslim traders were often tax collectors in agricultural areas. If peasants could not pay all of their tax on time, the traders lent them the money and then collected high interest rates on these loans, in spite of the Islamic doctrine against usury. This practice made the Muslim traders the most hated persons in agricultural regions such as China, but endeared them to the Mongol rulers as their most useful revenue collectors.

The merchants and the *ortoq* partnerships followed the path of Mongol expansion and they could be found in all the khanates. In the early years when Karakorum was the capital, merchants came carrying textiles from Iran and China and furs from Siberia for the Mongols' tents and clothing. Although the Mongols themselves produced *kumis*, a drink made from fermented mares' milk, there was also a strong demand for grape wine and mead, a drink made from fermented honey. Since grape wine was a rare commodity on the eastern steppe, the Mongols not only enjoyed it, but also associated its presence with their conquests of other lands, and thus its possession was for them a mark of high status. When a large amount of booty came in, such as after the sack of Baghdad or Kiev, the process of distributing it became quite complicated. Traders then flooded in with their trade goods, searching out the princes who had been on the receiving end of the gold, silver, and other valuables. Muslim traders were the most numerous, but traders from Constantinople and the western part of Europe also came.

After the Mongols had become settled in their khanates, the *ortoq* partnership prevailed throughout the Mongol-held regions, including the Mongol heartland, China, Central Asia, the Il-Khanate, and the region of the Golden Horde (the central and western parts of Russia). After the Mongols conquered southern China and became involved in the maritime trade on the Southern Ocean, the Yuan government provided the Muslim traders in the southeastern ports with investment capital and ships for their journeys to Southeast Asia and the shores of the Indian Ocean. The Yuan dynasty's share of the profits made from this capital was quite generous, given that the split was 70 percent for the Yuan government and 30 percent for the traders.

The patterns of trade on the South China Sea and the Indian Ocean were not disrupted, but reinforced by Mongol rule in China. In 1292 on his way home to Italy, Marco Polo's party took the sea route. In his account of the journey Polo says that he was also escorting a Mongol princess from the Yuan court to the court of the Il-Khanate in Tabriz on this voyage. (The official history of the dynasty says that the princess was sent to Tabriz at this time in order to marry into the family of the Il-Khan, but it does not mention who accompanied her on the journey.) According to Marco Polo, there were a few hundred people on the ship, including the three Polos, the princess, and three envoys from the Il-Khan Arghun to the Yuan court who were returning home. It took them two years to make their way from China, via Java and the Indian Ocean, to Iran. It was not an easy journey and many people died in route. Nevertheless Marco Polo was later able to describe the voyage and the ports of the various regions in great detail.

In many ways Polo's account of the journey and the trade, when compared to earlier accounts, indicates that not much had changed and that such journeys were still dangerous. Several decades later the Moroccan traveler Ibn Battuta (ca. 1304–1378) made his way from Morocco to the Muslim holy lands, India, and China and his description of conditions at sea also indicates that trade went on much as it had before the Mongol conquests. Nevertheless, there were some differences. One thing that was obvious was that the quantity of goods and the numbers and sizes of ships were even greater than they had been. There were also more fundamental differences, both on land and sea. The differences were in the commodities and the cultures embodied in those commodities.

TENT CULTURES AND TEXTILES

In the wake of the Mongol conquests across a wide swath of Eurasia, there came another wave of nomadic culture, settling over and transforming sedentary life. As the tent culture of the nomads, with its carpets, draperies, and various upholstered items, began to appear in the palaces and houses of the sedentary lands, textiles became an even greater component of wealth in all societies. This trend actually began during the time of the Muslim expansion from the seventh to the tenth century. Many Arabs were part of a tent culture, in particular, the Bedouin camel herders as well as the caravan traders who were based in the cities of the Arabian Peninsula but lived in tents when they were transporting goods across the deserts.

The importance of textiles on the peninsula is obvious when one considers the significance that the caliphates placed upon precisely who supplied the exquisite silk textile cover for the Kaaba, the sacred structure covering the black stone in Mecca. Also the Islamic practice of praying five times a day while facing towards Mecca created a demand for prayer rugs, since almost all Muslims used one. Nevertheless, the textile industry was just beginning to take off during the early days of Islam. The caliphates and sultanates had organized and encouraged textile manufacturing, especially the production of silk, by establishing the *tiraz* system, which ensured that there were "brand names" on textiles, indicating precisely where and when they had been made within the various domains of the Islamic world. By the eleventh and twelfth centuries, textile production in Eurasia, not only within the Muslim lands, but also in the regions surrounding them—in East Asia, South Asia, and Europe—increased to the extent that they were producing more than was required simply to clothe the general population. Although the military conquests of the Mongols did much damage and destruction to textile workshops in a great many places, the knowledge and skills of the producers survived and textile production revived not long after the conquests. In fact, it developed even further, stimulated by a new demand and the spread of a new textile culture.

Nomads on the steppe had always been proud of their tents, and the great tents of the chiefs represented the highest material culture on the steppe. Unfortunately there is little information on the tent courts of the early nomads such as the Xiongnu and the Yuezhi, and even details about the Arab tents are few in number. However, after the fifth century CE when Chinese Buddhist monks began writing about their travels to India on the overland routes that traversed the Eurasian steppe, descriptions of steppe rulers' tents became more numerous. This was especially true after the Turkish tribes became prominent in the seventh century. More specific information is available about them, indicating that the tents were covered with felt, a matted and compressed woolen textile. The interior walls of the courtly tents were decorated with silk draperies and their floors were covered with rugs. In the early seventh century, the Chinese pilgrim Xuanzang wrote the following about the tent court of Yabgu Khan of the Western Turks:

> The Khan lived in a great camp, decorated with golden ornaments. Its splendor was so brilliant it caused people to wince. All Advanced Officials

were seated on two long rugs. Their poly-chrome silk attire was impressive, while all the guards stand behind them with their weapons. Even though he was only a king living in a tent, his court was quite elegant. (Huili and Yanzong, *Da Ci'en Si Sanzangfashi Zhuan* [*Biography of Huanzang*], eds. Sun Yu-tang and Xie Fang, Beijing Zhonghua Shuju, 1983, p. 28)

The court tent of the Yabgu Khan was quite impressive, mostly because of the golden ornaments and the silk robes worn by the khan and his subordinates. In the early tenth century, Ahmad ibn Fadlan, an envoy from Khwarizm to the rulers of the Bulghars, an early Turkic people who lived along the Volga River, described the king's tent as follows:

They all live in domed tents (*qibab*); now the tent (*qubba*) of the King is so great that it can hold a thousand people or more. It is carpeted with Armenian carpets (*farsh*) and in the middle is a throne (*sarir*) covered with [Rum] brocade (*dibaj*). (Ahmad ibn Fadlan, *Rihlat*, ed. & trans. by A. Zeki Validi Togan as *Ibn Fadlan's Reisebericht* , Leipzig, 1939, reprint 1966, text p. 19, trans. p. 39, quoted from Peter Alford Andrews, *Felt Tents and Pavilions*, vol. 1, London, Melisende, 1999, p. 189)

This tent, located on the western section of the Eurasian steppe, was not only big enough to hold a large audience, it was furnished with Armenian carpets and had a throne that was covered with brocade from Rum (meaning Byzantium). Textiles made in sedentary societies, east and west, played a significant role in the tent culture. By the time of the Mongols, the courtly tents demonstrated the grandeur of the rulers. They not only had access to the materials of the sedentary societies, but also summoned the skilled workers to their camps on the steppe to construct the tents, or yurts, for them. The camp of Genghis Khan, no doubt, was splendid, but there is no visual record of it and little in the literary sources to verify this.

By the time the Mongol princes had carried out most of the conquests, their tents could be very elaborate. Rivalries among the khans encouraged demonstrations of their wealth and power through the grandeur of their camps and capitals, and thus a kind of competition arose over the beauty and the size of their tents. According to Marco Polo, when Hulegu, the founder of the Il-Khanate, went to fight with Berke, the Khan of the Golden Horde (on the Russian steppe), both sides set up their camps with many pavilions and tents decorated with cloth woven with threads of gold and silver and decorated with precious stones and pearls. This description was hardly an exaggeration. Nomadic rulers displayed their power and their wealth by means of their tents, and the material wealth, the craftsmanship, and the fashion of that time throughout Eurasia permitted them to make their tents extraordinarily splendid.

Before the Mongol conquests the Arab caliphs and the Turkish sultans were already focused on tents and textiles. Thus, when the Mongol conquerors took possession of the cities, especially Baghdad, they had direct access to numerous pieces of exquisite materials suitable for clothing and tents. These newly obtained materials embellished the tent culture of the Mongols and inspired further improvement in tent structures. There had been two distinct traditions of making tents on the steppe. The Mongolian yurt used a collapsible trellis to support the structure of the tent from the inside. The western Asia-type pavilions depended on outside guy ropes to hold up the structure. After the conquests both types of tents were in the camps of the Mongol rulers, and many artisans from sedentary societies came to do the carpentry and the metal work, and to make the ropes and textiles for the tents.

The Mongol rulers started a fashion of covering the inner walls of the tents with exquisite textiles, especially the *nasij* silks, the ones on which gold thread was used to make brocaded patterns. This was a technique developed in China, Byzantium, and Southwest Asia long before the Mongols carried out their conquests. The gold threads in Tang textiles look flat, since the gold was gilt on a paper base that flattened the threads. In Byzantine and Iranian textiles, the threads were round, since the thin sheets of gold were wrapped directly around the threads. The Mongol rulers admired the dazzling effect of gold on silk cloth and preferred the western style of rounded threads. They thus moved many Muslim weavers to the east and put them to work making the *nasij* silk.

Since the courtly tents of the khans were gigantic, demand for this gold brocade was also large. In particular, contemporary writers and travelers marveled at one of the courtly tents in Sira Ordo, a satellite camp founded by Ogodei near his capital of Karakorum. Although the capital cities were their administrative centers, the Mongol rulers had to have seasonal camps such as Sira Ordo to maintain their nomadic lifestyle, and to practice horse riding, archery, and hunting. Thus, they spent much of their time in these camps and spared no expense in decorating them. In this case, Chinese workers had made the wooden trellis that held up the structure of the tent, which could hold 1,000 people. The interior columns were plated with gold and the gold plates were fastened to the beams with gold-plated nails. Under the outside felt cover, the entire inside of the tent was lined with golden brocade. Given the scale of the Mongol rulers' courtly tents, these linings and coverings demanded more silk than the cathedrals of Byzantium and Western Europe ever had.

The Il-Khanate in Iran also maintained courtly tents in the seasonal camps. Ghazan Khan, the first Il-Khan born in Iran, spent much of his life in such camps. He was born in a winter camp near the Caspian Sea, and it was in another seasonal camp that he received his Mongolian education in the Uighur script from Chinese tutors. After he ascended the throne and converted to Islam in 1295, Islamic culture also entered the camps. A painting dated to the early fourteenth century shows two Mongolian Muslims in such a camp, each diligently reading a copy of the Koran in a tent mosque. (This painting of ink and color is from the previously mentioned book by Rashid al-Din, *Collection of Histories*. A reproduction of the painting is Figure 134 in *The Legacy of Genghis Khan*, which was published by the Metropolitan Museum of Art in 2002 and 2003.)

When the Mongol rulers settled at the centers of sedentary societies, they brought the tent culture with them. The Yuan emperors, for example, pitched tents just outside the palaces, and they also decorated the palaces with rugs and draperies, as if they were decorating tents. The Mongol tent culture depended largely upon the workmanship of the sedentary societies. Thus, their move to the centers of those societies actually improved the availability of the materials used to create the grandeur of the tents. The Yuan court in Dadu (now within the Beijing area) acquired a large bureaucracy just to manage the artisans who produced so many different items to serve the Mongol aristocracy and provide materials for construction. According to the official *Yuan History*, there were three offices in charge of producing felt. The one in Dadu had 127 households of felt makers under its charge, and the one in Shangdu, or Xanadu, the summer camp of Kibilai, had 97 households. There was also a high-level office in charge of the business of making tents and three offices in charge of making pile rugs, batik cotton cloth, and gold brocade and golden threads to be woven into silk brocades. In short, in the eastern part of the Mongol domain during the Yuan dynasty all the materials and production techniques that went into the making of the courtly tents were made or carried out by people in China working under dynastic supervision. The development of craftsmanship in the modern Beijing area as a result of the Mongol demand for tents and textiles also made it possible for the introduction of many elements of tent culture into the lifestyle of the sedentary population. One might also add that from the time of Kibilai Khan until the present, except for a relatively short interlude during the early Ming, the capital of China has remained in the Beijing area.

After the Chinese overthrew the Yuan dynasty in 1368 and the Mongol armies retreated to the steppe, tent culture in China persisted in the Mongol elite families who remained there, but otherwise it lost much of its significance. However, the situation in Iran and Central Asia was different.

In the Muslim areas rugs and tapestries had much deeper roots and had been well established even before the coming of the Mongols, and the Mongol-influenced tent culture continued to survive thereafter as a part of the local material culture. Some of the successor states to the Mongols, especially the Muslim Turkish powers, sustained this culture, and as a result of their conquests spread it even further afield. Indeed, it was only after one of the Muslim Turkish powers in Central Asia had invaded India and established the Delhi sultanate (1206–1526), that Chinese-style sericulture came to India, complete with mulberry leaf-eating silkworms and the steaming of the cocoons in order to get long filaments. Thereafter, the weaving of silk rugs and tapestries also developed in India.

When Ibn Battuta, the scholar and traveler from Morocco, was in India in the fourteenth century, he served one of the Delhi sultans, Muhammad Shah. He was thus entrusted with the responsibility of delivering a large quantity of gifts from the sultan to the emperor of Yuan China. The long list of gifts included a hundred good horses with full harness, a hundred male slaves and a hundred female slaves, and many kinds of textiles. Also, some of the gifts make it obvious that the Turkish sultans had carried the tent culture into India. These include one colored pavilion, six domed tents, and a hundred rolls of fine felt.

Today, when one views the buildings that have survived from the Delhi sultanate, they are all barren stone structures. Although there is no hint of it now, the sultans had decorated these stone palaces with silk tapestries and rugs. Also miniature paintings from the sixteenth century, for example, indicate that the emperors of India's Mughal dynasty (1526–1761), whose ancestors were both Turkish and Mongol, had colorful pavilions and canopies set up inside their marble or sandstone palaces. The roofs of the palaces often were supported by columns, and during the winter season, rugs and tapestries hung between these columns, functioning as interior walls and making the temperatures in the building more comfortable. In the hot season, the textiles were taken down to let the breeze in. Some palaces also were equipped with gutters that filtered water down from the eaves of the building, forming a water curtain around it. The water curtain cooled the palace since the falling water evaporated quickly, reducing the temperature of the surrounding air.

In addition to covering their courtly tents with gold-embellished silk textiles, the Mongol rulers also stockpiled a wide variety of exquisite textiles to robe their nobles and soldiers. In granting silk robes to subordinates the Mongols were following a long-standing tradition. Sasanid Iran, Byzantium, Tang China, the Arab caliphates, and the Fatimid caliphate all had

practiced robe granting. Not long after the conquests, the Mongols also began using robe granting to demonstrate the mutual recognition between
the sovereign and a subordinate. The difference in the Mongol period was
the amount of granting. During the period of the conquests, Genghis Khan
and his successors had enough silk robes and textiles from their war booty
to grant robes to the Mongol nobles, respected guests, scholars, and diplomats. Once the khans were settled in their khanates, the Mongol rulers
moved artisans to their camps and capitals to produce these silk robes.

Remarkably, as Thomas Allsen has pointed out, Mongol nobles sought
to distinguish themselves not by the number and quality of their horses,
but by the number and quality of their silks, especially the gold brocades.
Precious furs such as sable lined with gold brocade demonstrated that one
was at the highest rung of the status ladder. The rulers not only dressed
themselves and their courtiers in gold brocade, but even their maids and
musicians, and in the military forces it was not only the military commanders, but also the soldiers in the imperial guard units who wore these expensive clothes. Marco Polo reported that at the court of the Great Khan
Kibilai all the 12,000 barons who served as imperial guards wore costly
robes garnished with gems and pearls and other precious items. In addition, the Great Khan granted each baron thirteen sets of robes and boots,
each of a different color. And at each of the thirteen festivals held each year
all the barons wore robes of the same color. This must have been a spectacular sight. Perhaps the young Marco Polo exaggerated somewhat, but
the custom of clothing imperial guards in shiny brocade robes survived
the Mongol period and became the norm in China during the Ming and
Qing dynasties as well.

It was not only the Yuan dynasty in China that could afford so many
silk robes for the imperial retinue. On the western front of the Mongol domain, both the Il-Khanate and the Golden Horde expanded upon the robe-
granting custom of the Abbasid caliphate. Revealing their wealth and
power by displaying a retinue clothed in dazzling robes was part of the rivalry among the Mongol princes, and it was the same on the diplomatic
front when they met with statesmen who were not from the Mongol-held
lands. For example, one of the wives of Ozbek, the Khan of the Golden
Horde (then called the Khanate of the Qipchaq), was by origin a Byzantine
princess whom the Mongols renamed Bayalun. When she asked to return
to her father's palace in Constantinople so that she could have her baby
there, Ozbek agreed that she could go. Ibn Battuta, who was then visiting
her husband's royal camp on the Volga, asked if he could join the caval-
cade that would accompany her. Since Ozbek agreed to this as well, this

Moroccan traveler was with the party of thousands that departed in the summer of either 1332 or 1334. (The date is not clear.)

Ibn Battuta's account of the voyage indicates that the homecoming of this Mongol queen was a carefully staged production, showing the grandeur on both sides. Bayalun traveled by horse on a land route with a large retinue that included hundreds of the Byzantine, Turkic, and Indian servants of Ozbek's queen. When they reached a meeting place between the travelers from the khanate and the representatives of the Byzantine court, her brothers were there to escort her home. First, her younger brother came forward and met her at one of her father's seasonal palaces. This prince, riding a white horse and wearing a white robe, was at the head of a heavily armed cavalry. The princess, in contrast, was surrounded by about 500 servants, maids, and slaves, all dressed in gold-embroidered, gem-garnished silk robes. And the princess herself was surely covered with gold, silk, and gems. Later, her elder brother, the heir apparent to the Byzantine throne, arrived. It was only after a similar display of grandeur, that the elder brother and Bayalun entered a silk tent to meet personally. At the time of this early fourteenth-century encounter of the two cultures, the Byzantine court still maintained restrictions on who could wear silk clothing, according to a strict hierarchy, while the Mongol rulers showered gold and silk clothing on all members of their retinues. It is obvious that by this time the lands under the Mongol princes possessed more silk and more textiles in general than did Byzantium.

GROWTH AND DEVELOPMENT OF THE SEAFARING TRADE

The sea routes became increasingly more convenient for long-distance trade due to increases in the production and trade of commodities, as well as hostilities taking place among the various Mongol khans on the land routes. Among the four Mongol states, it was the Il-Khanate in Iran and the Yuan dynasty in China that had the best bilateral relations and the most frequent exchanges in culture and technology. This resulted in an obvious mutual influence upon each other in all spheres of cultural life, especially art and music. The exchanges between these two Mongol regimes were no doubt facilitated by their direct access to the overseas trade routes between southern China and the Persian Gulf. In China, under Mongol rule and Muslim management, the port of Quanzhou flourished even more than before. Its major exports were still silks, including Quanzhou's own satin, and porcelain ware. However, the celadon ware that had dominated Chinese porcelain exports during Song times gradually disappeared from the international trade. The most popular porcelain ware in overseas markets became pieces with a blue design painted on a white background. This blue pattern ware was produced in many places in China, but the best known was from Jingdezhen, Jiangxi, China's foremost porcelain-manufacturing city. The quality of the porcelain varied from Jingdezhen's finest thin, but hard translucent ware to rough-painted coarse ware fit for common use. They were priced according to their quality and all had good markets abroad.

The blue pigment used to paint the pattern was made from the mineral cobalt, which had to be imported from abroad. It came from either the mountains near Kashan in Iran, or from sites in Central Asia and eastern Europe. In the lands of the Il-Khanate cobalt had long been used to make the blue tiles that decorated the mosques, and in China the technique used to apply the blue pigment to the porcelain was quite similar to the technique used in the Il-Khanate to make the blue tiles. Given the timing of this technological transfer, it was most likely the result of interaction brought about by the increased traffic on the overseas routes between these two Mongol powers.

The Mongol takeover of the Chinese and Iranian ports did not disrupt the trading patterns on the Indian Ocean. The Muslim traders and officials under the Yuan government basically followed the old maritime pattern by skipping India's southeastern coast and sailing around the tip of the Indian Peninsula to its southwestern coast. After Ghazan Khan's conversion to Islam in 1293, the Il-khans themselves were Muslims, so it is not surprising that the old Muslim networks from India to the Mediterranean remained intact. However, in tandem with economic development in all of the coastal regions along these routes, the nature of the trade changed. The cargoes of the ships were becoming increasingly bulky. Blue-pattern porcelain, both the high quality and the ordinary varieties, had to be well packaged to prevent breakage, and the resulting containers were both heavy and large. From Hormuz, an Iranian port on the Persian Gulf, and Aden on the Arabian peninsula's Red Sea coast, ships carried an even more challenging cargo—horses destined for southern India. Marco Polo said 2,000 horses were shipped annually to the king of Maabar on the Coromandel Coast.

Polo reported that because the kings of southern India had no knowledge of taking care of horses, the horses died quickly. Horse traders thus could keep supplying large numbers of horses at exceedingly high prices. Apparently Polo did not realize that there are biological problems with keeping horses in southern India, or any place relatively near the equator, and that these problems are much more intractable than a lack of knowledge, which can usually be remedied. Horses, native to the Eurasian steppe, face a number of problems, when they are moved to places without large grassy pastures, especially places with densely cultivated rice lands.

One problem is that in order for horses to flourish, their food must supply ample amounts of beta-carotene, which green grass generally provides. Rice and most other grains available in densely cultivated lands like southern India do not provide beta-carotene, and rice straw has very little nutritional value of any kind. In addition, in places where horses are stabled and manure accumulates, they are much more susceptible to disease and infections than they are on the open steppe. If the imported horses in southern India did have a high rate of premature death, it may well have been due to these sorts of problems.

Even more likely, the problem was that the mares did not reproduce, a situation that would also require the rulers of southern India to continually import horses at exceedingly high prices. In order to get pregnant, mares must have high levels of beta-carotene. Also, proximity to the equator is a major problem. Ovulation in mares is stimulated by the lengthening of days that occurs after the winter solstice. In the case of almost all breeds of horses, if mares are too close to the equator, they do not ovulate since the length of daylight does not vary much throughout the year, if at all, in such places.

In various parts of the world, including southern India, there have been a number of places near the equator whose rulers have been willing and able to pay whatever was required just to have horses. The prestige that came from possessing them and using them in ceremonial displays in such locations was even greater than in places where horses were commonplace. Also, in some of these places the use of horses was more than ceremonial. In towns and villages where almost everyone is on foot, people on horseback, especially in the case of government officials, are very intimidating and pedestrians will quickly draw back and let the horses and their riders have their way. There have also been such places where rulers actually used the imported horses for military purposes with considerable success, especially when they could monopolize the importation of horses into the area.

Obviously the rulers of southern India had to have a way to pay for all the horses being delivered by sea. According to Ibn Battuta, who visited the region of Aden several decades after Marco Polo, ships carried high-quality horses to India and brought back large quantities of rice in return. Rice thus became a staple food in the coastal region of southern Arabia and in the Persian Gulf region. Both horses and rice took up a great deal more space on the ships than silk yarns, spices, aromatics, or even glassware and wine had in the ancient trade.

The horses also demanded much more attention on board. Horses do not have good sea legs, and due to the motion of the ships, broken legs are a major hazard. In southern India horses were used only by its rulers, and in southern Arabia and areas around the Persian Gulf, the imported rice most likely was used only in elite cuisines. Nevertheless, the trade in such heavy and less precious goods is yet another indicator of significant improvements in navigation and shipbuilding technology, both of which made such overseas transportation more affordable. It also indicates that there was a larger surplus of these products coming from agricultural and pastoral economies in Eurasia, a surplus that could be diverted onto long-distance trade routes.

Beginning in the late thirteenth century, Western European traders, especially the Italians, began to appear in the ports of the Indian Ocean and the South China Sea for the first time. Beginning in the Mongol period, there were many Italians going to Asia, not just the Polos, who became so famous only because of Marco Polo's account of their voyage. After leaving the eastern Mediterranean Basin, the Polos reached northern China by overland steppe routes. According to an Italian manual for traders that circulated in Florence around 1310–1340, some of these land routes were passable during the time of their journey eastward. The manual's advice to traders included the following information.

> The road leading from Tana, [near the northeastern part of the Black Sea] to Cathay is quite safe both by day and by night, according to what the merchants report who have used it—except that if the merchants should die along the road, when going or returning, everything would go to the lord [the Khan] of the country where the merchant dies, and the officers of the lord would take everything.... And there is still another danger, that is, should the lord die, until the new lord who is to rule has been sent for, in that interval sometimes a disorder occurs against the Franks and other foreigners. (Francesco di Balduccio Pegolotti, *The Practice of Commerce from the Italian*, reprinted *in toto* in Robert Lopez and Irving Raymond, *Medieval Trade in the Mediterranean World*, Columbia University Press, 1990, p. 357)

This is an accurate description of the conditions on the steppe routes to China. Much of the time they were relatively safe under the Pax Mongolia, but when there was a political dispute in progress, things could be quite dangerous. These were the times that merchants and missionaries turned to the sea routes. Also, by this time, the sea routes between the Yuan dynasty in China and the Il-Khanate in Iran had become the preferred routes of many merchants and officials, regardless of the conditions on the land routes. Thus, it is not surprising that the Polos, when contemplating their trip home, decided to begin with a sea voyage to the Persian Gulf.

Early missionaries from Italy and France such as Plano Carpini and Rubruck had reached Khara Khorum, the Mongol capital on the steppe, by land routes. The most successful missionary, John of Monte Corvino, was an Italian who first went to Tabriz, and then went by sea from the Il-Khanate to China in 1291. He oversaw the construction of two major churches in Dadu, Kibilai Khan's capital in the area of present-day Beijing. In his letters to the pope in Rome he estimated that he had baptized 6,000 Chinese. He also noted that his major rivals were the Nestorian Christians who had settled there long before him. In 1307, the pope gave Monte Corvino the designation of Archbishop of China and sent more assistants to him. Monte Corvino sent these priests to take charge of a church in Quanzhou, where many Italian traders supported the missionaries' activities.

The presence of Italians and other Western Europeans in Quanzhou, where they could trade directly for Chinese goods, is no doubt due to the growth and development of commercial and financial capacities in their homelands. Since the days of the crusades, some Western Europeans had become familiar with the ways of the Mediterranean's eastern shore. Through their encounters with Jews and Muslims the Italians learned to use paper and calculate with Arabic numerals instead of Roman ones. These basic tools paved the way for the invention of "double-entry bookkeeping," a great step in financial management that took place around 1300 in Italy. This bookkeeping system places the entry of all debits in the left column, and the entry of all credits on the right. Scholars differ about who actually developed it or where it was invented, but the leading contenders were in Venice, Genoa, and Tuscany.

The crusaders may also have been responsible for the growing use of the compass on Mediterranean ships in the thirteenth century. An early form of the compass was first developed in China, even before the emergence of the silk roads. As mentioned in Chapter Six, during the Song dynasty Chinese sailors started to use a new needle version of the compass, and it was this compass that was used for navigation on the South China Sea in the eleventh century. How the Europeans learned this technology is still a mystery. It has been suggested by George Hourani, an expert on Arab seafaring, that the Arabs transmitted the magnetic needle compass from China to the Mediterranean around the time of the crusades. In addition, because the Arabic literature about seafaring rarely mentions the compass, Hourani also suggested that the compass never played more than a subordinate part in Arab navigation of the Indian Ocean. However it happened, by the late thirteenth century the compass had become an essential part of the nautical revolution in Mediterranean seafaring.

Using records from frequently traveled Mediterranean routes, sailors studied the locations of ports and the distances between them, and carefully compiled this information. Sometime around 1250, they completed a book of ports that included the entire Mediterranean. Thereafter, all the information on ports and routes was charted on a large piece of parchment, called a portolan chart, which is actually a map showing all the ports on the Mediterranean's shores. Around 1270, when the portolan chart had just appeared, someone located in the Mediterranean area found a special way to use the compass. The needle compass was placed on a card showing the degrees and then attached to the ship in a straight line with the ship's keel, such that the magnetized needle revealed the direction that the ship was heading. All these technological breakthroughs had been completed by the end of the thirteenth century.

The immediate effect of this nautical revolution was to extend the season of navigation on the Mediterranean Sea. With the compass, sailors became less cautious about sailing during the stormy winters. During the eleventh and twelfth centuries, as described in the Geniza documents, ships in the Mediterranean stayed in their ports during all the winter months, and made only one major trip a year. In the fourteenth century, however, Venetian fleets began making two round trips a year. The first voyage left around February, and the second trip returned before Christmas. And the same was true of ships from Genoa and Pisa. After 1300, the compass spread out of the Mediterranean and was used on ships sailing the coastal waters along Europe's western shores. Voyages between the Iberian Peninsula and the English Channel became much safer, and the same was also true along the more northern shores of Western Europe.

Another century would pass before Portuguese sailors, relying on the compass, Arabic tables indicating the declination of the noonday sun at various latitudes, and the lateen sail (which apparently spread from the Arabian Sea to the Mediterranean), started sailing south to explore Africa's western coast. Almost two centuries had passed before Bartolomeu Dias, a Portuguese captain, rounded the southern tip of Africa and entered the Southern Ocean on a voyage of 1487–1488. The arrival of this Western European ship on the Indian Ocean was of momentous significance in world history. Previously European travelers, traders, and missionaries, on their way to ports in South Asia, Southeast Asia, and

China, had to go overland to either the Red Sea or the Persian Gulf and board Asian ships that would take them to their destinations. However, by the end of the fifteenth century, the new maritime technology would enable some Europeans to sail their own ships around the southern tip of Africa to the Indian Ocean, and soon thereafter to the South China Sea. Their arrival would have a profound impact on the well-established patterns of trade on these southern waters, and within a few more centuries, the long-standing commercial networks of the Southern Ocean were changed beyond recognition.

FOR FURTHER READING

Allsen, Thomas. *Commodity and Exchange in the Mongol Empire, a Cultural History of Islamic Textiles*. Cambridge, England: Cambridge University Press, 1997.

————. *Culture and Conquest in Mongol Eurasia*. Cambridge: Cambridge University Press, 2001.

————. "Mongolian Princes and Their Merchant Partners, 1200–1260,"*Asia Major*, third series, vol. II, part 2. Princeton, N.J.: Princeton University Press, 1989, pp. 83–154.

Andrews, Peter Alford. *Felt Tents and Pavilions*. London: Melisende, Publications 1999.

The Book of Ser Marco Polo, edited by Henry Yule and Henri Cordier. Reprinted in New Delhi by Mumshiram Manoharlal, 1993.

Dunn, Ross. *The Adventures of Ibn Battuta: A Muslim Traveler of the 14th Century*. Berkeley: University of California Press, 1986.

Marshall G. S. Hodgeson, *The Venture of Islam*, Vol. 2 *The Expansion of Islam in the Middle Periods*. Chicago: University of Chicago Press, 1974.

Hourani, George Fadlo. *Arab Seafaring in the Indian Ocean in Ancient and Early Medieval Times*, Expanded Edition. Princeton, N.J.: Princeton University Press, 1995.

Battuta, Ibn. *Travels in Asia and Africa*, trans. by H. A. R. Gibb. London: Routledge and Kegan Paul, 1929.

Komaroff, Linda, and Stefani Carboni (eds.). *The Legacy of Genghis Khan: Courtly Art and Culture in Western Asia, 1256–1358*. New York: Metropolitan Museum of Art, 2002 and 2003.

Lane, Frederic C. "The Economic Meaning of the Invention of the Compass." *The American Historical Review*, vol. 68, issue 3, (April 1963), pp. 605–617.

Marco Polo: The Travels, trans. by R. E. Latham. London: Penguin Classics, 1958.

Morgan, David. *The Mongols (Peoples of Europe)*. Oxford: Blackwell Publishers, 1986.

Rossabi, Morris. *Kibilai Khan, His Life and Times*. Berkeley: University of California Press, 1988.

◖ INDEX ◗